Second Edition

Making Sense

A Student's Guide to Research and Writing

Psychology

Margot Northey
Brian Timney

OXFORD
UNIVERSITY PRESS

OXFORD
UNIVERSITY PRESS

Oxford University Press is a department of the University of Oxford.
It furthers the University's objective of excellence in research, scholarship,
and education by publishing worldwide. Oxford is a registered trade mark of
Oxford University Press in the UK and in certain other countries.

Published in Canada by
Oxford University Press
8 Sampson Mews, Suite 204,
Don Mills, Ontario M3C 0H5 Canada

www.oupcanada.com

Library and Archives Canada Cataloguing in Publication

Northey, Margot, 1940-
[Making sense (2012)]
Making sense in psychology : a student's guide to research and
writing / Margot Northey, Brian Timney. -- Second edition.

(The making sense series)
Revision of: Making sense : psychology : a student's guide to research
and writing / Margot Northey, Brian Timney. -- Don Mills, Ont.
: Oxford University Press, © 2012.
Includes bibliographical references and index.
ISBN 978-0-19-901031-8 (pbk.)

1. Psychology--Authorship. 2. Report writing. I. Timney, Brian, author
II. Title. III. Title: Making sense (2012). IV. Series: Making sense series

BF76.7.N675 2015   808.06'615   C2015-900052-1

Cover images: (clockwise from top left) © iStock/AnthiaCumming; © iStock/pixologicstudio; © iStock/beemore

Oxford University Press is committed to our environment.
This book is printed on Forest Stewardship Council® certified paper
and comes from responsible sources.

Printed and bound in Canada

1 2 3 4 — 18 17 16 15

Contents

Preface

Although the rules of writing stay much the same over the years, a great deal has changed with respect to our ability to gain access to research materials and to prepare documents using computers. When the first edition of *Making Sense* was published in 1986, the personal computer was less than five years old and the Apple computer less than two. There were no laptops, the Internet did not exist, and almost every research resource available in a library was a hard copy. Only a small proportion of students had everyday access to a personal computer, so most papers were either typed on a typewriter or handwritten. Making simple corrections to text was inconvenient, and even a minor rearrangement of a few sentences or paragraphs might mean that several pages, or perhaps the whole paper, would need to be retyped. In such an environment, preparing an essay for a course was very different from today.

Now, you have complete control of what you write. There is no excuse for making a spelling mistake because there are spell checkers; if the order of topics doesn't seem quite right a quick cut and paste will let you see if the paper flows better; you can even check to see if your grammar is correct. Unfortunately, the quality of student writing has not automatically improved along with this technology. In a world of texts and tweets, students don't tend to think about how a written sentence can make you feel as if you were listening to someone talking to you. Despite (or maybe because of) all the technical aids to writing that we all take for granted now, many students pay little attention to the *craft* of writing.

In this book, I have tried to bring together all of the elements that will allow you to write a high-quality paper, whether it be an essay that reviews a body of literature, a short lab report, or an honours thesis. This is not just a "how to write well" manual. Rather, I have tried to provide you with a framework that will allow you to start with an idea for a project, do the research to gather the materials you'll need, and then write a paper that is not only "well written" in a formal sense, with respect to grammar and sentence structure, but is also organized in a way that lets your instructor know that you understand the material and can argue a case.

Writing is easy. Writing well can be very hard. Just as there are people who are naturally eloquent when they speak in front of an audience, there are some who can put together a piece of written work without having to think about it. Most of us cannot do that. However, most of us do have a good sense about the quality of the writing that we read.

There are three crucial elements to writing a high-quality paper. The first is **doing good research** before you start. If you are familiar with the material you are writing about, then you simply have to select what to include. The second, and perhaps the most difficult part of writing for a student, is **creating a logical structure** into which you can fit all of the pieces. You have to lead the reader through the research you have done and make her think that the paper hangs together very well. The third is **the writing itself**: the grammar and sentence structure, as well as choosing the right words and adopting the right tone. You also have to think about the formal style—that is, the format that ensures all papers are written in a consistent fashion for your discipline.

In this edition, I have provided you with information on each of these elements. I have given you advice on where and how to search for your materials, paying particular attention to online resources. I have devoted a complete chapter to the topic of keeping accurate data records and organizing your research and lecture notes, because these skills are so crucial to your studies.

It is difficult in a small book like this to give you enough advice to ensure that every paper you write is going to be a shining example of logical thinking and organized writing, but I hope I have provided enough information to start you thinking about the way that you write and to make you read your own work as if you were seeing it for the first time.

I've discussed several different kinds of assignments that you might have to complete in your career as a student, including giving an oral presentation and making a research poster. The ability to give a formal presentation is extremely useful at university or college, but it is also a valuable skill to have when you graduate and begin your own career. For this reason, I have included a chapter with guidelines on how to give effective presentations, including the use of graphic presentation software, such as PowerPoint.

I have also provided a fairly full discussion of the editorial style presented in the sixth edition of the *Publication Manual of the American Psychological Association*. This is not a substitute for using APA's own publications, but it should serve you for most of the writing you will have to do as an undergraduate.

Brian Timney
London, Ontario

Acknowledgements

I would like to thank Kim McPhee, who is the librarian responsible for psychology materials at Western University and who provided invaluable advice in the preparation of Chapter 2: Information Gathering. She told me about sources I wasn't aware of and corrected some of my own out-of-date thinking on some of these topics.

Steve Matson, my research assistant, spent a lot of time preparing figures and tables, proofreading, and correcting errors; all the important but tedious work that ensured that the final manuscript was in good shape. I appreciate all the work that he did.

Two of my former students, Denise Pitre and Amanda Carpenter, graciously allowed me to use and modify some of their own work as a basis for sample chapters.

My daughter, Meagan, whose direct experience as a former university student, and as someone working in electronic publishing, gave me added insight into what I needed to include in this book. She also prepared the initial draft of Chapter 3: Electronic Resources. Without her help, the book would have been much less comprehensive.

Finally, I would also like to acknowledge all those students whose writing, good and bad, gave me the motivation to prepare this book.

for Joanne and for Meagan
– B. T.

Communicating in Psychology

1

> **Objectives**
> - understanding scientific thinking and scientific writing
> - learning what is expected of you and how you will be graded
> - choosing initial strategies for research and writing
> - using electronic resources

Introduction

Most students enrolling in a psychology program think first about the content they will learn: about child development, or clinical assessment, or perhaps consumer behaviour. They probably do not think about how they will be expected to carry out research and communicate their findings to an audience. In the arts and humanities, undergraduate students will learn to do research and to write critiques of literary works. In the natural sciences, they will spend time in labs and will write up lab reports. In a discipline like history, they will collect and read through a variety of sources before writing an essay. As a psychology student, you may be expected to do any of these things, and you might also do more. The expectations with respect to research and writing placed on undergraduate psychology students are among the most varied of any discipline. In the course of your years as a psychology student, you may be asked to write a thought paper; you will almost certainly have to write a lab report; and you will probably have to prepare a literature review. Many students will also have to write an honours thesis and present their work orally, in front of an audience, or visually, by displaying research and results on a poster. This means that you will have to tailor your work to the needs of each course.

No matter the specific form and content of your writing in psychology, there is an underlying expectation that your writing will be scientific: that is, you will be expected to present an argument or a hypothesis and back it up with evidence. You will also have to make sure you are presenting a chain of evidence that leads to your conclusion, which usually means supplying the documentation to support your claims. In this book, we will provide you with the tools to produce good scientific writing. In the chapters that follow, we will provide you with guidelines about doing your initial research, organizing your thoughts and your notes, taking advantage of the variety of electronic resources available to you, and making sure that your work is not only organized but also well written.

Over many years, a set of implicit and explicit rules for scientific writing has been steadily developing. Minor details may vary between disciplines, but it should be possible for a physicist or a psychologist to read a biology paper and judge whether the science is reasonable, even if he or she doesn't understand all the technical details. The challenges of presenting research findings are not the same as they are when you have to write, say, an English paper on how Edgar Allan Poe's various substance addictions contributed to his poetry. While room for creativity exists in scientific writing, constraints exist too. For instance, when you are writing a lab report, you will be required to follow certain rules about how to organize that report. Your professor or lab instructor may give you those rules, or the rules may be standard for the discipline of psychology. Even if you're writing a review paper, you will have to follow guidelines for organization, as well as for citing and listing references. In psychology, you will almost certainly be required to follow the guidelines set out in the *Publication Manual of the American Psychological Association*, currently in its sixth edition (American Psychological Association, 2010). We will discuss this style guide in Chapter 10.

Having a clearly defined format makes your writing task easier. But don't forget, you are still responsible for all of the other aspects of the writing process. Even when the topic is assigned, your first step will be to decide what to include in your paper and how to organize your thoughts. After that you will need to gather your background materials and make notes in preparation for writing. Only then will you actually put fingers to keyboard to write the paper itself and submit it for grading.

One of your most frustrating experiences as a student may occur when you get back an essay or lab report and find that your grade is lower than you had expected. When you ask your instructor why you received such a low grade, he or she might say something like, "It didn't hang together very well" or "You seemed to know the material, but you didn't get your points across as well as some other students did." Often an instructor will not go into detail about the specific ways you might have improved your paper, so you are thrown back onto your own devices. In fact, many instructors may recognize good writing when they see it but are not very good at explaining why a paper is not well written. This can be especially irritating if you are a psychology student who has not had a lot of experience writing papers, or if your background is in the humanities or the natural sciences. It may seem unfair that someone who knows less about the material than you do gets a better mark because the instructor gives what might seem to you to be unnecessarily strong emphasis on "writing style."

In fact, many instructors do place a premium on style, so you should realize that there is more to good writing than correct grammar and spelling. These things make a difference, but expressing your ideas in a clear and logical way is just as important. Your instructors are not mind readers, so you cannot leave out essential parts of an argument and still expect to get credit. Nor should you take it for granted that just because your instructors know the topic, they will understand the ideas you are trying to communicate. They may, but their job is to evaluate what you have actually written, not what they think you meant to say.

Expressing yourself clearly and effectively is especially important in scientific writing because much of the time you will be trying to convey complex information. To convince your reader that you know what you're talking about, you have to ensure that he or she can understand what you've written. The best science writers have the ability to describe a complicated theory or procedure in a way that not only makes it easy to understand but also conveys their enthusiasm for the material. For example, take a look at *Hallucinations* (2012) written by Oliver Sacks, a well-known neurologist who writes about psychological topics with ease and engagement. This skill is not something that certain people are just born with. Almost anyone can learn to write in a way that will convince the reader that he or she is scientifically literate and has a good grasp of the subject.

The main purpose of this book is to give you the tools to develop your scientific research and writing skills. Because writing in science typically requires you to deliver information in a particular way, you should always begin by considering the needs of the scientific reader. If you know what your reader will be looking for, you are likely to produce a better paper. In the next section, you will find suggestions to help you craft papers that are suitable for a scientific audience. The section also explores some of the conventions of scientific communication and shows you how to follow them so that you can produce an interesting and effective piece of work. Finally, you will find suggestions to help you improve any kind of writing or presentation you will have to do.

Scientific Thinking and Scientific Writing

Whether you are writing an essay for an English course, a review paper for a microbiology course, or a lab report for a psychology course, you are not likely to produce clear writing unless you have first done some clear thinking. This means that you must first decide what you want to say and then organize your thoughts before you commit them to paper. Content and organization are independent entities.

For the most part, the ability to write in a clear manner does not depend on the subject matter, but there are occasional exceptions. Sometimes a student will produce excellent essays but disastrous lab reports. Different rules apply to different kinds of writing, so you should be aware of these rules to be sure that your essays will be as strong as your lab reports and research papers. In some ways, though, the distinction between the kinds of writing required for an essay for a history course and a lab report for a psychology course is artificial. After all, each is designed to tell a story based on evidence that has been gathered, sorted, and evaluated in a logical, systematic way. The only differences lie in the kinds of evidence examined and the specific principles used to evaluate that evidence. In fact, you can be scientific in your approach to almost any academic discipline; all you have to do is ensure that your evidence is strong and your analysis of that evidence is systematic and logical.

On the other hand, it is also possible to approach even scientific subject matter in a way that is quite unscientific. Perhaps the best way to see the difference between scientific and unscientific writing is to compare the descriptions of a particular finding in a tabloid newspaper and a scholarly journal. In a tabloid, claims by scientists are typically presented as established facts, with no attempt to evaluate how the data were gathered or whether the conclusions are justified. The story may be written in correct English, but no science instructor would be satisfied with it.

For example, a tabloid story might proclaim that a new drug treatment for cancer is the cure everyone has been searching for. If you were to look up the original report in a medical journal, however, you might find that the treatment worked only for certain types of cancer, that the number of patients whose condition improved was quite small, and that the authors put all kinds of qualifiers on their conclusions. Although the tabloid article might lead you to think that a cure for cancer had been found, the journal article would likely lead you to conclude that this was just another small step in ongoing cancer research. To be scientific, a report must not only present the author's own evaluation of the evidence but also provide enough information for readers to draw their own conclusions.

What Is Expected of Me?

One of the most frustrating things for an instructor is to receive a paper that is well written but that is not what she has asked for or is expecting. In these situations, the instructor may mark a paper harshly because she feels that it misses the point. If this situation arises, it does so because of a failure of communication between the instructor and the student, and the fault may lie on either side. Some instructors are not very good about communicating what they want, and they might not inform students, say, that they were looking for a *critical* review paper, rather than one that simply describes a group of studies. On the other hand, you might end up writing the "wrong" paper because you haven't paid enough attention to the instructions. So, your first task is to find out what your instructor wants.

Instructor expectations

If you are writing a lab report, typically you will be given quite explicit instructions as to how it should be prepared, down to the format of individual sections. If you are writing a major research paper, there is the potential for a lot more flexibility in what to present and how to present it. Most instructors have in mind the "ideal" paper, and you should know what this is before you begin. In most cases, if you have to write a review paper for a course that will be worth a significant portion of your grade, then you will be expected to do a *literature search* to find the relevant papers for your topics and write a paper that describes and comments on the work that has been done. But if the instructor does not give you specific guidance, you should ask about how she would like to see the paper written. These are some questions you might want to ask:

1. How long should the paper be and how much variation in length is acceptable?
2. Approximately how many sources should I consult and write about?
3. Am I expected to criticize the work I review or simply have a commentary on the findings?
4. To what extent am I allowed to use secondary sources rather than original articles?
5. How should my paper be organized and formatted?

This list is not exhaustive, and much will depend on the specific course and the instructor you have. Just be sure that you understand what is expected of you and that both you *and* the instructor are in agreement about these instructions. If you are going to write a book report or a thought paper, the specific questions may differ, but the principle will be the same: find out what is expected of you.

How will I be graded?

There are probably as many answers to this question as there are instructors, so it will be helpful to you if you know a little about how your grade will be determined. Some instructors may not be willing to provide you with a detailed breakdown or a grading rubric, but at the very least they should be able to tell you how much emphasis they place on style versus content, how strict they are with respect to your use of APA style, and what the penalties are for late submissions. If you have this information, then you can decide how much time to devote to different aspects of the paper.

Where Do I Start?

Even if you have been assigned a topic for your research report or essay, you may have difficulty just getting started. We've all stared at a blank page for much longer than we would like to, thinking, "What am I going to write?" In some cases, this initial writer's block turns into an excuse to procrastinate until you have only enough time left to throw together a paper with minimal planning.

It is always worthwhile to step back a little before you put your fingers to the keyboard. If you've done some background reading, you should already have an idea of what information the paper will contain; your problem will be deciding what material to include and in what order. If nothing springs to mind immediately, it can help to take some leisure time to think about the assignment without any pressure. Taking a walk, going to the gym, or even just sitting quietly away from your desk will give you a chance to let ideas percolate and coalesce. Relaxation in this context does not mean watching TV or going out with friends; you need some quiet time to reflect on what your paper is going to look like. You may not always have a major inspiration, but most of the time you'll find a starting point.

Sometimes the problem lies in coming up with an idea for a topic; other times, you may have decided on the topic but you aren't sure of the approach you should take. We will talk about this in Chapter 4, but for now you may find it most useful to start by developing an outline. Initially, this may be a simple list of potential topic headings, but gradually you will see some common themes emerging. You can then begin to rearrange the list and add subtopics. Soon you will reach a point where you have a detailed outline of the paper itself and all you have to do is add the content.

Initial strategies

What is the purpose of this piece of writing?

Two related issues that you should consider before you begin to write are the *purpose* of your writing and the *approach* you should take to achieve this purpose. Writing a review of a body of literature requires a different approach from the one you would take to write a paper considering the merits of two opposing theories. Sometimes you will be asked to *discuss* a particular topic, and sometimes you will be asked to *compare* different theoretical viewpoints. At other times, you may be writing a lab report or a thesis. Each of these assignments will require a different approach. Therefore, you must have a clear idea of the purpose of your paper.

Even if you select your own topic, you must decide what you are trying to accomplish. Depending on the assignment, your purpose may be any one or more of the following:

- to describe and interpret an experiment you have done;
- to show that you can do independent library research;
- to demonstrate your ability to evaluate primary or secondary sources;
- to show that you understand certain terms, concepts, or theories;
- to demonstrate your knowledge of a topic; or
- to show that you can think clearly and critically.

Although there is some overlap among these goals, an assignment designed to see if you have read and understood specific material will certainly call for a different kind of paper from one that is meant to test your critical thinking or research skills. Starting to work on an assignment without setting a goal is like setting out on a journey with no destination: your writing will be aimless, and you will never know when you have arrived at the end.

Formulating your ideas

In some ways, this is the most difficult part, because what you do here will determine what kind of paper you will end up with. As we have said, you should use this time to reflect, to do some informal browsing of the literature, to talk about the paper with your instructor, or even to bounce ideas off your friends. Keep in mind, though, that there is not necessarily a perfect topic. There are many potential topics that you can write about if the area is well defined. Your goal should be to select a topic that you will find both interesting and enjoyable to research and write about. Once you have thought of one or two topics, you should do some informal research to see if they are manageable. Look at the available literature and ask yourself these questions:

1. **Is there sufficient material available for me to write about?** If you have restricted the scope of your topic too much, there may not be enough relevant research available for you to write a whole paper. Or you may find that the most important references that you want are not in your library and you cannot download them.

2. **Is there too much material available? Will I be overwhelmed?** If this is the case, then think about refining your topic.

3. **How technical are the papers?** If you are not very good at statistics and you see that most of the papers on a topic have detailed statistical analyses, then you should probably stay clear of that topic. Similarly, if you find it difficult to understand the methodology, for example if there is a great deal of anatomical or physiological material that you are unfamiliar with, then you might want to look elsewhere.

4. **Is there any scope for me to be original?** Contrary to what you might think, being original does not mean doing something that has not been done before. Rather, it means starting with a topic that raises questions in your own mind. This will motivate you to search for answers and can lead to a much more compelling paper than one for which you have no enthusiasm. Most instructors do not expect undergraduate students to come up with something completely new, but when they see a paper that is more than a simple recitation of facts, they will enjoy it more.

What approach should I take?

The way you approach your paper will be determined both by your purpose and by the context of the course you are taking. How did your instructor describe the purpose of the course at the beginning of classes? What aspects of the course materials does your instructor emphasize, and how has he or she approached them? How does this particular assignment relate to key concepts and themes of the course? Has your instructor been mainly descriptive, or analytical, or critical in each lecture? Your instructor's approach is probably a reflection of his or her own preferences about the subject matter. We will discuss the different approaches in Chapter 4.

Who is my real audience?

Even if the only person who will read your paper is your instructor, don't think of that one individual as your target audience. If you do, you're likely to leave out important explanatory points because you assume your instructor will know them already and will understand your argument without this essential information. Instead of writing specifically with your instructor in mind, try to think of your reader as a stranger who has knowledge of the discipline but doesn't know everything about your specific topic. The person who reads your paper can read only what is on the page, not what is in your head. Don't take detailed knowledge about your topic for granted. Remember, your task is to convince the reader that you know what you are talking about and that your arguments have merit.

Thinking about the reader also means taking into account the intellectual context in which he or she operates. If you were to write a paper on human sexuality for a biology course, it would likely be quite different from one on the same topic submitted for a psychology course. You have to make specific decisions about the background information you will supply, the terms you will need to explain, and the amount of detail that is appropriate for a given situation. When you are writing a lab report, you need to give much more procedural detail than you would if you were writing a review of the same topic. If you don't know who will be reading your paper—your professor, your tutorial leader, or a marker—just imagine someone intelligent, well informed, and interested, who is skeptical enough to question your ideas but flexible enough to accept them if your evidence is convincing.

If you are giving a seminar or an oral presentation, then you will have a real audience in front of you. You will have to take into account a much greater variation in background knowledge, so you must be as clear as possible and avoid leaving important details out of your descriptions and explanations. Never underestimate the lack of knowledge of your audience.

How long should the paper be?

Before you start writing, you will also need to think about the length of the assignment in relation to the time available to you. If both the topic and the length are prescribed, it should be fairly easy for you to assess the level of detail required and the amount of research you need to do. If only the length is prescribed, that restriction will help you decide how broad or how narrow your topic should be. You should also keep in mind how much the assignment is worth. A paper that is worth 50 per cent of your final grade will need more of your time and effort than one that is worth only 10 per cent.

What should the tone of the paper be?

Everyday written communications, including texts, blogs, and emails, almost always take a casual tone, but academic writing is usually more formal. The exact degree of formality will depend on the kind of assignment and instructions you have been given. In some cases—for example, if your psychology professor asks you to keep a journal describing certain personal experiences—you may well be able to use an informal style. However, in lab reports and review papers, where you need to express yourself unambiguously, a more formal tone is required.

On the other hand, you should also avoid the other extreme of excessive formality. You must resist the temptation to fill your work with long words and high-flown phrases, which will only make your writing sound stiff and pretentious. Finding a suitable tone for academic writing is a challenge for many students. You will find some guidelines for setting the tone of your paper in Chapter 11.

How do I write in an online course?

As more and more courses are offered as e-learning options, you may find that you spend a lot more time producing written output in the form of online posts. Although the formal writing requirements of an online course will be the same as those taught in a regular classroom, very often you will be required to be part of a chat room, or you will be expected to make posts and respond to questions and comments from your instructor or your classmates. In some cases, you will be graded for participation and for the quality of your posts. Most, if not all, of these posts will be written and available for everyone to see. What you write, and how you write it, has the potential to make a big impression, good or bad, on your instructor and classmates. Writing online posts should not be taken lightly because it will give you an opportunity to shine. You should keep in mind that a post is not a text, and that the rules of good writing still apply in this context, even though the style may be less formal than when you are writing a paper.

Use Your Computer Wisely

It is difficult to overestimate the role played by computers and the Internet in all areas of academic research. We take it for granted now that we will be using a computer to prepare a paper for a course or to make an in-class presentation. Further, almost every student is familiar with software suites, such as Microsoft Office, that allow for word processing, data analysis, and even the preparation of slides for visual presentations. It is also a given that we will use the Internet while researching and preparing a paper. In the following chapters, we will discuss how you can take advantage of this technology, both in the initial stages of your research and in the final preparation of an assignment, a paper, or a talk. While you are likely familiar with the most common electronic tools, you may not know about the many other resources available to help you prepare an outline or take notes. You can also collect your reference citations online and format them as you go along, and we will talk about the software that allows you to do this. In our experience, most students use their laptops for almost all of their coursework. So we have couched our advice about note-taking, organizing, and writing in terms of computer files and software. But the same principles apply even if you do all of your initial work by hand, for example by making sure that your notes are kept in a format that will allow you to rearrange them in a different order as your ideas develop.

Using a computer simplifies many of the tasks of writing: you can correct mistakes before they show up on paper, experiment with the structure of your writing by cutting and pasting blocks of text, check your spelling, create tables and graphs, and prepare a clean and professional final copy. However, using a computer also presents a number of potential problems. Here are a few things you should always keep in mind.

Don't let the system rule your thinking

Seeing something typed out neatly on screen or on paper certainly looks professional. But don't be fooled into thinking that fancy graphics and a slick presentation can replace intelligent thinking. Thoughtful arguments, careful analysis, and clear organization will impress your professor more than the range of fonts and graphics used. Also, remember to proofread your work carefully, even when your program has not pointed out any errors. While your program's spell checker might catch obvious mistakes, it will not know that you meant to type *kind* instead of *kid* or *lead* instead of *led*.

Save regularly and back up your files

There is nothing worse than spending all day working on a paper only to lose everything because of a system crash or a power outage. Don't just rely on your software's auto-save function. Take the time to save your work in regular intervals. It's also a good idea to save your work occasionally to a location other than your hard drive. This could mean saving it to a USB drive, a CD, or a local network. If you have backed up your files regularly in an external location, damage to your hard drive will have a minimal impact on your writing. An alternative is to use *cloud storage* systems, such as Dropbox, that allow you to keep your files on web-hosting sites so that they are accessible from any computer. We will describe this facility in Chapter 3.

Don't discard your files

Be sure to keep a copy of your writing, at least until your paper has been graded and returned to you. The resolution of many cases of alleged plagiarism has been dependent on whether the student was able to produce an electronic version of the paper. Some universities now use specialized software to check for plagiarism and may therefore require you to submit an electronic version of the paper as well as a printed copy. In this case, you should always keep an electronic version in case something happens to your instructor's copy. If you want to go even further, you can use the note-taking software that we will describe later to keep track of exactly where you got your references from. Then you will have a complete record of how you constructed your paper.

Summary

In this chapter, we have tried to give you a bird's-eye view of what is involved in preparing assignments for a psychology course. We have attempted to show you how to look at your work not only from your own perspective, as the person who will be submitting the assignment, but also from the perspective of your instructor, who will be marking it. We have touched upon the broad issues of what is expected of you as a student, as well as how to get started on your assignments. We hope that we have set the stage for you to think about research and writing not just as a required task that you have to do to get a grade but as a true intellectual exercise that involves many elements. If you can move away from the content of any particular assignment and think about the process behind it, you will have developed an important skill set that you will be able to use in many different contexts.

References

American Psychological Association. (2010). *Publication manual of the American Psychological Association* (6th ed.). Washington, DC: Author.

Sacks, O. W. (2012). *Hallucinations*. New York, NY: Knopf.

Information Gathering

2

Objectives

- asking questions
- developing answers
- obtaining information
- figuring out where to start
- using the Internet as a research tool
- using the library

Introduction

Doing research means different things depending on your academic discipline. In this book, we focus on two different kinds of research: what you do in the library or on your computer, and what you do in a lab. Although these types of research may seem very different, they have a great deal in common. The goal of any research project is to answer a question that you have set yourself. To do that, you will need to take a particular approach to the topic you are working on. It makes little difference whether you begin by reading and making notes from a book in the library or by recording a person's responses to stimuli presented on a computer screen; the same general rules will apply.

No matter what kind of research project you are working on, you will go through the same three stages:

1. obtaining information;
2. organizing that information; and
3. presenting the information to an audience.

If you are writing an essay, you will obtain your information from a variety of sources, either in print or online. If you are in a lab course, or if you are working on a thesis, you may be conducting an experiment as well as doing some background reading. Although these are quite different activities, one thing they share is the need for organization.

If you have to do a lot of reading, you will need to take notes in such a way that they can be easily rearranged, depending on how you decide to organize your paper. If you do an experiment in a lab, you want to be sure that you have tabulated your data in a way that makes it easy to organize your analysis and the final write-up of your lab report. The final product of your research may be an essay, a lab report, or a thesis; it could also be a seminar or a more formal presentation at a conference. But no matter what format you're using to present the results of your research, the rules are the same: you must be clear, concise, and coherent. In this chapter, we will provide you with some guidelines that will help you to organize the way you do academic research, with an emphasis on how to collect information.

Asking Questions

The ability to ask intelligent questions is one of the most important—albeit underrated—skills that you can have, whether at university or at college or in the outside world. Sometimes, the most elegant research comes from asking some very simple questions. In the 1950s, Kenneth Roeder (1998) studied the behaviour of moths as they tried to avoid bats that were hunting them. His hypothesis was that moths could hear and react to high-frequency sounds that bats emitted as they flew about. Beginning with a simple experiment in which he recorded the responses of nerve cells in a moth's ear as a bat flew by, he then went on to ask if there was a relationship between the proximity of the bat and the response of the moth. Then he asked if the nerve cells responded in a way that could identify the direction the bat was coming from. Each answer led him to another question, so that over a period of many years, he was able to describe the whole predator–prey relationship between bats and moths.

This example shows that asking the right questions is an essential part of scientific investigation. Even if you are given specific instructions by your professor, you will still have to limit your project by posing a series of questions about your topic and how you should approach it. The kinds of questions you ask will depend in large part on the specific content of your work and on the approach you decide to take.

Developing Answers

Research begins with asking questions, followed by the collection of information, and then by the evaluation of that information in order to draw a conclusion. We will discuss methods for gathering information in the next section, but first we will look at ways to draw conclusions from the information you have gathered. One way to draw conclusions from the results of your research is by adopting the *scientific method*. You can think of the scientific method as a systematic way of approaching the questions you ask. In doing this, you will use two of the basic principles of logical reasoning: *induction* and *deduction*.

Induction

This method allows you to start with the study of individual observations and arrive at a general conclusion. For example, you would be using induction if you reviewed a number of experiments on a particular topic, each of which was quite different, and then developed a hypothesis that would allow you to explain the results of all the experiments. You start with the data and move to the theory. Imagine your instructor describing only the results of a series of experiments:

- In the first of these experiments, participants are shown two photographs that alternate every half second or so. The pictures are identical photographs of an airplane, but in one photo, the engine hanging from the wing is not present. Most people, when asked if there is anything different about the pictures, fail to notice the missing engine, even after many presentations.
- In a second experiment, students are shown a video clip of a pickup basketball game and are asked to count the number of times the ball is passed between players. At some point, a person in a gorilla suit walks across the court. About half the observers fail to notice the gorilla.
- In a third experiment, participants are asked to judge the lengths of lines flashed briefly on a screen. The participants typically don't notice the shape of small objects presented at the same time during some of the trials.

These are very different experiments, but you could use induction to look at what is common to them. The hypothesis you generate might be that human observers are not good at noticing changes if they are not actively looking for them.

This example is fairly clear-cut, but you should be aware when using an inductive approach that your conclusions will only be as reliable as the information they're based on. The reasoning process itself does not include any way to evaluate the specific cases you consider, and if the data are not accurate or representative, you might draw an incorrect conclusion.

Deduction

In the situation we've described for inductive reasoning, you examine some sets of data and then come up with a hypothesis based on the observations you've made. That is, when you start your experiment, you have no preconceived notion about the results you might expect. However, this is not usually what happens in science. More often than not, we *begin* with a hypothesis about something and then look for evidence to support or (more formally) reject the hypothesis. This is the process of deduction. Deductive reasoning is not a source of new information; rather, it is a way to uncover relationships as the researcher moves from the general to the specific. It depends on the assumption that the initial generalization is correct, which may not always be the case.

By themselves, induction and deduction do not establish truth. They are tools that allow you to evaluate the evidence available to you, and they operate best when used together in the context of the scientific method. The scientific method relies on a set of orderly procedures, combining aspects of both induction and deduction to allow you to answer the questions you ask. Although the precise path you take will vary with the specific project you are working on, for an experimental research project you would normally proceed through a logical sequence of steps such as the following:

1. deciding on the problem you want to address;
2. reviewing the related literature;
3. developing a theoretical framework;
4. formulating hypotheses;
5. selecting a research design;
6. specifying the population that you will study;
7. developing a plan for data collection;
8. conducting a pilot study and revising your research plan;
9. selecting the sample to be tested;
10. collecting the data;
11. preparing the data for analysis;
12. analyzing the data;

13. interpreting the results; and
14. sharing the findings with others.

Research bias

Ideally, as a researcher, you should be entirely neutral and objective with respect to the subject matter at hand. However, this is not always as simple as it may seem. Let's say that you are a university scientist and that a major pharmaceutical company funds all of your research. You are asked by the editor of a prestigious medical journal to write a literature review on the effectiveness of a particular drug that is made by your sponsor. How do you go about selecting the studies to include in the review? How do you interpret the results of the experiments that you describe? While you may wish to be as objective as you can, is it possible that you might be subject to some unconscious bias? Sometimes, even though you feel that you've been completely objective and neutral, questions may be raised about the validity of your work simply because you are associated with the industry. Biased research doesn't just occur in controversial situations such as this. Someone doing basic research may also be more willing to accept a result that is consistent with his or her hypothesis than one that seems to refute it. The best way to avoid bias is to make your research procedures as rigorous as possible so that your conclusions are indisputable.

Obtaining Information

When writing a scientific paper, one of the most important rules is that everything you say must be supported by documentary evidence. This rule applies whether you're writing a lab report for a classroom project or a review paper for publication in a professional journal. For example, if you go looking for information on the effectiveness of a particular dieting strategy, you may come across a number of online articles or blog posts that give examples of individuals who have tried the diet and lost a great deal of weight. This is considered to be *anecdotal evidence*. As a student in a scientific discipline, you are expected to read through articles in reputable psychology journals and to base your conclusions on the data you find there. This is *evidence-based research*, and it is considered the standard way to obtain information in science. If you're going to pursue a career as a researcher in psychology, you will find out quickly that you must be able to back up your arguments with facts. Once you've learned how to track down information efficiently, you'll find that this skill is a powerful asset in many different situations.

Collecting information from various sources is fundamental to the research process. However, you may tend to overlook another essential part of research: the way you gather and organize your research materials. This may even make the difference between an average paper and an excellent one. For many years, research meant going to the library with a notepad, and perhaps index cards, and making notes from books and journal articles. You needed to be careful to write down every source of your information, especially if you were quoting an author. Sometimes, you would discover that you had lost track of an important source because you had written down the incorrect reference. Often, you would need to photocopy materials and keep everything in file folders and binders until you had finished writing your paper. Although a few students still prepare for writing their papers this way, there are now much more efficient ways for you to collect, organize, and store your research materials electronically. We will describe some of these methods in the next chapter. No matter how you manage the information you gather, some basic principles apply whenever you have to summarize information.

Nothing is more frustrating than discovering that you aren't sure where a piece of information came from. Each time you read an article in a journal or a chapter in a book, keep a record of its citation in case you want to find that reference again or in case you need to list it in the *References* section of your completed paper. If you are working with books, it may be helpful to also put down the library call number. For journal articles, much of the time you will be searching for and retrieving them online. Even if you print them out to read, get in the habit of keeping an electronic record of each citation. In fact, many databases allow you to download the citation directly into a citation management package such as RefWorks or Reference Manager, which makes it very easy to keep track of your references. For more discussion on these programs, please see Chapter 3.

If you do not have online access, it is best to use an index-card system. You can either use real index cards on which you write down your reference, or you might use note-taking software on your computer to save virtual index cards. The main thing is to keep all your reference citations as separate elements so that you can rearrange them and add or subtract items as you develop your paper. If you are not using a citation manager, write the full reference in the format that you will use for your reference list—typically in APA style—so that it will be easy to copy and paste them into your paper's *References* section. Whether you use real index cards or an electronic system, if you keep track of every source you may use, you can start to build up your own database of references. This may come in handy for other papers on similar topics.

Where to Start

Let's assume that you have already selected—or been assigned—a topic to write about. (More details about planning a paper and finding a topic are given in Chapter 4.) Your first task is to find out something about the topic, as well as the names of the major authors in your field. Once you have this information, you can begin to look more systematically for relevant papers by these and other authors. If you have absolutely no knowledge about your topic, perhaps the best way to start is to take the shotgun approach: cover a wide area, but do it superficially.

There are quite a few ways to get at least a general idea of what is going on in a particular subject area. First, consider simply asking. Many students don't think of taking advantage of their principal resource: their course instructor. Although you should not expect that he or she will provide you with all the information you will need, your instructor, or a graduate teaching assistant if you have one, should be able to give you some names and references to get you started. Similarly, if you have friends who have taken the course before or who may be more knowledgeable than you about a particular topic, don't be afraid to ask for their advice on how to approach your assignment. You can also get very useful information from your textbook or the materials in your recommended readings.

Armed with this information, you can begin your research. At first, you should be seeking general information about your topic so that you can become more familiar with the names of some of the authors in the field and get a sense of the important issues. This used to mean going to the library to look for books and articles on your topic. Now, your first step almost certainly will be to turn on your computer. Even if you want to use the library catalogue, you will likely access it online. However, you may also want to take a look at your library's reference collection. Often, they will have specialized encyclopedias and scientific dictionaries that may help direct your search. Later in this chapter, we will offer some advice on familiarizing yourself with your college or university library, but first, we will consider the Internet as a tool for scientific research and offer some suggestions on how to use it most effectively.

The Internet as a Research Tool

Over a relatively short period of time, the Internet has changed the way we do research. Even as recently as twenty years ago, searching for and collating research materials was a fairly arduous process that involved spending a great deal of time in the library. Much of your research time was spent looking through card catalogues, wandering through the stacks, and physically collecting the books and articles you needed for your paper. The library is still a place to gather your information, but the whole search process has been speeded up enormously through the Internet. Now, every institution has its catalogue online, and many of the articles, and even some of the books you need, are available electronically. If they are available through open-source journals, or if your library owns a subscription, you will be able to download them without charge. And just by typing a few words into a search engine, you may find references to sources you didn't know existed. Your task as a researcher is no longer limited by the physical availability of materials. Instead, you must decide what is relevant and reliable, and from there you must select what is going to be most important for your project.

Although the Internet has made the gathering of information much easier, it has also created a new set of issues that you must deal with. The most important of these is the reliability of the data available. For example, *Wikipedia* is a great place to gather some preliminary information about a topic, but because anyone can write or edit articles, even if that person has no expertise in the area, you have no way of knowing how accurate it might be. For this reason, you will need to verify the information from *Wikipedia* or other sites that contain materials that have been "contributed" without passing through some kind of evaluation process.

When you begin a search, you should always make a conscious effort to assess the academic quality of your sources. In some cases, this is not a problem. Articles in scholarly journals are still peer-reviewed, even when they are available online. This means that when an author submits a manuscript to a journal, the editor sends it to independent experts in the field for evaluation before deciding whether it should be published. When the article is published and becomes available online, it is identical to the original hard copy. All that has changed is your ease of access. You will come across many other websites that discuss your topic and here you must be very careful to sort out fact from opinion. As a general rule, although you might cast a wide net initially to get a sense of what the major issues are and what kinds of research have been done, when you actually come to write the paper, you should rely on the traditional sources: books and journal articles.

Having said that, you can find a huge amount of legitimate information by using the online tools available. The way research is gathered has changed significantly over the past 20 years; today, the Internet is the first place you think of starting when you begin a research project. Further, you have probably found a growing number of your instructors are putting course materials online. This may range from a few lecture notes to a complete course. The amount of material available online will continue to increase, so it is essential that you become comfortable working in this electronic environment. You will also need to know about some of the pitfalls associated with online information.

Online search tools

You can use the Internet for research in two ways: first, as a simple and fast method of accessing materials that you could also find by other means; and second, as a tool for finding information not available elsewhere. In the first case, you may consider the Internet simply as a tool for boosting your productivity, rather than as a source of new information. Depending on your own particular library system, you will have varying degrees of access to materials. At a minimum, you will have access to the library catalogue and a number of databases, but in some cases you may also have access to many thousands of journals electronically. We will describe these later in the chapter and provide you with a list of search resources that are available through most libraries. For now, let's consider how to use the Internet to find information not available anywhere else.

Search engines

A search engine is a tool that uses the Internet to find specific information and then provides you with a list of everything it has found, including websites, images, and other types of files. Most search engines operate using search algorithms to seek out the keywords you've specified, and these algorithms are different for each search engine, meaning they will generate different search results. From the perspective of someone researching a topic, the way these algorithms work will have a significant impact on the kinds of hits that come back. Google is the search engine that everyone is familiar with, but there are many others, and we'll talk about a few of them below.

Some search engines also "mine" for information contained in certain databases. Such databases may belong to a publisher and contain electronic copies of a number of journals. Or, they might be more extensive repositories like PubMed, which is owned by the US National Institutes of Health (NIH), and is a free digital archive of biomedical and life sciences journal literature. You may access a database like this directly through its URL or through your own library system, or you can use a search engine that seeks out such databases.

Google and Google Scholar

For most of us, a basic search engine, like Google, is our first step in finding information about a particular topic. Simply type in a search term and look at the enormous list of hits that is returned. Much of what you find may be irrelevant, but you will get a chance to see what has been said about a topic from a variety of different sources. A search engine is an excellent place to start when looking for non-academic information, but it is not always the best for an academic search. Search algorithms cannot guarantee that the information on the pages they return is factual and accurate, which is a problem when you are looking for scientific information. Much of the material you'll need will be housed in databases that are not indexed by non-academic search engines. You will be much more successful if you use an academic or scientific search engine. These engines index the full text of scholarly articles and can provide you with much more comprehensive information.

One such search engine is Google Scholar (http://scholar.google.ca). Google Scholar allows you to do very broad searches of the scholarly literature, although its coverage is best in the life sciences and social sciences. This search engine can mine certain open-source databases and is not confined to any one discipline or area. This means you may find items that are in less obvious places, where you wouldn't normally look. Google Scholar also gives you access to a wide range of different kinds of scholarly work, including books, articles, theses, conference abstracts, professional society publications, and online repositories. It has access to the contents of many journals, although very often only the abstracts are available. You can do very wide searches, or you can use the advanced search function to restrict your searches and target your topic. If you are logged into your university or college network, Google Scholar will even locate copies of articles that your library has access to. It can also locate free versions of papers or articles anywhere on the Web. Another reason to use Google Scholar is that each hit it displays is linked to other sources that have cited that paper. This means that when you click on the "cited by" link, you will be taken to other references that may be relevant for your project.

However, you should be aware of the limitations of Google Scholar. One difficulty is that Google provides very little information about its source content or how its search algorithms work, which makes it difficult to know how comprehensive or up to date it is. So, you may miss important research articles if you don't use any other search tools. The advanced search functions of Google Scholar are not nearly as sophisticated as those for MEDLINE/PubMed (described below), and its coverage of older material may be somewhat limited. Nevertheless, Google Scholar is an excellent place to start.

MEDLINE and PubMed

A very important online search engine for psychology is PubMed (http://www .ncbi.nlm.nih.gov/pubmed). PubMed allows users to search various journals and books, as well as the massive MEDLINE database, which contains over 21 million journal citations for the biomedical and life sciences literature going back to 1946. A PubMed search returns citations to the majority of the current and historical research that has been done on many topics related to psychology. Along with these citations, a PubMed search also generates links to the full text of articles, many of which are available without charge, especially if you are searching via your institution's library. PubMed is more effective for psychology research than Google Scholar is because of PubMed's use of "Medical Subject Headings" (MeSH), which allow you to access all the information on a topic even if different terminology has been used to describe the same concepts. Another advantage is PubMed's sophisticated advanced search features, which are explained in free tutorials on the PubMed website.

Other online search engines

While Google is the search engine that most of us are familiar with, there are a number of scientific search engines to help you find what you are looking for. We have described two of these below, but you can do your own Google search for "scientific search engines" to discover others. Because each engine has its own way of searching, sometimes you will find a reference in one that you will not find in another. Therefore, it is definitely worth using more than one search engine.

- **OJOSE** (http://www.ojose.com). OJOSE (**O**nline **JO**urnal Search Engine) describes itself as "a free powerful scientific search engine enabling you to make search-queries in different databases by using only one search field. With OJOSE you can find, download or buy scientific publications (journals, articles, research reports, books, etc.) in up to 60 different databases." The most useful feature of OJOSE is that you can type in your search phrase and then choose any one of a range of different databases, including those hosted by the American Psychological Association.

- **Q-Sensei Scholar** (http://scholar.qsensei.com). Q-Sensei is a privately owned software company that has developed technology for searching through data on the Internet. One of their products is Q-Sensei Scholar, an engine that searches for citations from several different databases, including the National Library of Congress and the National Library of Medicine. This search engine has access to over 40 million records in many different fields. It has a particularly helpful feature: once you enter your own search phrase, it will suggest alternative search strategies so that you can narrow your focus on the most relevant topics.

You can choose from a wide range of search engines to help you with your specific topic. You should also be aware of the difference between a search engine and a *searchable database*. The search engines we've described here will look for information in a variety of different places, including databases. Search engines are general in their approach and cast a wide net, meaning they may return references from places you might not have thought about searching. Searchable databases, on the other hand, allow you to browse only within their own holdings, although these can be extensive. Some of these databases will charge a fee for access, so you should always check to see what is available through your library. We will describe some of the more important databases when we discuss your use of libraries later in this chapter.

Online encyclopedias and dictionaries

Although we do not recommend that you use encyclopedias as major research tools, they are a good starting point. You can consult many different scholarly, subject-specific, scientific dictionaries if you want to get more than simply an extended definition. Specialized online encyclopedias can be great starting points for areas that you are not familiar with. Your librarians can show you how to find these.

Wikipedia

Wikipedia is a go-to website for many students when they begin their research. Unfortunately, for some it is also a place where they *end* their research, and we've seen numerous cases where student essays plagiarize a large amount of content lifted directly from *Wikipedia*. *Wikipedia* is a controversial resource because anyone can contribute or edit an article. This is its greatest advantage but also its most severe limitation. Articles for *Wikipedia* may be written by professional scientists or by people with no formal background in a particular area. The articles are not peer-reviewed, which means that they may contain errors (unintentional and sometimes intentional) and are not subject to any oversight except by other members of the public who might correct errors they find in articles. Many instructors do not allow the use of *Wikipedia* as a citable resource, so be sure to check before you cite it in research you are submitting. It's our view that *Wikipedia* should only be used as a guidepost to send you in the right direction for further research.

Other online encyclopedias

Most encyclopedias are now available in an electronic format. In some cases, there is a subscription fee to access the content, which may be covered by your library, but there are several encyclopedias where all of the content is offered free of charge. One useful tool that your library may have is called Reference Universe (http://reference.paratext.com). This search tool allows you to enter your search term once, and it will then find references to the term in any of the encyclopedias in your library's reference collection. Depending on your needs, you may also want Reference Universe to look at handbooks, indexes, bibliographies, and subject guides. The portal to access Reference Universe will be different at different institutions, so check with your library's reference desk.

Online academic searches

No single search engine will provide complete coverage of every source article you might need. Database size, relevancy rankings, search results, features, and commands vary from engine to engine, so you will probably want to use several of them in the course of your research. Even if you use the same keywords as you go from one search engine to another, you'll get different results. You should also be aware that some Internet service providers limit the range of sites you can visit. For example, some universities now block access to sites from which students might download copyrighted materials, and other providers may block on the basis of content. The following points may help you make your search more effective:

- **Remember alternative spellings or synonyms.** Search engines look for only what you type in. For example, if you use upper-case letters, the engine may only look for sites where the terms are capitalized, whereas if you use lower-case letters, all sites will be considered. Similarly, there may be multiple spellings of a word. Even a plural *s* at the end of your search term can make a difference. So you should always try to include alternative spellings and to search for synonyms of your term. If you are looking for information on gender differences, you might want to use *woman, women, female, feminine, girl*, or even *womyn* to catch as much as you can.

- **Use an advanced search to gain access to the most pertinent sites.** Most search engines permit you to do advanced searches. This type of search allows you to select certain search limitations, such as language, period of time, or types of occurrence. You can also use *Boolean* operators (i.e., AND, OR, and NOT) to restrict your terms. Check the "Help" section on the site to see the format for entering these terms. You should also check to see whether the engine treats your terms in the OR or AND mode by default. We will discuss this in more detail in the Search Strategies section below.

- **Consider limiting by domain.** Most of the time, you will get hits back from a whole range of information providers, including commercial operations whose primary goal is to sell a particular product. You can restrict your search by specifying that you only want hits from a particular category of top-level domains, that is, the last part of a URL, which specifies the origin or type of the host site. The most familiar is *.com*, which usually specifies a commercial site. There are others: *.edu* is used by educational institutions in the United States, *.gc.ca* indicates government of Canada websites, and *.gov* designates American government institutions. In Google, you can restrict your search simply by appending "site: .edu" or ".gc.ca" to your search terms.

- **Consider searching by phrase.** How you put your search terms together can make a big difference to the number and the relevance of the hits you get. If you are looking for a topic best described as a phrase, such as "attention deficit disorder," most engines will search the words as a phrase (i.e., in AND mode), but sometimes each word will be considered separately and you will get large numbers of hits on each of the terms. To be sure you get exactly what you want, enter your terms as a single phrase by putting them in double quotes. Try this with terms like "attention deficit disorder" or "fetal alcohol syndrome" and look at how the number of hits changes.

- **Know when not to use the Internet.** Remember that not everything is available online. A great deal of information can be found only in printed sources. When in doubt, seek guidance from your instructor and your reference librarians.

- **Save particularly useful websites.** When you find a website you plan to visit again, be sure you bookmark it in some fashion. If you use a tool such as Citation Manager or Zotero, you can keep a snapshot of the page as well as the URL information.

Search strategies

When you are doing an online search, you don't want to miss any relevant information, but you also don't want to be overwhelmed with lists of sites that have little or nothing to do with your topic. Try this simple experiment: imagine you are writing a review paper on the visual abilities of different species of animal, one of which is the Australian marsupial rat. Go to one of the search engines and type in "marsupial." You will get a huge list of hits. Now try a Boolean search: type in "marsupial AND rat AND visual acuity." This time the list is much more manageable, and most of the hits will seem relevant to your topic. The Boolean "logical operators" AND, OR, and NOT allow you to broaden or narrow your search by including or excluding specific words to look for. In some search engines, you can also use NEAR to require that both terms are in the same sentence, or you can use ADJ if you want words that are adjacent to each other. For example, if you search for "alcohol NEAR abuse," you would pick up topics like "child abuse is often associated with alcohol consumption," but if you used "alcohol ADJ abuse," you would only find pages with those words in sequential order.

You should be aware that different search engines take different approaches to Boolean terms. Google, for example, assumes that if you enter more than one word, they *all* have to be in the page (implicit AND), whereas other search engines will look for sites that contain *any* of the keywords you enter (implicit OR). Click on the Advanced Search or Help link to get more advice for a particular search engine.

When you do plan a search, you should think about both the set of keywords and the *exclusionary* words that will keep your search manageable while still procuring the best results. However, it's probably a good idea to cast your net wide to begin, look at the kinds of hits that you are getting, and then refine your search to get exactly what you want.

Evaluating web sources

Later in this chapter, we will describe some of the databases that allow you to search for relevant references. These include peer-reviewed journal articles, that is, articles that have been reviewed by professional experts in the field before they were accepted for publication. If you do a general search online, the situation is a bit different. Most online material is not peer-reviewed, which means that you must be extra cautious about evaluating the accuracy and the bias(es) of what you find. The first thing you should do when you come across a website that has information relevant to your research topic is consider the source. Is the site credible? Was it created by an academic institution; a recognized research centre; a group with no professional affiliation; an individual?

Let's say that you have been asked to write a paper evaluating the contribution of animal research to clinical psychology. In your Internet search, you find a site belonging to a group called Understanding Animal Research, which strongly defends the use of animals in research and the contributions animal research has made. You also come across the website of PETA—People for the Ethical Treatment of Animals—an animal rights organization that vociferously opposes the use of animals in medical research and denies that animal research has made any positive contribution. Both of these organizations have clear credentials, and you understand that what they say must be interpreted in the context of what they believe.

Now suppose you come across another site representing the Physicians Committee for Responsible Medicine. The description of this group suggests that it is an independent body that has evaluated the literature and concluded that the application of animal research to humans is fundamentally flawed. When you read this material, you conclude that it is quite persuasive in its argument that using animals in research is ineffective. But what if you discover that this organization has a number of links to PETA? Would this influence your interpretation of its arguments?

You must be very careful about accepting what you find on the Internet at face value. There is certainly a tremendous amount of information out there, much of which may be useful to your research project. However, it's always best to approach a site you don't know with a fair degree of caution and skepticism, and you should carefully evaluate what you read before you try to incorporate it into one of your papers.

Here are some tips for evaluating websites:

- **Check the URL.** As we discussed above, you can get quite a lot of information just by looking at the top-level domain name of the URL. You can determine the trustworthiness of the sites you come across based on their domains. Along with our earlier examples of *.edu*, *.gc.ca*, and

.gov domains, many other domain types exist. Universities in the United Kingdom use *.ac*, such as the website for Durham University (http://www.dur.ac.uk). Note that the country might also be represented, for instance, *.uk* for the United Kingdom. Many non-governmental agencies may use *.org*. Personal sites within larger organizational sites are often signified by a tilde (~). By looking at a domain name, you can get a sense of the possibility for bias in the material you find.

- **Look for a statement identifying the site host.** Such a statement might also give the author's qualifications and contact information.
- **Check to see how current the information is.** While this may not be crucial in all cases, if you are looking for something that is completely up to date, you should check when the page was posted to the website or when it was last updated. Some pages will have a footnote providing this information but others may not. Remember that setting up a website is easy, but that it needs to be updated regularly in order to be useful. There are lots of websites that have been abandoned, displaying information that has become quite out of date, yet they remain on a server. University professors are often guilty of having out-of-date personal websites.
- **Evaluate the accuracy of the information by checking facts and figures with other sources.** Data published on the website should be documented in citations or a bibliography, and research methods should be explained.
- **Be wary of blogs.** Although some institutions have official blogs that can offer accurate information on a variety of academic subjects, many are simply online diaries published by a rapidly increasing number of people who are expressing personal opinions. Using such unverified material can seriously undermine your essay, as many students have discovered.
- **Don't trust everything you read.** Many websites will look like—and will claim to be—authentic, reliable sources of information, but that doesn't guarantee they are infallible. *Wikipedia* is an example of a site that, while generally reliable, does require that you verify the information available there before using it for academic purposes.

If you still have questions about the reliability of a particular website, ask your instructor about the organization or group the site represents; he or she will probably have some idea of their reputation in the academic community and how legitimate the information they present is likely to be. If your instructor isn't familiar with the organization or group, it's probably a good sign that the organization isn't well established, and you may be better off not using their information in your work.

Using the Library

We started our discussion of how best to do your research by talking about the Internet. The huge amount of information available on the Web makes it a great starting point for a quick search. By starting online, you can see if your chosen topic is really the one you're interested in and if there is sufficient material readily available. But doing scholarly research is a little like going to a department store to buy a high-quality sound system. The department store sells lots of different items, but you are only interested in a few of them. If you want a sound system, you don't need to look at refrigerators or go to the cosmetics counter. In fact, high-end systems may not be offered at a department store at all. If you want to go for quality, then you should go to a store that specializes in audio technology, where they will have the best products and knowledgeable staff. The library is your academic specialized store. Many online databases that are offered for a fee to private individuals may be available without charge through your library. And perhaps most important, there will be a group of experienced staff, many of whom specialize in specific areas, who can guide you through everything the library has to offer and give you advice on where you might be able to find information. So, although you might use the Internet to get an idea of what is available, you should begin your systematic research by using the library.

These days, a visit to the library will not necessarily involve walking in through the doors, although we strongly recommend you do so for the reasons we list below. Many libraries have, to a large extent, become "virtual," and you can think of them as sophisticated portals to the scholarly material that is online, with a lot of help and guidance available. This means that if you are planning serious online searches, you are almost always better off by going through your library system.

But even if you do most of your searches online, it's important to become familiar with the physical library at your institution. Some larger universities have more than one library, each containing materials for a particular area, such as law or education, and you should get to know what their holdings are. This is particularly important for students of psychology, because some of the material you need might be located in the science and medical library, some in the education library, and some in the arts and social sciences library. If your college or university offers library orientation tours, it's well worth taking one. You will learn a great deal about useful reference sources that are not in the book and periodical stacks: you may be introduced to bibliographies and guides to literature, dictionaries, encyclopedias, government documents, and online databases. Once you know what is available and where the materials are, your literature searches can be much more efficient. You should also take advantage of the knowledge your librarians have; their jobs involve finding these materials, cataloguing them, and making these resources accessible. Their assistance can be invaluable.

It's also a good idea to make yourself familiar with the cataloguing system your library employs. This will enable you to go to the general area containing materials that may be relevant to your topic. The two main cataloguing systems are the *Library of Congress Classification* system (the most common one in university libraries) and the *Dewey Decimal Classification* system (more common in public libraries). As you can see in Table 2.1, psychology is broken down into a number of subcategories in each cataloguing system. So, if you are interested in, say, special education, you could go directly to the shelves to look for call numbers beginning with "LC" if your library uses the Library of Congress system or "37" if it uses the Dewey Decimal system.

Computer-based searches

Today, almost every library's catalogue is accessible on its computers. In addition, many libraries allow remote access to their catalogues from your home computer or laptop. Using your library's catalogues online offers several advantages:

- you can find materials quickly and efficiently;
- you can search for materials by keyword, by author, by title, by call number, or by subject, which gives you much more flexibility in your search; you can also do both basic and advanced searches;
- you can access the catalogues directly from your home or residence room;
- you can find out whether the book you need is available in one of the university's libraries or whether it has been checked out;
- you can recall material that has been checked out so that you will be next in line when it is returned; and

Table 2.1 Common library classification systems

	Library of Congress Classification		Dewey Decimal Classification
BF	Abnormal psychology	00-	Artificial intelligence
	Child psychology	13-	Parapsychology
	Cognition	15-	Abnormal psychology
	Comparative psychology		Child psychology
	Environmental psychology		Cognitive psychology
	Motivation		Comparative psychology
	Parapsychology		Environmental psychology
	Perception		Industrial psychology
	Personality		Motivation
	Physiological psychology		Perception
	Psycholinguistics		Personality
	Psychological statistics		Physiological psychology
HF	Industrial psychology	30-	Family
	Personnel management		Psychology of women
HM	Social psychology		Social psychology
HQ	Family	37-	Educational psychology
	Psychology of women		Special education
LB	Educational psychology	40-	Psycholinguistics
LC	Special education	51-	Statistics
Q	Artificial intelligence	61-	Psychiatry
	Physiological psychology		Psychotherapy
QA	Mathematical psychology	65-	Personnel management
RC	Abnormal psychology		
	Psychiatry		
	Psychotherapy		
T	Personnel management		

- if the source you're looking for is not available in your own library, you may be able to access the catalogues of other libraries to see where it is available and use the interlibrary loan service to borrow it.

To get the information you need efficiently, you should know a little about the logic underlying database searches. When you are searching databases and indexes, you should use the same Boolean logical operators we recommended for searching websites. Although each database has its own rules, they all require you to enter relevant keywords in order to carry out a search. These words may be contained in the title or the abstract of the paper, or they may be part of a list of *descriptors* assigned to the paper by an indexer. When you do a search, you should use enough keywords to ensure that you do not miss too many references, but you should not use so many that you come up with too much irrelevant material.

For example, suppose you have been assigned a paper on some aspect of domestic violence. One database that you might try searching is PsycINFO, which we will describe later in this chapter. If you type in "domestic violence" as a search term, you will get back over 12,000 hits, which is way beyond what you can browse through. Adding "women" to the search terms reduces that number to about 5,000, but this is still much too big. If you decide you want to narrow your focus to violence in dating relationships, just adding "dating" as a search term drops the number to around 100 sources, a much more manageable list. By including further requirements, such as looking only at adolescent relationships, or searching for data from a particular country, you can find a list of journal articles that you should be able to use as the basis for your paper. By selecting the appropriate combination of search terms, a skilled researcher can usually come up with a manageable list of useful references. If you are having trouble establishing an appropriate search strategy, be sure to consult the reference librarians at your institution; they have a lot of expertise in this area.

Systematic searching

Although an online search is often your first step, another excellent way to get an overview of a topic is to browse through the library stacks, particularly for secondary sources that review the body of work you are interested in (we will discuss the differences between primary and secondary sources in the next section). Let's say that you want to write an essay on congenital insensitivity to pain. You know that the literature on pain is vast, and you also know that there is relatively little information on congenital insensitivity. You might try the following approach:

1. Have a look for your general topic, in this case "pain," by doing a keyword search in your library's online catalogue. You might find that "pain" as a general term yields too many results, in which case you could try to narrow your search by looking at terms such as "pain" and "insensitivity" together, or by looking for the terms "hypoalgesia" or "analgesia." A quick glance will probably show you that most of the books on pain have similar call numbers.

2. Once you find the appropriate stack, browse through some of the books. You don't have to look for specific titles: just go through the indexes of different books for any reference to pain insensitivity. Even if you don't find a book devoted to your specific topic, you should find a few relevant references; you'll also begin to see how different authors have discussed the topic. If you do find a book that looks relevant, check the copyright page; often there will be a list of subject headings that correspond to those in the Library of Congress catalogue. By going to the Library of Congress website, you can search using those keywords to find additional material.

3. Be sure to look at the specialized journals dealing with your topic. Much of the research on pain is published in the journal *Pain*. Go to the current periodicals section of your library, or access the journal online, and skim through the contents pages of all of the issues for the past year or so. This technique doesn't always work, but often you will find something relevant. Not only will you become familiar with this up-to-date reference on your topic, but the reference list at the end of any relevant papers you come across should provide other recent references.

The strategies outlined above will help you get some basic background information on your topic. If you are writing a review of a body of literature, however, you will need to obtain a much more extensive list of references. You can develop your list of references in a variety of ways, either by examining relevant secondary sources or by searching through the various databases and indexes that are available, either physically within the library or online.

Primary and secondary sources

You'll find lots of different sources of information available when you are writing a paper, so you need to think about what kinds of sources will be most appropriate for the paper you will be writing. The most important distinction is between primary and secondary sources:

- A *primary source* is one written by the individual(s) who did the original research. In psychology, primary sources are usually journal articles, or in some cases book-length monographs, which describe research work first hand.
- A *secondary source*, in contrast, is written by someone who has read the primary material and is providing a summary and comments on

the original material. A secondary source could be anything from a scholarly review published in a scientific journal, to a book that gives an overview of a wide range of literature.

- You should be aware that a third kind of source lies somewhere in between: a *meta-analysis*. A meta-analytic paper is one in which the author takes the data from several primary sources and reanalyzes them to help draw a broader conclusion. You should consider a meta-analysis to be a primary source if you are looking at the results of that analysis, but as a secondary source if you are looking only at the descriptions it provides of other papers.

Reviews and handbooks

When you are searching for reviews, one of the best sources is the *Index to Scientific Reviews*, a serial publication listing review articles and chapters that have appeared in the recent scientific literature. Sources are filed under different subject headings and are extensively cross-referenced, so if you are not sure of the best way to describe what you are looking for, you can find alternative headings. PsycINFO also allows you to limit your search to reviews.

Another useful source is the *Annual Review* series. These are books of reviews that are published each year and provide detailed summaries of current research. The series includes the *Annual Review of Psychology*, the *Annual Review of Neuroscience*, and the *Annual Review of Physiology*. All of these volumes may contain reviews that are relevant to psychology. They are particularly helpful because they cover most of the sub-areas of a discipline, and new reviews on each topic (and on some new topics) are commissioned every few years.

In psychology, a number of publications will help you begin your search, whether for topics or for references. If you are looking for a topic to write on, you could consult a handbook, such as the *Handbook of Social Psychology* (DeLamater, 2006; Fiske, Gilbert, & Lindzey, 2010), *Stevens' Handbook of Experimental Psychology* (Pashler, 2002), or the *Handbook of Psychological Assessment* (Groth-Marnat, 2009). Each of these gives a broad overview of the field and may provide you with ideas for topics to write about. Note that several of these handbooks are now available online and your library may allow you to access them at no cost.

Dictionaries and encyclopedias

If you want more general background information about a subject area before you start reading literature reviews, you might look at subject dictionaries or encyclopedias. Your library will have access to a number of these, and we have listed a few of them in Table 2.2 below.

Table 2.2 Dictionaries, encyclopedias, and testing manuals

Title	Comment
Dictionaries	
A Student's Dictionary of Psychology	A good starting place to find out about an unfamiliar area.
Biographical Dictionary of Psychology	A useful resource if you're researching a prominent figure in the history of psychology. This dictionary features short entries, a list of that person's principal publications, as well as a list of sources for further reading.
Cambridge Dictionary of Psychology	Surveys the broad discipline of psychology from an international, cross-cultural, and interdisciplinary focus.
Dictionary of Theories, Laws, and Concepts in Psychology	Provides an excellent overview of theories, laws, and concepts. Each entry includes a list of references for further reading.
Encyclopedias	
Encyclopedia of Cognitive Science	Consists of four volumes with detailed entries and diagrams on a wide variety of cognition topics.
Encyclopedia of Counseling	A four-volume set that aims to cover all major theories, approaches, and issues related to psychological counselling.
Encyclopedia of Industrial and Organizational Psychology	A useful resource for those studying psychology, management, or human resources.
International Encyclopedia of the Social and Behavioral Sciences	Contains in-depth entries on a wide range of topics. Provides useful background information on unfamiliar topics, as well as references for further reading. Available online.
Learning and Memory: A Comprehensive Reference	An online, four-volume encyclopedia with in-depth articles on a variety of topics. Each entry has linked references, and the entire encyclopedia is searchable.
Psychological Testing Instruments	
Health and Psychosocial Instruments (HaPI)	Covers a wide variety of evaluation and measurement tools for health and psychosocial studies. Includes questionnaires, checklists, index measures, rating scales, project techniques, tests, interview schedules, and a variety of other means of evaluation.
Mental Measurements Yearbook	Contains full-text information about and reviews of English-language standardized tests covering educational skills, personality, vocational aptitude, and psychology.
Test Critiques	Contains detailed critiques describing the practical applications and technical aspects of psychological tests.

Bibliographic databases and citation indexes

Once you have narrowed your study topic to a manageable thesis statement, you are going to be most interested in books and journal articles that review or report original research. Bibliographic databases and citation indexes are the best places to look for such sources. Some are open access so that anyone can search them, while others require you to go through your library to gain access. Libraries usually subscribe to the most important databases and indexes that you will need to find your references.

Bibliographic databases

There are now many databases available that can be accessed through your library. Some of these are electronic versions of, or replacements for, print-based volumes. For example, PsycINFO is the online (and more extensive) replacement for *Psychological Abstracts*. There are two kinds of bibliographic databases:

- The first type contains the bibliographic information about a particular reference, including all of its publication information, and sometimes its abstract and links to other sources that have cited this paper. A *bibliographic database* will not contain the full article. PsycINFO is an example of this kind of database.
- The second type is called a *full-text database*. Full-text databases contain not only the bibliographic information but also the entire text of the paper that you can download and print or simply search through on your computer. PsycARTICLES is a full-text database.

But even simple bibliographic databases, while not containing the articles themselves, may give you access to the full text of articles elsewhere. For example, if you are searching PsycINFO while connected to your school's network, you may be able to download a PDF file containing the full text of the article so that you can print a copy of the article in the same form that it was published in the journal.

In Table 2.3, we list various bibliographic databases. In psychology, PsycINFO and the related services PsycARTICLES and PsycBOOKS will likely be the most valuable. These will give you access to most of the psychological literature, going back many years. PubMed, as we have mentioned, provides extensive coverage of the medical and health literature, with lots of material of relevance to psychology. The databases we have listed are only a few among many, so you should check with your own reference librarians to see what is available where you are studying.

Table 2.3 Bibliographic databases

Name	Comment
ERIC (Education Resources Information Center) http://www.eric.ed.gov	Bibliographic database. Offers extensive coverage of journal articles and other materials related to education.
ingentaconnect http://www.ingentaconnect.com	Bibliographic database. Gives access to a large number of publications in different fields.
JSTOR http://www.jstor.org	Full-text database. Coverage includes both life science and social science journals.
PsycARTICLES http://www.apa.org/pubs/databases/ psycarticles/index.aspx	Full-text database. Provides access to articles in journals published by the American and Canadian Psychological Associations, among others.
PsycBOOKS http://www.apa.org/pubs/databases/ psycbooks/index.aspx	Full-text database. Coverage includes books and chapters published by the American Psychological Association, including many historic texts. It also contains over 1,500 entries from the APA/ Oxford University Press *Encyclopedia of Psychology*.
PsycEXTRA http://www.apa.org/pubs/databases/ psycextra/index.aspx	Mostly full-text database. Covers the "gray" psychological literature compiled by the APA. Supplements PsycINFO with less technical content (magazines, newspapers, government reports, etc.).
PsycINFO http://www.apa.org/pubs/databases/ psycinfo/index.aspx	Abstract database. Includes every abstract from APA journals back to 1887 and also covers a wide range of books.
PubMed http://www.ncbi.nlm.nih.gov/pubmed	Bibliographic and abstract database. Covers the biomedical and life science literature, including psychology. The citations may include links to full-text articles from PubMed Central or publisher websites.
SCOPUS http://www.scopus.com/home.url	Abstract and citation database. Includes peer-reviewed literature and "quality" web sources.

Citation indexes

Some bibliographic databases, as well as Google Scholar, will provide you with a list of other articles that have cited the one you've just found. But you can do a much more systematic search of citations by using *citation indexes*. These indexes let you search forward in time: if you know of an important paper written by a certain author, you can find out what other articles have referred to that paper since it was written. Two of these indexes will be especially relevant to you: the *Social Sciences Citation Index* and the *Science Citation Index.*

Of course, not all of these citing articles will be directly relevant to your topic, but you will certainly learn what kind of work has followed the original article. You may also discover the names of other researchers working in the same area, and you can then see who has cited *their* work. In this way, you can build up a collection of core references that will allow you to make progressively wider searches (which is especially important if you are preparing the introduction to a thesis).

These databases offer several valuable tools to help with your research. Many of them will allow you to download citations for the references you find directly into a reference management program (see Chapter 3 for a discussion on these). In some cases, you can also include the article's abstract. If you have access to one of these databases, then you won't have to go to the trouble of transcribing your citations, and you can format them and insert them automatically into your paper. The best strategy when using this tool is to create a subfolder within the reference management program that will contain all the references for your current paper. Then you can easily access the articles you want to use without having to search continually for them. Once you have completed your paper, you can merge the references into your main database. This way, if you are working on a similar topic later, you will be able to easily find these references again.

Checklist

As you gather information about a research topic, ask yourself the following questions to ensure that your research strategies are effective and comprehensive:

- ☐ Am I familiar with my institution's library? Do I know how to find what I need?
- ☐ Have I explored the full range of databases, library search tools, journal searches, dictionary articles, and indexes available to me?
- ☐ Have I been careful and selective in using the Internet for online searches, and have I ensured that my sources are reputable?
- ☐ Have I documented the citation information for the sources I will use?
- ☐ Are my notes clear, appropriately referenced, and organized? Do they contain enough information to be useful when I'm writing?

☐ Have I ensured that I understand when to reference a source in my paper or when I am relying on another person's ideas? Do I understand plagiarism? Are my notes clear about what is my own writing and what belongs to others?

Summary

In this chapter, we have shown you what options are available when you need to gather information about a research topic that you have been assigned. As we mentioned earlier, the days of the solitary student searching the stacks for material are long gone. Now, your greatest challenge is to be able to evaluate the quality and the importance of the material you find. You should also remember that you now have the ability to create a personal "library catalogue" of your research materials. This can be of tremendous value and a great time saver if you are progressing to a career in psychology. Although you can do much of the research you need on your own, do remember that professional librarians complete a graduate degree to learn how best to find and catalogue research materials. Seek out someone working in your library if you need help finding material for a paper.

References

DeLamater, J. (Ed.). (2006). *Handbook of social psychology.* Boston, MA: Springer.

Evidence-Based Medicine Working Group. (1992). Evidence-based medicine: A new approach to teaching the practice of medicine. *Journal of the American Medical Association, 268*(17), 2420–2425.

Fiske, S. T., Gilbert, D. T., & Lindzey, G. (Eds.). (2010). *Handbook of social psychology* (5th ed.). Hoboken, NJ: Wiley.

Groth-Marnat, G. (2009). *Handbook of psychological assessment* (5th ed.). Hoboken, NJ: Wiley.

Pashler, H. E. (Ed.). (2002). *Stevens' handbook of experimental psychology* (3rd ed.). New York, NY: Wiley.

Roeder, K. D. (1998). *Nerve cells and insect behaviour.* Cambridge, MA: Harvard University Press.

Vine, R. (2006). Google scholar. *Journal of the Medical Library Association, 94*, 97–99.

Electronic Resources

Introduction

Almost all students these days rely on computers for just about every aspect of their academic lives. Information for assignments is mostly obtained online, essays and lab reports are written using Microsoft Word or a similar word-processing package, and seminar presentations are usually prepared using PowerPoint. We recognize the ability to use these tools as basic skills that students possess. However, you may not be familiar with a number of other electronic resources that can make your research and writing much simpler and more efficient. There are software packages available to help you do the following tasks:

- take notes and store information you gather from the Internet;
- collect and organize reference citations as you find them;
- construct an outline and fill in individual sections of your paper, or rearrange ideas as you need to;
- construct attractive graphs and tables; and
- keep backup files of your work.

Some of these programs are freeware and can simply be downloaded. Others charge a nominal fee for a fully functional software package. Your institution may also have licences for some of these software packages so that you can use them when you are logged on to your university's network. Explore what options are available to you at your institution. This book was written within an outliner, with a note-taking program open, and we organized our references using a citation manager. The figures were prepared using graphics software. Because there are a number of packages in each of these categories that will do these tasks, we will simply provide an overview of their functionality, with a few specific examples, in the following sections. In later chapters, we will provide you with additional suggestions on how to use them.

Information Managers

In the previous chapter, we talked about how you would go about looking for the information you need for your research project, and where you might find that material. The next step is to gather the information together and sort it for efficient use. Information management programs—such as Evernote, Intellinote, or Microsoft OneNote—can make this task much easier.

You can think of information management programs as digital filing cabinets that allow you to store virtually anything you can put into your computer, to organize this material, and to search through the content in a very efficient manner. They also save all of the material to *the cloud* (see page 51), so that you can access it from anywhere online, even from your smartphone. You can drag and drop many different file types (PDFs, Word and Excel files, etc.) and web pages directly into the programs for storage. These programs also help you keep snippets of information that you might otherwise lose. For example, if you come across a book that you might need from the library, rather than scribbling down the reference information on a scrap of paper, you can take a photograph of the title page with your smartphone and upload it for safekeeping.

Information managers have many other features, but you can see how a tool like this gives you a place to store and organize all the information you are collecting from many different sources.

Mind-Mapping Software

The next step in your journey towards writing a paper is to think about how you are going to organize all the material into a logically coherent structure. This should result in an outline that you can follow when you write, but sometimes at the beginning of a project you may feel that you will benefit from some brainstorming. That is, you might want to lay out a summary of all of the information you have gathered to date and see how it fits together. You could just write the information out as a list and try to think about what order to arrange the content for your paper. Alternatively, you might use mind-mapping (or concept-mapping) software (such as MindMaple, XMind, or Coggle).

Mind maps facilitate the brainstorming process by allowing you to visualize connections between different pieces of information in the form of a diagram or flow chart. Typically, you will begin with one central idea (the core element of your paper) and then link all of the other elements to the centre using arrows and lines. No matter what your project is about, you will see that your research materials start to naturally fall into distinct subcategories. Once you have those in front of you, you can start to think about how the topics are related to each other, and which topics should be considered as primary or secondary. Mind-mapping programs allow you to rearrange the elements, which can help you see new connections and draw out your research questions and ideas. Figure 3.1 shows an example of a mind map created for a paper on social perception. You can see that there are lots of content possibilities in writing such a paper, but by setting out your thoughts graphically, you can start to see which ideas might connect together and which would be main topics or subtopics.

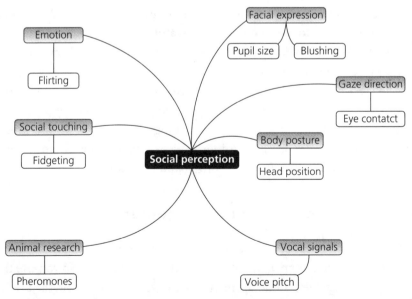

Figure 3.1 A sample mind map on social perception

Mind maps help you visualize multiple ways to organize the content of your paper.

Outlining Software

Once you have created a skeleton structure for your paper, the next step is to flesh that out with some of the information you have collected on the topic. The best way to do this is to create an outline that contains each of your ideas in a logical order. Putting your paper together in small steps like this is much less of a challenge than trying to write your whole paper at once. And you can reorganize as you go along. Outlining software can be a very useful tool for this step because you can begin with the headings you created in your mind map and then insert content for each section. If you decide that your original structure is not the best, then it is very easy to rearrange the sections.

An outlining program is simply a word-processing editor combined with a "tree" organizer that allows you to create a series of subject headings (or *nodes*). When you click on a node, anything you write in the edit box will be kept within that node. By using the hierarchical structure of the tree, you can move nodes around to make them into major or minor headings or to place them in different parts of your paper. Although there are a number of third-party outline programs available, if your needs are very simple you might consider the outliner that is built into Microsoft Word. Microsoft provides an online tutorial that gives you all of the information you need to create a document outline. If your project is large and you need a more sophisticated organizer, consider a program like ActionOutline (see Figure 3.2). This program is very simple to use and has many features to help you construct your documents. For example, by creating new tree nodes, you can keep your comments or research notes in a separate area, which gives you easy access to them while you're working, but you can easily take these out for the final version of your paper. In fact, you can write your whole paper in the outliner by entering your text into the edit boxes for each heading. Then, when you've finished developing your paper in the outliner, you can export the file to a regular word-processing program for final editing and proofing.

Reference and Citation Management

Proper documentation of sources is fundamental to any research paper. You should have a system to manage all of your references and to help you cite them correctly in your paper. A management system will help you avoid the problem of not having on hand all of the pertinent source information you will need to reference an article or study. At best, incomplete documentation can mean

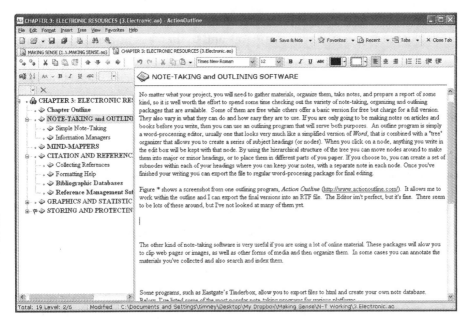

Figure 3.2 Note-taking and outlining software

This image shows our first draft of Chapter 3 laid out in ActionOutline software.

wasting your time with another trip to the library or the Internet to track down the information. At worst, it can mean that you don't have proper documentation for one of your sources when it comes time to turn your paper in.

Managing your documentation involves several steps:

1. identifying the source;
2. transcribing the citation accurately;
3. developing a list of references;
4. matching up the citations in your paper with the references in your reference section;
5. preparing a properly formatted reference list; and, if you know you are going to continue to do research in that area,
6. developing and maintaining a database of references.

There are two aspects to the documentation process. The first, *reference management*, means having a system to keep track of and retrieve the materials you have collected. If you only have a few references for a short paper, you can probably keep the materials you have collected in a couple of folders or binders and the sources will be easy to find. But, if you continue on to do an honours thesis or go to graduate school, you will start to accumulate a large number of references very quickly. So, you need a system that will allow you to file the references in a systematic way and to then keep track of where they are stored so they are easy to retrieve.

The second aspect is *citation management*, that is, a system that allows you to refer to your sources as you write your paper and then create a reference list when you're finished. This reference list will include the correct publication information for each document you have cited. Keeping an accurate list can be challenging if you have a major paper with a large number of references because you may add or remove citations as you are working on the paper. Any time you make a change like this, you will have to go back and cross-refer each citation with a reference in the final *Reference* list. When reading a published journal article, you may occasionally notice that a reference is missing or that a reference in the list has not been cited in the text.

Fortunately, a number of electronic tools are available that greatly simplify both the reference and the citation management processes, usually in the same software package. Some programs even allow you to store your source materials electronically, helping you keep your sources organized and conveniently available to you as you are writing.

Reference management

The simplest reference management system will allow you to enter the publication information into its database using a template for different forms of publication. If you organize the hard copies of the papers you've collected by keeping them in folders, you can include keywords with each reference so that you know where to look for them. Once the information is entered, you will be able to search for specific items or groups of similar papers. Most reference management systems are actually much more sophisticated than that, though. They will allow you to connect to the Internet to access bibliographic databases, such as PsycINFO, in order to search for references on your topic. Once you find the references you want, you can download the publication information automatically so that you don't have to enter it by hand.

In the past, your reference manager was simply a way to keep track of reference citations and to allow you to find the hard copy in your collection. Now, when so much material is available electronically, you can use your reference manager to keep virtual PDF copies of the papers you find. One of the best reference managers in this regard is Mendeley. It is simple to use, and it is free, although you can subscribe for a small fee to get additional storage space. You begin by downloading the program to your desktop, where you can use it to manage your references. But if you are online, you can gain access to your library of references from any computer by going to the Mendeley website.

If you have been using other reference management software, it is very easy to import the citations into Mendeley. The program also allows you to add any PDFs that you have on your computer and it will automatically extract the citation information if it can. Alternatively, you can organize your references into folders and search through the text using keywords. You can also highlight and annotate the articles, just as you would if you had paper copies. What distinguishes Mendeley from other reference managers is that it incorporates social networking. Using the "Group" feature in the program, you can work collaboratively with others and share your citations and documents.

Citation management

The other important aspect of the documentation process is citation management; that is, putting citations in your text and matching them up with your reference list. Most reference management programs, including Mendeley, can automate this process. When your paper is complete, you can use the program to create a reference list in your preferred format. This feature is particularly helpful if you use the same references for papers that require different reference formats; you only have to enter the references into the database once, and they will be there the next time you need them. If you revise your paper and take out or add references, your citation manager will automatically adjust your reference list.

Graphics and Statistics

If you have conducted an experiment for a lab or for a thesis and you have finished gathering all of your data, your next step will be to analyze those data and summarize them in a form suitable for a *Results* section. Typically, this will involve calculating descriptive statistics, such as means and standard deviations, for each of your conditions, and conducting inferential statistical tests, such as an *analysis of variance*. You may then want to present your data as tables or graphs. You should be aware of the software available to help you analyze your data and to prepare professional-looking graphics.

Graphics software

For many experiments, you may want to present your data in the form of graphs to illustrate relationships between variables. And even when you are writing a research essay, you may want to illustrate your points with a figure—a flow chart or a diagram perhaps. Although you could do this using graph paper or with freehand drawings, you should consider taking advantage of software with graphics capabilities. You will almost certainly have access to such programs on your own computer or through your school's network. Or, if you have more complex needs, you can use any of a number of specialized graphics programs to create both graphs and diagrams.

You can draw a simple graph using Microsoft Excel or a similar program. These programs can take the data you enter into a spreadsheet and convert the data to line graphs or bar charts, for example, depending on what you need. If you want to create a simple illustration, you can often do that using PowerPoint. Simply use the drawing tools to create the illustration you want, and then save the whole slide as a JPEG file that you can insert into any document. In Chapter 7, we will give you some advice on how to create attractive looking graphs and other kinds of figures.

Statistical packages

As a psychology student, you will have to take at least one statistics course. That course will teach you how to carry out the calculations necessary for particular statistical tests. When you are actually carrying out a research project, however, you are much more likely to use statistical software that will do those calculations for you. Many institutions make these packages available to their students. If you are lucky, you may also be taught how to use one of the standard statistical packages, such as SPSS, to run the tests for you. Even if you do not have access to statistical software at your institution, you have dozens of software options that will do the kinds of analysis you will need as an undergraduate student. Some of these you would need to purchase, but others are available as freeware. One note of caution: be sure that you understand the principles behind the analysis before you consider using a statistical package. If you choose the wrong analysis, or enter the data incorrectly, your output will be invalid.

Storing and Protecting Your Work

The days of handwriting all your notes and then typing up a single copy of a paper are long gone, so the "dog ate my homework" excuse for losing your work isn't convincing anymore. But, instructors now hear all kinds of stories about computer crashes, memory stick failures, or misplaced computer files.

Although some students may use these mishaps as an excuse for not having done their work, the possibility of data loss when you are working with a computer is very real. For that reason, it is essential that you take measures to avoid losing your data. It's so easy to put your trust into your hard drive. While most of the time you will never have a problem, it is a terrible feeling to discover that something you've been working on for a long time has disappeared irretrievably. Sometimes this can be annoying but relatively minor, for example if you somehow write over a file you had been working on, or a power outage causes you to lose several hours' worth of work. Or it could be catastrophic, like if you realize that the hard disk that contains not only your honours thesis draft but also all the research notes you've compiled is irrevocably damaged, or if your computer has been stolen. This doesn't happen often or to more than a few people, and you shouldn't let it happen to you.

You can guarantee that you won't run into this difficulty by having a systematic data backup and storage plan, and now there are lots of tools that make backup easy. In the following sections, we will describe a backup strategy you might follow and then tell you about some of the resources that are available to simplify the procedure.

Backing up your work

You should always keep a backup copy of your work. But have you worked out a backup plan to follow automatically every time you carry out a piece of research or write a paper? We've made some suggestions here, but the details are probably less important than the plan itself. Your backup plan should have two components: one to deal with storing material that will not change, or at least not change often, and one to take care of the files that you work on and change regularly. This second type includes drafts of your papers as you write them.

No matter how you do your backups, you should always follow these three principles:

1. **Backup often:** The longer you go between backups, the more work you will have to reconstruct if something goes wrong. Most of the programs you work with can create backup files automatically. The first thing you should do when you use any program is go to the Preferences or Options menu and set the automatic backup to occur every 5 or 10 minutes. That way, if the power goes off when you are working, you will lose very little.

Even if you are using the automatic backup option, you should make a full backup copy of your crucial work every day. You should keep this backup in a separate location from your working files.

2. **Make redundant backups:** It may seem like overkill to keep multiple backups of a piece of work, but it's a small investment for a large return in security. If you're just working on a 500-word essay, backing up your work is obviously not so important, but if you're a Ph.D. student writing your dissertation, you should have at least two independent backups of your work in different locations so that you always have a reasonably up-to-date version.

3. **Keep track of your versions:** If you are conscientious about making backups, then you also need to ensure that you know which versions are the most current. The same rule applies if you are working on multiple computers. For example, if you use a laptop at school and a desktop at home, you probably have a copy of your work on a USB drive that you use to transfer the files between your computers. But you might also have copies on the hard disk of each computer. Be sure that you have an annotation on your master file to indicate that it is the most current version. We will talk more about how you can avoid this kind of problem in the sections below.

Storage

While the kind of backup system you use is less important than having a routine for backing up and storing your work, we will take a few moments to look at some ways to make the storage process easier.

Media storage devices

Copying your work onto a USB flash drive is the simplest and quickest way to keep a backup copy. But do keep in mind that USB drives, especially the cheaper ones, can become corrupted. If your work is important, keep more than one copy. That will also protect you if you happen to lose your memory key.

If you use your institution's IT network, you will likely be given disk space on that system. If that is the case, then you can keep a copy of your work on the network drive. Because your IT department makes backups of all its systems every day, a copy kept there is very safe.

We mentioned the difference between work that gets updated regularly and research materials that may not change once they are collected. These latter materials should be archived. Keeping copies of these kinds of data on your school's network is a good way to ensure that they don't get lost.

Email

Email is an underused but powerful backup tool. Gmail is particularly useful because of its labelling and text-search capabilities. You might consider getting into the habit of emailing your files to yourself when you finish your work each day. If you use the same subject heading (with a note to indicate the version), those emails will be very easy to keep organized. This allows you to keep track of different versions and to return to them if you decide that you are not satisfied with the most recent writing you've done. If you are consistent in emailing your files to yourself, you can always search for an earlier version to work with.

Cloud computing

A fairly recent innovation to the storage and backup problem is known as *cloud computing*. In its full form, cloud computing is Internet-based computing where software applications and information are kept remotely on an Internet server, and individuals at multiple locations have access to the same resources. In some ways, it is like having access to Microsoft Office through your school's network, without needing an individual copy on your own computer. In this case, the network is the Internet.

If you simply want to protect your files and access them from multiple locations, you can use cloud computing for storage. Cloud computing has two important advantages. First, you can store all of your material in a single location but still have access to it whenever you are on the Internet. If you want to work on your paper in the library at school, or at your apartment off-campus, or when you go home for a weekend, you don't need to take all your files with you. If you've saved them on a cloud server, the most up-to-date version will be available to you anywhere. You should still keep a separate backup somewhere else, but you don't have to keep track of whether you brought home the most current version.

Cloud computing's other major advantage is its ability to update in real time. That is, if you are working on a joint project and several of you are making modifications to the same document, you do not have to keep sending a revised version to your partners and hope they haven't been working on the now-outdated version. Instead, each of you can work on the same file independently and it will update automatically in the cloud.

Numerous companies provide access to Internet storage. Often, they will offer a certain amount of storage space for free (which is usually enough for most student purposes) and then charge a fee if you want multiple gigabytes of space. There are several of these providers, but we will describe one typical one, Dropbox. When you sign up for Dropbox, you are provided with an initial 2 GB of storage space (although you can earn additional space by inviting friends to sign up). Once you install the program, a "My Dropbox" folder is created on your desktop. Any files you put into this folder are kept on your own computer so that you can work on them offline, and the files are updated on a central server whenever you are connected to the Internet. This allows you to access the most recent version from any computer. You can even get apps for your Android and iPhone that give you direct access to any files in your cloud.

You can also invite people to share any of your folders. This means that they have access to and can work on any files you place in the shared folder. And Dropbox provides protection if two of you are working on the same document simultaneously. It recognizes this and creates a "conflicted copy" version from which you can retrieve the changes and add them to the master copy.

Summary

Almost every technical aspect of writing a paper has been simplified by the introduction of electronic aids. None of these will help you to write better, but they do permit you to concentrate on the writing process itself, rather than having to spend a lot of time working on the mechanics of putting the paper together. In this chapter, we've provided you with examples of programs available for each of the major components of writing a paper. Many other packages do more or less the same thing; some are free, others you may have to purchase. But if you are likely to be writing or presenting materials in your chosen career, either in an academic setting or in the business world, you should consider all of these options.

Writing an Essay or Research Paper

4

> **Objectives**
>
> - planning your paper
> - finding your topic
> - choosing your sources
> - deciding on an approach
> - creating an outline
> - writing your paper
> - editing your paper

Introduction

Unlike students in the humanities, psychology students don't always get a lot of practice writing essays, especially in their early years of study. It is not unusual for students in upper-level psychology courses to admit that they have rarely had to write an essay in university. If you are one of the many students who dread writing an academic essay or research paper, you will find that following a few simple steps in planning and organizing will make the task easier—and the result better.

A scientific essay is usually a review of a body of literature, written to summarize what is known about a particular topic or to support a particular theory. The trick to writing a good scientific essay is to organize your material well and provide a good storyline. Try to avoid writing a paper that is nothing more than an annotated bibliography of what you have read: "Solway (2009) studied . . ."; "In 1973, Misener reported . . ."; "One interesting result (Singh & Rajaratnam, 2008) . . ."; and so on. Such papers are not only tedious to read but often difficult to follow. The solution to this problem is to begin with a well-organized outline and to stick to it when you actually write the paper.

The Planning Stage

Some students claim they can write essays without any planning at all. But even for these students, their writing is usually not as spontaneous as it seems: almost certainly they have thought or talked a good deal about the subject in advance and have come to the task with some ready-made ideas—they've just not put them on paper. More often, students who try to write a long essay without planning just end up frustrated. They may find it difficult to start; or they may get stuck in the middle and don't know how to finish; or they may drift off in the wrong direction (with or without realizing it). The result is something that has no organized structure. No matter how comfortable you feel about a topic, you will not be able to write an excellent paper unless you have a plan for how you are going to write it. If you leave things until the last minute, you will miss this crucial stage, and as a result, it will be quite obvious to your instructor that you have just thrown things together. Even if you are not good at spelling or grammar, a well-organized paper is easy to recognize.

Most good writers say that the planning stage is the most important part of the whole writing process. Certainly, the evidence shows that poor planning usually leads to disorganized writing. For the majority of student papers, the single greatest improvement would not be better research but better organization. This insistence on planning doesn't rule out exploratory writing, however. Many people find that the act of writing itself is the best way to generate ideas or overcome writer's block. The hard decisions about organization come after they've put something down on the page. Nevertheless, whether you organize before or after you begin to write, at some point you need to make a plan.

Every paper you write should go through the same stages:

1. finding a topic (or having a topic assigned);
2. looking for sources of information on the topic;
3. gathering and organizing the information you will need;
4. deciding on the approach you will take and refining your topic;
5. creating an outline that you can follow when you begin to write;
6. writing a first draft; and
7. editing and proofreading.

Finding Your Topic

Whether the subject you start with is one that has been assigned by your instructor or you have chosen it yourself, it is bound to be too broad for a single essay topic. You will have to analyze your subject in order to find a way of limiting it. The best way to do this is to ask questions about the topic.

Because every essay is different, there are no formal rules on the questions you should ask. However, questions about the *context* and the *components* of the situation you are discussing are relevant to almost every essay or research paper.

Context:
- What is the larger issue surrounding the topic?
- What tradition or school of thought is relevant to the topic?
- How is the topic similar to, and different from, related topics?

Components:
- Is the topic amenable to being broken up into manageable sections?
- Can these main categories be subdivided further?

When you ask about the *context*, you are trying to develop a conceptual framework into which you might fit the whole essay. So, if you are writing an essay on a topic relating to mental illness, one of the first things to ask is where your topic will fit with respect to the various theories about causes and treatment. Then you can decide how to approach the topic.

When you ask about *components* and how the topic might be broken down into different sections, you are forcing yourself to consider what the structure of your paper might eventually be. This should start you thinking about how you will organize your essay. Suppose, for example, that your assignment is to write about the localization of function in the brain—that is, which parts of the brain are responsible for different kinds of behaviour. You may decide that the main components of this topic are: (1) the historical origins of nineteenth-century phrenology; (2) the contributions gained from the study of brain-injured patients; (3) the anatomical and physiological brain-mapping experiments that identified the function of particular brain centres; and (4) the recent imaging techniques that allow researchers to study ongoing brain activity while a subject engages in specific tasks. You could write an entire essay about each one of these components. Once you have broken down the topic in this way, however, you can decide whether to write a brief overview of each of the components, or to examine the way in which the development of technology within these component areas led to current advances, or to break down one of the components further and discuss its different aspects in greater detail.

Choosing your own topic

Although at times your instructor will assign you a topic to write about or give you a specific question to answer, on other occasions your instructor will not restrict you at all. You will be limited only by the subject matter covered in the course. In such cases, it is important to select a topic that you can deal with comfortably. At the same time, remember that the purpose of writing a paper is to learn more about a topic, so you shouldn't be overly familiar with the one you pick. Here are some guidelines for choosing a suitable topic:

- **Choose a topic that interests you.** You won't be able to work up much enthusiasm for reading or writing about a topic if it doesn't interest you, and your lack of enthusiasm is likely to be reflected in the quality of your work. You will find it easier to spend time and energy working on a topic that interests you, and you will do a better job as a result.
- **Choose a topic that has sufficient material readily available.** However fascinating a topic may be, you won't get far if you aren't able to access the most important books or journals in that subject area.
- **Don't choose a topic that is too difficult.** Although this may seem obvious, students are sometimes drawn to topics that look interesting but turn out to be more technical than they had anticipated. If you decide to write a paper that requires detailed knowledge of a specific field—for instance, neurophysiology or statistics—be sure you have sufficient background knowledge, or you will not understand the literature.
- **Limit your topic to something manageable.** Beware of subject areas that are very broad: you don't want to put yourself in the position of having to deal with too much material. A cursory review of a large subject may appear thin and inadequate to a reader. If you do choose an area with a very large body of literature, limit your scope and be sure to indicate in your introduction that this is your intention.
- **Check with your instructor.** If you have any doubts about whether the topic you have selected is appropriate for the course, check with your instructor.

Once you decide which general topic to write about, look for a distinct subtopic that you can manage in the time and space available to you. For example, under the general topic of "neural plasticity" you would have an enormous number of potential paper topics. To narrow the field, you might begin by drawing a tree diagram of some of these possibilities. Obviously, you have many more options than this, and some topic areas may overlap, but such a diagram can help you narrow your choices down to a number you can handle comfortably. An alternative is to use the mind-mapping software that we described in Chapter 3.

Dealing with an assigned topic

Even if your essay topic is supplied by your instructor, you still need to analyze it carefully. Try underlining key words to make sure that you don't overlook anything that is asked for. Distinguish the main theme of your paper from the subordinate ones. A common error in dealing with prescribed topics is to emphasize one portion while neglecting others. Give each part its proper due and make sure that you follow all of the instructions; if you don't, you may receive a low grade, no matter how good your writing is. For example, *discussing* a subject is not the same as *evaluating* or *tracing* it. Here are some of the most common instructions you'll be given:

outline	state simply, without much development of each point (unless asked).
trace	review by looking back: examine the stages or steps in a process or the causes of an occurrence.
explain	show how or why something happens.
discuss	examine or analyze in an orderly way. This instruction allows you considerable freedom, as long as you take into account contrary evidence or ideas.
compare	examine differences as well as similarities (see pages 69–70 for a discussion of comparisons).
evaluate	analyze strengths and weaknesses to arrive at an overall assessment of worth.

These and other verbs tell you how to approach your topic; be sure that you know what they mean, and follow them carefully.

Choosing Your Sources

We described how to go about obtaining materials relevant to your topic in Chapter 2. The next step is selecting which references you want to read. If you are writing a review paper, or if you are preparing an introduction to an honours thesis, then your instructor will almost certainly expect your paper to be based on primary sources. But before you go to those sources, you may want to get an overview of the work that has been done on a topic. To gain an overview, you should look at secondary sources, such as book chapters and review articles. However, in disciplines such as English or philosophy, where students might be asked to provide an interpretation of what they have read, instructors may discourage the use of secondary sources. Students may be less willing to develop their own ideas if they rely too heavily on commentaries written by major figures in a field. In psychology, however, your first task is to find out what is known about a particular topic. Therefore, secondary sources can give you a quick overview of your topic. In fact, it is usually a good idea to read recent literature reviews on the topic you have chosen so that you can learn about the most recent work in your area.

When you do write up your own paper, you may want to refer the reader to these reviews to show that you are aware of the literature, but primary sources should be the basis for your own review. You shouldn't rely too heavily on secondary sources because literature reviews may be biased. If an author is reviewing the literature to find support for his or her own point of view, he or she may emphasize one set of findings but completely ignore another. In such a case, you should be prepared to evaluate whether the author's interpretation of the primary source is the same as your own. Remember that although secondary sources are an important part of background research, they can never substitute for your own active reading and analysis of the primary material.

When you do read primary sources, begin by skimming them in order to get an idea of their content. Don't start by reading every article from beginning to end. Read the introductory sections or abstracts of several papers to get a sense of the questions the authors are asking. Once you have an overview, it will be easier to formulate your own questions for a more analytic second reading. *You will have to work through the material carefully a second time.* An initial skim followed by a focused second reading will give you a much more thorough understanding of the material than trying to digest it all at once.

Deciding on an Approach

If your assignment is simply to write an essay on a particular topic, then it is up to you to decide how you will approach it. Whatever approach you take, you must make sure that the reader understands what you are trying to achieve in your paper. You should have a central, controlling idea that will lead the reader through the paper so that he or she will never have to ask, "What is the point that this paper is trying to make?"

You can take one of two general approaches. The first is to organize your essay around a *theme*, which will bind your ideas and information together. This approach is particularly useful for reviewing the literature on a particular subject, discussing recent findings in a particular area, or exploring research trends in a certain discipline. A good strategy for this kind of approach is to write a single-phrase statement of your theme to serve as an anchor before you begin writing—for example, "factors that determine performance on intelligence tests" or "the development of speech perception in infants." This phrase may become the title of your final paper. Once you have defined your topic, you can go on to discuss or explain it in whichever way you choose. With this type of approach, you are not necessarily arguing a point of view but rather providing the reader with a summary of your understanding of a subject or the available literature on it.

An alternative approach is known as the *argumentative form*, in which you develop and defend a *thesis*. It is usually easier to organize this type of essay, and it often produces more forceful writing. This approach certainly makes for a more interesting essay, if it is done well. For example, if you were writing on intelligence, you might take the position that cultural bias invalidates the results of many intelligence tests. Or, you could argue that intellectual ability is inherited and that IQ tests are the most valid measurements we have. It doesn't really matter what position you take as long as you make a convincing case for it. Your instructor may not agree with you, but if you provide a well-thought-out argument, you should get credit for it. A note of caution, however: "argumentative" in this context refers to the strategy of presenting reasoned arguments, not of being aggressive or dismissive of your sources. Good writing is dignified, not belligerent or abusive.

Once you have decided upon one of these two approaches, the next step is to select the single theme or thesis that will serve as the focal point around which you will organize your material. Although you may start with a particular *working thesis*, it doesn't have to be the final one; sometimes you will change your opinion as you work your way through the literature. A working thesis simply serves as a way to hold together your information and ideas as you organize your research materials.

At some point in the writing process, you will probably want to make your working thesis into an explicit statement that can appear in your introduction. A working thesis will help you define your intentions, make your research more selective, and focus your essay. Therefore, you should take time to develop your working thesis properly. Use a complete sentence to express it, and make sure that it is limited, unified, and exact (McCrimmon, 1976).

Make it limited

A limited thesis is narrow enough to be examined thoroughly in the space you have available. Suppose, for example, that your general subject is sexuality and adolescence. Such a subject is much too broad to be dealt with in an essay of two or three thousand words; you must limit it in some way and create a line of argument for which you can provide adequate supporting evidence. For example, you might want to discuss factors that influence contraceptive use, or the role of TV and movies in setting models for sexual behaviour and attitudes.

Make it unified

To be unified, your thesis must have one controlling idea. Beware of the double-headed thesis: "Adolescent sexual attitudes in the 1960s were permissive because children were rebelling against their conservative parents, but now their attitudes are more conservative because of concerns about sexually transmitted diseases." What is the controlling idea here? Is it parent–child relationships or the way that external threats can influence behaviour? It is possible to have two or more related ideas within a thesis but only if one of them is clearly in control, with all the other ideas subordinate to it. For example, "Although concern over the spread of AIDS resulted in sexual conservatism among adolescents in the 1990s, experts fear this caution is giving way to a growing sense of fatalism and the abandonment of 'safe sex' practices in the early 2000s."

Make it exact

It is important, especially when you are defending a position, to avoid vague terms such as *interesting* and *significant*, as in "Freud's distinction between the ego and the superego was a significant contribution to the study of neuroses." Was this distinction a positive contribution or was it one that slowed progress in this field because it became such a widely accepted model of mental life? Remember to make your thesis as specific as possible in order to focus your essay. Don't just present an assertion: give the main reasons for it. Instead of saying, "Freud's psychoanalytic theory impeded the scientific study of mental illness," add something like, "because it contained logical circular arguments that could not be tested easily through experiments." If you are concerned that these details make your thesis sound awkward, don't worry: a working thesis is only a planning device—something to guide the organization of your ideas. You can change the wording of it in your final essay.

Creating an Outline

In Chapter 3, we described software for developing outlines. Here, we will provide you with some practical guidelines on how to create an outline that will form the basis for your essay.

As we mentioned earlier, a paper that you write without any planning will simply not be as good as one for which you first spend some time organizing and constructing an outline. Although it may feel as though you are not making much progress when you are "only" working on an outline, this can be the most effective use of your time. If you can organize all of your thoughts and develop them into a series of headings and subheadings, you may not have to do much more than fill in the blanks when the time comes to do the actual writing. Having an outline also allows you to switch between sections with ease if you get bogged down on one particular topic or if you realize you can't go further on a section without more research.

If you use outlining software, you can set up your outline as a series of headings and subheadings. You can start by listing the main topics you are going to discuss, which will give you a sense of the overall structure of your paper. Then, you can insert subheadings under each topic as you do more research. Because these subheadings are nested under a main heading, you can also make sure that you have constructed a logical sequence within each section. Once you have the headings, you can begin to fill in the body text under each one. The advantage of this approach is that your work is broken up into a series of manageable chunks, and you can add to each section as you find and build your reference list. Also, it means that you don't have to work from beginning to end. If you are someone who struggles with opening paragraphs, you don't have to worry about that; you can develop the paper piecemeal and leave the toughest parts until you're ready. Of course, you will need to read through the paper carefully at the end of the process to make sure the transitions between sections are smooth. If, as you develop your themes and learn more about your subject, you realize that some material is in the wrong place, it is easy to move the content under a single subheading to another section of the paper.

The essentials of an outline

In its simplest form, an outline is just a list of the topics that you will cover in your essay. But you can make it much more than that. By successively refining your outline, you can get to the point where the actual writing of your paper becomes just a matter of filling in the blanks. A useful strategy is to begin the outline with single keywords that you can gradually expand into topics and then subtopics. When you first start this process, you may have a lot of ideas about the different things you want to talk about. Jot them down. At first, they don't have to be in any particular sequence, and you don't need to think about their relative importance, that is, what will be a large topic and merit a separate section and what will be a small subsection that might not even need a heading. Once you have an idea of the topics you might want to cover, you can move on to the next stage—constructing the outline.

Think of this process as analogous to building a house. You start off by creating a firm foundation (your research). Next, you construct a floor and build the wall that will support the rest of the house (thesis and supporting evidence). You put the roof on to protect the house from the elements and to hold the walls together (overall themes and conclusion). After that, you can work on the electrical, plumbing, and decorative elements (graphs, charts, diagrams, appendices, and so forth). The way that you construct the frame is going to determine what the house will look like and how strong it will be, so this is where you need to concentrate your major effort. You can always change the fittings at a later time, but if you don't have a good base structure, you won't have a strong building.

The frame that supports your essay is its logical structure. When you start to think about what you are going to write, you should also be thinking about how everything will come together. Although there is a tendency to see scientific writing as somehow different from writing in the arts and humanities, all writing is, in fact, about telling a story. You have written a good paper on a complex topic if the reader ends up thinking "that makes a lot of sense" or "that seems obvious to me, even though I hadn't thought of it before." To do that, you need to consider three things:

1. What is my goal in writing the paper, and how will my intended reader describe what my paper has accomplished?
2. What topics do I need to cover to achieve this goal?
3. How do I move from one topic to the next so that I can tell a story?

Once you have decided on your goal, your outline gives you a way to deal with items 2 and 3.

Let's say you have been assigned to write a 1,000-word paper in a course on the psychology of deafness. Your instructor has left the precise topic open but has suggested that the broad theme should be "the deaf person in society." You have a huge range of options, and you could look at the subject from many different perspectives. You could take a medical approach by looking at deafness as a physical impairment. Or, you could examine language learning in deaf children and how that affects their social development. You could even take a historical approach by exploring how views about deafness have changed over time. Each one of these would require you to draw from different literature and probably look at research from several disciplines. Your problem, then, is not going to be finding material but deciding what to include and what to leave out. Further, you will find that there are many controversial issues in the study of deafness. You may decide to advocate for a particular position, and that standpoint will influence how you treat the material you collect.

First, you should go to the library or simply Google "deafness." You will see that deafness is multi-faceted; the first few Google hits are about hearing impairment, causes of deafness, deaf culture, and sign language—any one of these subjects could be a paper topic in itself. From here, you should begin to make a list of potential topic headings. These may be very different from your final version, but they will give you a sense of which topics and subtopics are related. These headings should also give you a more manageable amount of material to work with. Your list of topics might look something like this:

Deafness Topics

What is deafness?	Cochlear implants
How do you measure hearing loss?	Sign language
Causes of deafness	Oral vs. manual communication
Kinds of deafness	Scholastic achievement
Deaf vs. hearing impaired	Speech pathology
Pre-lingual/post-lingual deafness	Gallaudet University
History of deafness	Prejudice
Alexander Graham Bell	Deaf and dumb
Deaf education	Language learning
Big "D," little "d" deafness	Noise and deafness
Deafness as a disability	Deaf families
How do you define cultural difference?	Incidence and prevalence of deafness

This is a long list, but it shows you the range of topics you could cover. However, there's no common thread that you can use to tell a story, so next you should think about how to take the paper beyond a simple recitation of facts. Perhaps you begin by considering what it means to be deaf. You decide that being deaf must be like having the volume control in your ears turned down. So, you think, hearing impairment could be treated by finding a way to "turn up the volume." You know about hearing aids, but you come across a few references on cochlear implants, devices that are surgically inserted into the inner ear to directly stimulate the auditory nerve. On the face of it, this looks like an excellent way to help deaf people hear, but the story is more complicated than that. At the Canadian Association of the Deaf's website (2014), you read the following statement in their section on cochlear implants: "The argument commonly made by proponents of auditory-verbal therapy and cochlear implants, that learning Sign language inhibits hearing and speech development in deaf children, is contrary to everything that is known about language acquisition and bilingual development."

Through your research, you realize that deafness is a controversial topic and that you can write a paper that explores deafness as a medical condition versus a cultural difference. Now, at last, you can begin to build the outline of your essay. The assigned length of the essay will determine what topics you can cover and in how much detail. Now you can reorganize your initial list to see what is essential and what can be left out. Your next outline will be more focused.

Using outlining software, as previously discussed, you can create a preliminary outline that might look like this:

Is Deafness a Disease or a Cultural Difference?

Introduction

Technical Background
- Hearing impairment and deafness
- How do you measure hearing loss?

Consequences of Hearing Loss
- Communication difficulties
- Language development

Fundamental Questions—The Oral/Manual Debate
- Teach speech—integrate children into the hearing world
- Teach to communicate by any means

History of Deaf Education
- Early approaches—(Ponce de León?)
- Nineteenth century—Alexander Graham Bell
- Early twentieth century—oral ascendancy
- Late twentieth century—the rise of sign language

Big "D" / Little "d" Deafness
- Sign as an "ethnic" language
- The revolt against the oral tradition

The Philosophical Dilemma
- Speech or communication
- Medical vs. cultural model
- Cochlear implants

Conclusion
- Deafness is far more complex than simple hearing loss
- Need to consider a deaf person in the context of her/his social environment

You might have noticed that this outline is extremely ambitious for a short paper. It will need to be trimmed quite substantially. However, it is better to start out with too much material rather than too little. It is much easier to trim content than it is to try to build on to something that is already self-contained. At the end of this chapter, we will show you the final version of the essay that resulted from this preliminary outline.

To summarize the outlining stage, here are some of the general principles that you should follow in developing your paper:

- **Arrange your outline according to themes.** In the example above, there are three main themes: (1) What is the nature of deafness? (2) What are the consequences of being deaf for an individual, and how can the problems that arise be alleviated? and (3) How have these approaches developed into a philosophy of education? You could make your first section quite short, giving only enough information for the reader to understand that hearing loss is much more than a loss of the ability to hear sounds. Later sections could discuss the controversy associated with various approaches to deaf education. Arranging your material in a logical sequence of themes will produce a much more readable essay than, say, simply describing how deaf children are educated.

- **Use headings and subheadings to organize your material.** Begin with the broadest category, and then move down to the subtopics. You can follow APA formatting for different levels of heading to help you organize this material in your final write up (for more on APA, see Chapter 10). You can do this most efficiently with an outlining program.

- **Categorize according to importance.** Make sure that you arrange your headings and subheadings in a way that reflects the importance of the topics in your paper. So, a main heading could refer to the general topic of deaf education, with subheadings on the oral approach and on the use of sign language.

- **Check lines of connection.** Make sure that each of the main sections is directly linked to the central thesis or theme, and then check that each subsection is directly linked to the main section under which it falls.

- **Be consistent.** In arranging your points, be consistent. You may choose to move from the most important point in each section to the least important or vice versa, as long as you follow the same order in every section.

- **Use parallel wording.** Phrasing each element in a similar way makes it easier for the reader to follow your train of thought. For example, each bullet point in this list begins with a similarly phrased sentence telling you what you should do.

- **Be logical.** In addition to checking for lines of connection and organizational consistency, make sure that the overall development of your work is logical. Does each heading, idea, set of data, or discussion flow into the next, leading the reader through your material in the most logical manner?

A final word

Be prepared to change your outline at any time in the writing process. Your initial outline is not meant to constrain your thinking but to relieve anxiety about where you're heading. A careful outline prevents frustration and dead ends—that "I'm stuck, and where can I go from here?" feeling. But since the very act of writing will usually generate new ideas, you should be ready to modify your original plan. For example, you might find after you've written several sections that the original proposed order no longer flows naturally because you now want to use a concept in a later section that you haven't introduced in an earlier section. So, you may decide on a different, better topic order after you have written some of the sections. You should never think of your outline as being unchangeable, especially when cut and paste functions are available. Your outline helps you organize your thinking, and your thinking may change once you begin to write your paper.

The Writing Stage

Writing the first draft

Most writers find it easier to compose the first draft of an essay as quickly as possible and do revisions later, rather than try to produce a polished final version on the first pass. This is probably the best way to proceed because you will almost certainly want to make changes after you've read over the first draft. It is also more satisfying to see that you have something written on all of your sections so that there is "only" editing to do. But no matter how you begin, you shouldn't expect the first draft to be the final copy. Skilled writers know that revising is a necessary part of the writing process and that the care taken with revisions makes the difference between a mediocre essay and a good one.

As we mentioned, you don't need to write your sections in the order in which they will appear in your final draft. In fact, many students find that the *Introduction* is the hardest part to write. If you face that first blank page with a growing sense of unease, try leaving the *Introduction* section until later. Look instead at your outline to see which section you feel you can make a start on. Don't be tempted to procrastinate. Instead of surfing the Web or running out for a snack, try to get something written. Don't worry too much about grammar or wording: at this stage, the object is to put something down on paper or into your computer.

Developing your ideas: Some common patterns

The way you develop your ideas will depend on your topic, and topics can vary enormously. Even so, most research papers follow one of a few basic organizational patterns. Here are some common patterns, along with tips for using them effectively.

Defining

Sometimes a whole paper is an extended definition or description, explaining the meaning of a concept that is complicated, controversial, or simply important to your field of study: for example, the *superego* in psychoanalytic writings; the relative roles of genetic and experiential factors in child development; or the modular organization of the visual system. Rather than make your entire paper an extended definition, you may decide to begin your paper by defining a key term and then shift to a different organizational structure. In either case, make your definition exact; it should be broad enough to include all the things that belong in that category but narrow enough to exclude things that don't belong. A good definition builds a kind of verbal fence around a word, bringing together all the members of the class and cutting off all outsiders.

For any discussion of a term that goes beyond a bare definition, you should give concrete examples. Depending on the topic of your paper, these could vary in length from one or two sentences to several paragraphs or even pages. If you were defining the superego, for instance, you would probably want to discuss at some length the theories of leading psychoanalysts.

In an extended definition, it's also useful to point out the differences between the term you are working with and other terms that are connected or perhaps confused with it. For instance, if you were discussing the concept of the superego, you would have to bring in the related concepts of ego and id.

Classifying

Classifying means dividing something into separate parts according to some principle of selection. There are many ways to divide a topic into separate sections. If you are describing the effects of various forms of brain damage, for example, you could classify these effects according to the location of the damage *or* the kinds of symptoms they produce. Or, if you are examining the stages of infant development, you could classify the stages in terms of perceptual, social, personality, and so on. If you are organizing your essay by a system of classification, remember the following guidelines:

- **All members of a class must be accounted for.** If any are left over, you need to alter some categories or add more.
- **Categories can be divided into subcategories.** You should consider using subcategories if there are significant differences within a category. For instance, if you were classifying the effects of brain damage according to the site of the lesion, you might want to create subcategories for memory deficits, language problems, perceptual difficulties, and so on.

- **Any list of subcategories should contain at least two items.** In the example above, your main category would be "the site of the lesion," but you wouldn't need to create a subcategory list if you were only going to talk about memory deficits for one site and perceptual difficulties for another.

Explaining a process

This kind of organization shows how something works or has worked, such as the photochemical reactions of the eye, or the way in which children learn a second language. Remember to be systematic when breaking down the process into a series of steps. While the organizational structure you choose will vary depending on the topic, typically it will be sequential, so you should make sure that you lay out the steps in a way that is accurate and easy to follow.

Tracing causes and effects

When you trace causes and effects, you are explaining a process, emphasizing how certain events have led to or resulted from other events. You usually use this organizational scheme when you want to explain why something happened. Showing how certain events have led to or resulted from others is a complex task, and you must be careful not to oversimplify a cause-and-effect relationship. If you are tracing causes, distinguish between a *direct cause*, that is, one that directly influenced the outcome, and a *contributing cause*, which may have had an indirect effect. For example, if you are writing about psychological factors related to teenage pregnancy, individual personality characteristics may be the most important factor in determining the behaviours, but variables like socio-economic status or family religious affiliation may also play a role.

Comparing

Many successful essays are based on comparisons. Even if it is not specifically part of your assignment, by choosing a limited number of items to compare—theories, neural mechanisms, or factors that might influence behaviour, for example—you can create a clear focus for your paper. Just be sure that you deal with differences as well as similarities.

When you prepare your outline for this kind of paper, you will have to decide how best to set up your comparisons. Perhaps the easiest way of comparing two subjects is to discuss the first subject in the comparison thoroughly and then move on to the second. This is not always the best approach, however, because you may end up with something that reads like two separate essays slapped together.

A more effective approach is to integrate the two subjects, first in your introduction (by placing both in a single context) and again in your conclusion, where you should bring together the important points you have made about each. When discussing the second subject, you should always refer back to your discussion of your first subject (e.g., "Unlike honey bees, bumble bees have a much looser social organization. . . ."). This method may be the wisest choice if your subjects seem so different that they would not fit logically into common categories, that is, if the points you are making about X are of a different nature from the points you are making about Y.

If you can find similar criteria or categories for discussing both subjects, however, it is most effective to make all of your comparisons within one category before moving on to the next. This way, you can discuss both subjects category by category. Because this kind of comparison is more tightly integrated, it is easier for the reader to see the similarities and differences between the subjects. As a result, the essay is likely to be more forceful.

Introductions

The beginning of a research paper has a dual purpose: to introduce your topic and the way you intend to approach it, and to whet your reader's appetite for what you have to say. One effective way of introducing a topic is to place it in a context, that is, to supply a kind of backdrop that will put it in perspective. The idea is to step back a little and discuss the wider area into which your topic fits, and then gradually narrow your focus to your specific subject. Baker and Gamache (1998) call this the *funnel approach*, where you make a general statement at the beginning of your essay and then narrow it down to the particular issue that you explain and develop in the body of your essay. For example, suppose your topic is the specific action of certain neurotoxins on the nervous system. You might begin with a general discussion of the effects of some naturally occurring neurotoxins, such as the one produced by the puffer fish (also known as fugu, which is served in many Japanese restaurants). You would then narrow the focus of your discussion to the specific topic you plan to discuss, namely the effects of neurotoxins on the nervous system. The funnel opening is applicable to almost any kind of paper.

You should aim to catch your reader's interest right from the start. You know from your own reading how a dull beginning can put you off a book or an article. The fact that your grader has to read on anyway makes no difference. If a reader has to get through thirty or forty similar essays, it's all the more important for yours to stand out. However, it's also important that your lead-in relates to your topic: never sacrifice relevance for catchiness. Finally, whether your introduction is one paragraph or several, make sure that by the end of it, your reader knows exactly what the purpose of your essay is and how you intend to accomplish it.

Conclusions

Endings can be painful—sometimes as much for the reader as for the writer. Too often, the feeling that one ought to say something profound and memorable produces either a pompous or a meaningless ending. You know the sort of thing:

> This is not to say that the research of the last decade has been in vain, to the contrary, we have learned a tremendous amount. Critical and conflicting evidence does tell us, however, that we still have a long way to go before we can deal in absolutes.

Even if you ignore the grammatical difficulties in this example, it easy to see that these two sentences could easily have been omitted without affecting the substance of the paper. Experienced editors say that many articles and essays would be better without their final paragraphs: in other words, when you have finished saying what you want to say, usually the best thing to do is stop. This advice may work for short papers, where you need to keep the central point firmly in the foreground and don't need to remind the reader of it. However, for longer pieces, where you have developed a number of ideas or a complex line of argument, you should provide a sense of closure. Readers welcome an ending that helps tie the ideas together so that they don't feel as though they've been left dangling. And since the final impression is often the most lasting, it's in your interest to finish strongly. Simply restating your thesis or summarizing what you have already said isn't forceful enough. Here are some of the alternatives.

The inverse funnel

The simplest conclusion is one that restates the thesis in different words and then discusses its implications. Baker and Gamache (1998) call this the *inverse funnel approach.* In this type of conclusion, the specific arguments made in the body of the essay widen to a more inclusive final statement. The danger in moving to a wider perspective is that you may try to embrace too much. When a conclusion expands too far, it tends to lose focus, as in the example above. It's always better to discuss specific implications than to trail off with vague generalities. So, in the conclusion to your paper on neurotoxins, you would begin with a summary of the effects of neurotoxins on the nervous system, followed by a brief comment on the advisability of eating fugu fish as a delicacy.

The full circle

If you began your essay by relating an anecdote, citing some unusual fact, or raising a rhetorical question, then you can complete the circle by referring to it again in your conclusion. At this point, you can relate it to some of the insights revealed in the body of the essay. This technique provides a nice sense of closure for the reader.

The stylistic flourish

Some of the most successful conclusions end on a strong stylistic note. Try varying your sentence structure to make the conclusion stand out from the rest of the text. If most of your sentences have been long and complex, make the last few short and emphatic. Be careful not to overdo it, though. If you're not comfortable modifying your style, you might be better off playing it safe and sticking with a method that's more suited to your writing style.

The Editing Stage

Often the best writer in a class is not the one who can dash off a fluent first draft but the one who is the best editor. To edit your work well, you need to see it as the reader will, and to do that, you have to distinguish between what you meant to say and what you have actually put on the page. For this reason, it's a good idea to leave yourself some time between drafts so that when you begin to edit you will be looking at the writing afresh, rather than reviewing it from memory. This is the time to go to a movie or do something that will take your mind off your work. Without this distancing period, you can become so involved in your paper that it's hard to see it objectively.

Editing doesn't mean simply checking your work for errors in grammar or spelling. It means looking at the piece as a whole to see if the ideas are *well organized*, *well documented*, and *well expressed*. It may mean making changes to the structure of your essay by adding or deleting paragraphs or sentences, and moving others around. Experienced writers may be able to check several aspects of their work at the same time, but if you are inexperienced or in doubt about your writing, it's best to look at the organization of the ideas before you tackle sentence structure, diction, style, and documentation. As you read through your paper, ask yourself whether it flows properly: is the rhythm comfortable, or do some passages slow you down because they're awkwardly constructed? Such problems can often be corrected just by shuffling the word order a little.

When taking on the role of your reader in the editing stage, keep asking yourself whether your explanations are sufficiently clear. Would they make sense to a reader who is less familiar with the material than you? Are there places where you have assumed the reader would know what you're referring to when you make a statement? Remember that you should think of your reader as someone who is intelligent and educated but who does not necessarily share your level of expertise in the subject you are discussing.

The next section lays out two checklists of questions to ask yourself as you begin editing. These are not all-inclusive but focus instead on the first steps: preparing to write your paper and then examining the organization of your work. Because you probably won't want to check through your work separately for each question, you can group some together and overlook others, depending on your own strengths and weaknesses as a writer.

Checklists

As you prepare for and write your essays, checklists can be helpful tools. Below are some pre-writing and post-writing questions that you should ask yourself as a guide during the writing process. Please refer to the sample research essay at the end of this chapter to see how to employ these strategies.

A pre-writing checklist

- ☐ Have I given myself enough time to prepare this paper, and have I made a timetable to work through each of the preparation stages?
- ☐ Do I have a clear understanding of what is being asked for this paper?
- ☐ Have I identified the main question or issue that I will address?
- ☐ Have I decided on the approach I will take (e.g., explain, compare, evaluate)?
- ☐ Have I found enough material to do some preliminary research?
- ☐ In my preliminary research, have I identified key themes, components, and ideas to serve as main points for my outline?
- ☐ Have I established a thesis statement to serve as a controlling idea for the essay?
- ☐ Is my thesis restricted enough? Is it unified and precise?

A post-writing checklist

- ☐ Is my title concise and informative?
- ☐ Are the purpose and approach of this essay evident from the beginning?
- ☐ Are all sections of the paper relevant to the topic?
- ☐ Is the organization logical?
- ☐ Will the subheadings be meaningful to the reader? Do they clearly identify the various sections of the paper?
- ☐ Do the paragraph divisions give coherence to my ideas? Have I used them to keep similar ideas together and signal movement from one idea to another?
- ☐ Do any parts of the paper seem disjointed? Should I add more transitional words or logical indicators to make the sequence of ideas easier to follow?
- ☐ Do my transitional words really link two ideas with a logical connection or are they just filling in space?
- ☐ Are the ideas sufficiently developed? Is there enough evidence, explanation, and illustration?
- ☐ Would an educated person who hasn't read the primary material understand everything I'm saying? Should I clarify some parts or add any explanatory material?
- ☐ In presenting my argument, do I take into account opposing arguments or evidence?
- ☐ Have I been accurate and fair in my representation of what my sources say?
- ☐ Have I cited all the sources I used? Is the style of in-text citations consistent and appropriate?
- ☐ Do my illustrations and figures add anything to the paper? Do they present information in the clearest, most effective way? Have I described or discussed each one clearly and completely?
- ☐ Have I checked the illustrations and figures for spelling and content? Have I cited their sources?
- ☐ Are the tables complete and correct, with the sources noted?
- ☐ Do my conclusions accurately reflect my argument in the body of the work?
- ☐ Is my reference list accurate and complete? Is it in the correct format?
- ☐ Have I backed up my work, both electronically and as a hard (paper) copy?

Another approach would be to devise your own checklist based on comments you have received on previous assignments. This is particularly useful when you move from the overview of your paper to the close focus on sentence structure, diction, punctuation, spelling, and style. If you have a particular area of weakness—for example, irrelevant evidence, faulty logic, or run-on sentences—you should give it special attention. Keeping a personal checklist will save you from making the same mistakes repeatedly.

Summary

Writing is an individual activity, and each of us has a way of working that produces the best results for us. However, many students, especially in psychology or in other sciences, have not been exposed to the basics of writing. What most students in the arts and humanities take for granted may be quite new for a psychology student who has not taken a writing course. We hope the tools we have given you will help you get started on any writing project.

References

Baker, S., & Gamache, L. B. (1998). *The Canadian practical stylist* (4th ed.). Don Mills, ON: Addison-Wesley.

Canadian Association of the Deaf. (2014). Cochlear implants [Online statement]. Retrieved from http://www.cad.ca/cochlear_implants%20.php

McCrimmon, J. (1976). *Writing with a purpose* (6th ed.). Boston, MA: Houghton Mifflin.

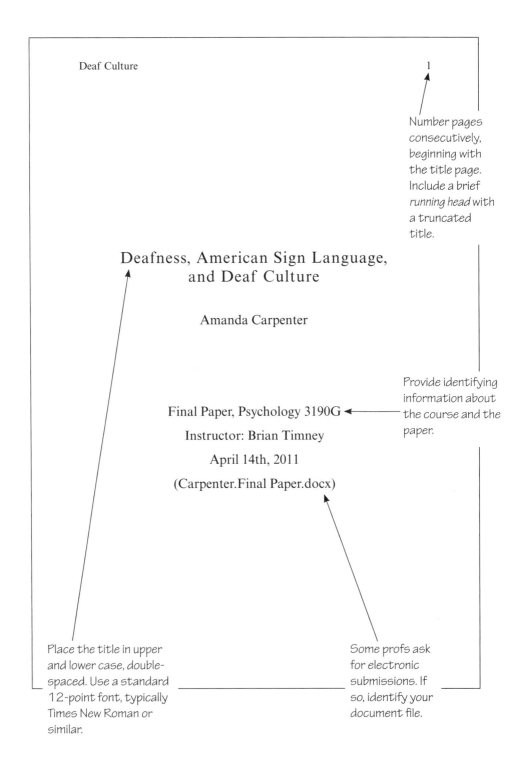

Deaf Culture   1

Number pages consecutively, beginning with the title page. Include a brief *running head* with a truncated title.

Deafness, American Sign Language, and Deaf Culture

Amanda Carpenter

Final Paper, Psychology 3190G ◄— Provide identifying information about the course and the paper.

Instructor: Brian Timney

April 14th, 2011

(Carpenter.Final Paper.docx)

Place the title in upper and lower case, double-spaced. Use a standard 12-point font, typically Times New Roman or similar.

Some profs ask for electronic submissions. If so, identify your document file.

The introductory paragraphs
should set the context for the
rest of the essay.

2

Deaf Culture

Deafness, American Sign Language, and Deaf Culture ← The
essay
begins
on a new
page and
repeats
the title.

Most of us who live in a hearing world have a concept of
hearing impairment and deafness that is almost certainly incorrect.
We tend to think of hearing impairment as no more than that—a
reduced ability to hear that can be fixed, at least partially, with
a hearing aid. But deafness is very different from that. It is not a
medical condition; it is a cultural debate (Lane, 1984).

Leave at
least
2.5 cm
margins
around
the text
to allow
for your
instructor
to write
comments.

The most serious form of hearing impairment is a sensori-
neural loss. This occurs when the cells in the inner ear that
transmit information about sound to the auditory nerve are
damaged. The damage is irreversible. Once these cells are gone,
the acoustic connection to the outside world is lost. In many
cases it is not possible to restore that connection with a hearing
aid because the receptors are no longer functioning. Until fairly
recently, this meant that a child born with a profound sensori-
neural loss would never have the experience of hearing sounds.
Now, with the development of cochlear implants, devices that
stimulate the auditory nerve directly, it is possible to restore some
auditory sensation, but as we shall see, this is a controversial issue.

Many children with profound hearing impairments have a
great deal of difficulty in learning to use spoken language. If they
are children of deaf parents, it is very likely that they will learn
American Sign Language (ASL) as their first language. But if their

In situations where there
is a well-recognized body of
knowledge, a reference is not
essential; or, you could include a
reference to a textbook.

If you are going to use a term
repeatedly and there is an
abbreviation, show that in
parentheses immediately after
your first reference.

Deaf Culture   3

parents are hearing, this is less likely, and it is possible that great efforts will be made to help them develop normal speech and vocal language by teaching them to make use of their residual hearing and other cues, such as lip movements. In this essay I will explore the differences between those who advocate for the integration of the deaf child into the hearing community and those who celebrate deafness as a cultural difference.

Two Concepts of Deafness

Perhaps the greatest challenge faced by parents whose child is born deaf is that of communication. How does a child who has never heard a sound learn how to speak words and understand sentences? How does she learn language so that she can express her wants and needs? The answer to these questions has been a source of controversy for well over 100 years, and has led to two very distinct schools of thought and very different approaches to deaf education.

Oralism

For the greater part of the twentieth century, the predominant conception of deafness was that it was a medical condition that needed to be treated (Myklebust, 1964). What followed from this idea was that a deaf child should be helped to become "normal,"

Using "he or she" can be awkward if you are going to make several references of this type. It is acceptable to refer to a single sex in this case.

This is a Level 2 heading. Note that you would only have a subheading if there is more than one subsection.

Use the APA levels of headings in ascending order. This is Level 1.

4   Deaf Culture

in the sense that she should learn to communicate verbally using
spoken words. Proponents of this view, known as *Oralism*,
argued that the most important thing is to integrate a child
into the normal hearing world, and that every effort should
be directed toward teaching oral speech by encouraging the
use of residual hearing, lip-reading, and intensive speech
therapy. The prevailing attitude toward deaf individuals was
paternalistic, with most educators taking the position that they
knew best, and that "best" was to develop spoken language to
the exclusion of everything else (Lane, 1984). Education for
deaf students, even at early ages, often involved being housed in
residential schools, away from their families. To reach the goal
of achieving normalcy, social interactions among deaf people
were discouraged on the grounds that they might resort to
other forms of communication that would interfere with their
progress toward being able to speak and their integration into a
hearing society.

The Manual Approach

The other school of thought stressed that the paramount
need of a deaf child is to be able to communicate, and that there
may be other, non-vocal, avenues that may lead to successful
communication. For the most part this involved the use of Sign
Language. For many years the use of Sign among deaf people was

This is the second
subsection at the same
level as **Oralism** above.

seen as primarily a way to communicate among themselves, and it allowed for a degree of social interaction within the community. Many deaf social clubs were formed, and after a period of time it was recognized that there was a significant deaf culture. A more complete historical perspective may be found in Lane (1984).

American Sign Language

Lacking the ability to speak, deaf people have long used gestures in order to communicate. Sign language is a language that, instead of sound patterns, uses visually transmitted hand patterns to convey meaning. Sign language incorporates hand shapes, orientation, movement of the hands, arms, or body, and facial expressions to convey the speaker's thoughts. Wherever communities of deaf people exist sign languages have developed. Hundreds of signed languages are in use around the world and are at the core of local deaf cultures. ASL is the dominant sign language of deaf Americans.

In the early 1800s Thomas Gallaudet travelled to Europe to study the methods used to educate the deaf because he had heard of the successful reports. Gallaudet met Laurent Clerc, a very well-known educator of the deaf and persuaded him to return to the United States with him to help him establish schools for the deaf (Moores, 1982; Shaw & Delaporte, 2010). Clerc advocated the use

If you are restricted in the number of words allowed in your essay, cite a more complete review source to show that you are aware that there is more to be said.

6   Deaf Culture

of sign language and introduced the French educational methods
in the first American schools. This relationship between Gallaudet
and Clerc laid the groundwork for ASL in America. Gallaudet had
learned French Sign Language in Europe, but when he returned
to America he was exposed to the signs of North America and
incorporated the two styles to develop what is known today as
American Sign Language. This relationship was confirmed in a
historical study by Shaw and Delaporte (2010), who collected data
from a number of historical sources to show the lexical connections
between the two. The term *sign language* is an important one. For
many years, one argument against the use of ASL in an educational
setting was that it was a primitive form of gestural communication
and not a true language. It was not until the 1960 that William
Stokoe demonstrated unequivocally that ASL was indeed a true
language, with formal lexical properties that could be analyzed
in the same terms as any spoken language.

    ASL quickly became the natural language of the deaf in
North America (Lane, 1984). It was most frequently used among
families in which there were deaf children with deaf parents, and
within their social groups. This occurred despite the fact that, by
the end of the nineteenth century, the Oral approach had become
the one taken by most educators of the deaf (Moores, 1982). As

When referring to two authors in the text, use "and."

If you have a date and the author's name in proximity like this, you don't need to repeat the reference in parentheses.

mentioned above, children were often sent to Oral residential schools for their education. In these schools, not only was signing frowned upon, it was actively forbidden. Children were punished for attempting to sign among themselves, even outside of class (Lane, 1984) and were made to feel that to use signs was somehow to be inferior. In her novel *In This Sign*, which chronicles the repression of the signing culture through the eyes of deaf family, Joanne Greenberg (1970) describes one character who associates signing with the smell of urine, because the only place that children could sign was in the washrooms of the school they attended.

Deaf Culture

This active repression of manual communication by the hearing community was an important factor in bringing the deaf community together to fight for their rights, and ultimately to change the shape of deaf education in the United States. For most people in the hearing world, the distinction between "deafness" and "Deafness" is not a familiar one. However, these two terms define the difference between the Oral and the Manual communities. The "big D" Deaf reject the view that hearing impairment is a medical condition that needs treating (Lane, 1995). Instead, they argue that people with hearing impairments belong to a cultural and

You can paraphrase a quote from a book like this. If you had given an actual quotation, then you would use quotation marks and include a page number.

8   Deaf Culture

linguistic minority, with ASL as the natural language. Reagan's
(1995) sociological study of Deaf culture in the U.S. supported
the view that ASL was the binding force for the community,
because it defined their world view and provided them with
a sense of identity. Deaf culture arose out of a need to give
a voice to those who could not hear. Today, being Deaf is
considered a badge of honour by large numbers of people with
hearing impairments. An excellent review of Deaf culture is
provided by Padden and Humphries (2005).

The Cochlear Implant Debate

Being unable to hear does not automatically confer status
as a Deaf person. Even within the deaf community, there is an
ongoing discussion as to whether children should be raised as
Deaf or be integrated as much as possible into a hearing society.
One of the best examples of the intensity of the feelings in this
regard comes from the advent of cochlear implants.

Cochlear implants were introduced in the 1980s to provide
some direct auditory input to profoundly deaf individuals. A
cochlear implant is a surgically implanted auditory prosthesis
that bypasses damaged hair cells, applying electrical stimulation
directly to the auditory nerve (Spencer, Bruce, & Knutson, 2004).
Although the range of auditory sensations created by an implant

If multiple authors are
cited in parentheses, use
an ampersand.

is quite limited, the implant can improve a deaf individual's understanding of spoken words (Spencer et al., 2004). The use of such implants was established as effective and safe in the early 1990s (Dowell, Dettman, Blamey, Barker, & Clark, 2002).

However, in spite of the abundant research demonstrating the effectiveness of cochlear implants, there is a raging debate as to whether they are "beneficial" for deaf people and the proponents of each position are divided along the deaf/Deaf dimension. Those who support implants argue that they provide deaf children with a new opportunity to join the hearing community and to learn spoken language. The available scientific evidence strongly supports this position (Beadle et al., 2005; Francis, Koch, Wyatt, & Niparko, 1996).

In contrast to this position, a large segment of the Deaf community is strongly opposed to the use of cochlear implants. One argument is an ethical one, concerning freedom of choice. Some Deaf advocates argue that a parent should not force an irreversible surgical procedure and device on a young child who does not have the ability to give his/her consent (Kluwin & Stewart, 2000). The other, and perhaps more forceful, arguments are more concerned with the cultural implications of a device that might move a child from a Deaf to a hearing community. The view of many in the Deaf community is that cochlear implants are a

In a multi-authored paper with up to five authors, list all surnames in the first citation. In subsequent citations to a paper with three or more authors, include only the surname of the first author followed by "et al.," and the publication year.

If there are six or more authors, cite only the first author, followed by "et al.," and the year.

threat to their culture. They argue that the use of implants validates the concept of deafness as a medical condition, implies that the Deaf are of lesser worth, and that implants signal the end of Deaf culture. In his 2002 paper Levy addresses each of these claims. He is sympathetic to the first two claims. However, he rejects the third claim, that implants are a threat to the Deaf culture. First he argues that Deaf culture is intrinsically and strong enough to withstand this incursion. His second argument is more telling. He suggests that because most implants are done on prelinguistic children of hearing parents, the burden of banning the implants would affect people who are not members of the Deaf culture.

Conclusion

The purpose of this paper was to provide a brief overview of the different ways in which Deafness is viewed in North America. I used the cochlear implant as an example of the strength of feeling associated with these different views. This debate also highlights the role that language plays in a community. Those who advocate for an exclusive Deaf culture are arguing essentially that belonging to a linguistic community, even though it is small and may lead to some degree of isolation from broader society, is more important than being able to become a fully functional member of the hearing community. Fortunately, this extreme position is not held

Begin with a brief summary of the purpose of the paper.

Do not be afraid to inject your own position into a paper about a controversial topic.

The conclusion should bring together the elements of a paper to show the reader how they relate to each other. It should go beyond being a simple summary.

by everyone. Over the past few decades there has been a steady transition from an almost exclusively Oral approach in education to one that embraces ASL as a crucial vehicle for communication and the basis for success in school. Although most schools will also provide instruction in speech and spoken language, it has been recognized that the basis for a successful education is the ability to communicate, and that the avenue for communication is ASL. The fact that ASL is used so extensively is a validation of Deaf culture and perhaps will extend, rather than inhibit, the Deaf community. Without diversity of culture, language, and different ways of seeing the world, we would never have learned what we now know about the ways that humans live. The linguistic and social lives of Deaf people have given us unique and valuable ways to explore the vast potential for human language and culture.

Consider the value of ending with a passage like this. Would the ending be stronger if the student had stopped at the end of the previous sentence?

12   Deaf Culture

References

Beadle, E. A. R., McKinley, D. J., Nikolopoulos, T. P., Brough, J., O'Donoghue, G. M., & Archbold, S. M. (2005). Long-term functional outcomes and academic-occupational status in implanted children after 10 to 14 years of cochlear implant use. *Otology & Neurotology, 26,* 1152–1160.

Dowell, R. C., Dettman, S. J., Blamey, P. J., Barker, E. J., & Clark, G. M. (2002). Speech perception in children using cochlear implants: Prediction of long-term outcomes. *Cochlear Implants International, 3,* 1–18.

Francis, H. W., Koch, M. E., Wyatt, R., & Niparko, J. K. (1996). Trends in educational placement and cost-benefit considerations in children with cochlear implants. *Archives of Otolaryngology Head and Neck Surgery, 125,* 499–505.

Greenberg, J. (1970). *In this sign.* New York, NY: Holt, Rinehart and Winston.

Kluwin, T. N., & Stewart, D. A. (2000). Cochlear implants for younger children: A preliminary description of the parental decision process and outcomes. *American Annals of the Deaf, 145,* 26–32.

Lane, H. (1984). *When the mind hears: A history of deafness.* New York, NY: Random House.

Comma before the ampersand. Use ampersand rather than "and" in the reference list.

Italicize the journal name and volume number. Capitalize the journal name.

The References section begins on a new page. It is not a heading level, so don't set it in bold.

Only capitalize the first word of the article title. Do not italicize.

For books, include place of publication and publisher.

Only capitalize the first word of a book title, and any proper names. Lower case any other words in the title. For books, include place of publication and publisher.

Include the city, followed by the province or state abbreviation.

Capitalize the first word of a subtitle.

Deaf Culture   13

Levy, N. (2002). Reconsidering cochlear implants: The lessons
    of Martha's Vineyard. *Bioethics, 16*, 2, 134–153.

Moores, D. F. (1982). *Educating the deaf: Psychology, principles
    and practice* (2nd ed.). Boston, MA: Houghton Mifflin.

Myklebust, H. (1964). *The psychology of deafness: Sensory
    deprivation, learning, and adjustment* (2nd ed.). New York,
    NY: Grune and Stratton.

Padden, C., & Humphries, T. (2005). *Inside deaf culture*.
    Cambridge, MA: Harvard University Press.

Reagan, T. (1995). A sociocultural understanding of deafness:
    American sign language and the culture of deaf people.
    Intercultural Relations, 19, 2, 239–251.

Shaw, E. & Delaporte, Y. (2010). New perspectives on the
    history of American sign language. *Sign Language Studies,
    11*, 2, 158–204.

Spencer, L. J., Bruce, J. G., & Knutson, J. F. (2004). Outcomes
    and achievement of students who grew up with access to
    cochlear implants. *The Laryngoscope, 114*, 1576–1581.

Stokoe, W. (1960). Sign language structure: An outline of
    the visual communication systems of the American deaf.
    Studies in Linguistics Occasional Papers No. 8. Washington,
    DC: Gallaudet University Press.

Include information about the edition
number following the title number.
Use "ed." for edition. If you are citing
an edited volume, then use "(Ed.)"
following the editor's name.

Ethical Issues in Research and Writing

Objectives

- understanding ethical issues in the conduct of research
- understanding ethical issues in writing

Introduction

All academic work starts with an assumption of integrity. This concept is crucial in scientific and biomedical research where the implications of misrepresentation can be profound, which is why this chapter appears early in the book. You should recognize the significance of integrity very early in your career as a student. Surveys have shown that as many as 50 per cent of students admit to some form of academic dishonesty, which can range from something as simple as copying a few lines from an Internet source, through to the falsification of data in a thesis. Scholastic dishonesty is taken very seriously in colleges and universities and can result in severe penalties. Unfortunately, students do not always realize the seriousness of their actions, and sometimes they are not even aware that what they are doing is unacceptable. In this chapter, we will place the whole issue of academic ethics into a broader context so that you can understand the importance of holding yourself to the highest standards.

Until fairly recently, there was a strong tendency for the average person to think of science as a "pure" endeavour and of scientists as disinterested individuals in pursuit of nothing but "truth." This view of science is certainly promoted by those TV commercials in which an actor wearing a white coat points to a set of "clinical studies" showing how effective a certain product is. In fact, science is not always driven by idealistic motives. While most scientists are interested above all in their research and take great care in the way they go about it, others, seeking primarily wealth and glory, may be willing to cheat to achieve those ends.

Outright scientific fraud is uncommon, but it is of sufficient concern that the US National Institutes of Health has a special office devoted to investigating research integrity. Even *Science* magazine, one of the most prestigious journals in the scientific literature, now requires that researchers who submit a paper for publication both have colleagues review it beforehand and make their data and materials available for verification. Further, the American Psychological Association has developed a set of reporting standards (Cooper, 2010) detailing what information should be included in any paper that presents new data, regardless of the way in which the study was carried out.

With the advent of online storage capability, many journal publishers, including the APA, encourage authors to provide supplemental materials along with their studies, including detailed data files that can be accessed by readers. Requiring such material to be available makes it more difficult for an author to make spurious claims about his or her data.

In general, the public finds out about only the most glaring frauds through the media—usually when people are discovered to have falsified a significant part of their data. Stories of major scientific fraud or unethical behaviour emerge from time to time. If you would like to learn more, Broad and Wade (1982) document several early cases of scientific dishonesty. We'll look at a more recent example. One of the most shocking cases is a study from 1998 led by Dr. Andrew Wakefield that claimed that certain components of the measles, mumps, and rubella (MMR) vaccine caused colitis, which in turn led to developmental problems that are part of autism spectrum disorder. This study had a huge impact worldwide and led many parents to decide against having their children vaccinated. As a consequence, there was a noticeable rise in the incidence of these diseases. No one else was able to replicate the results of this study. But there was no public outcry until the discovery that the lead author had received funding from lawyers who were seeking evidence to use against vaccine manufacturers in civil litigation. Further investigation brought to light serious flaws in the conduct of the study, and in February 2009, the renowned British medical journal the *Lancet*, which had originally published the study, formally retracted it. Wakefield was stripped of his medical licence. But the damage has been done. Unfortunately, even now some parents believe, despite all the evidence, that there is a conspiracy to discredit Andrew Wakefield, and so they refuse to allow their children to be vaccinated.

The effects of all of this bad science are now well documented. The possibility that the work was fraudulent was first raised by an investigative reporter for the *Sunday Times* of London (see http://briandeer.com/mmr-lancet.htm), who published the complete story in a series of articles in the *British Medical Journal* (Deer, 2011). More extensive accounts of the whole anti-vaccine movement can be found in two recent books (see Mnookin, 2011; Offit, 2010).

The vaccination–autism case is a particularly egregious one, but most cases of questionable scientific behaviour are more prosaic. For example, a researcher may discard data from participants who do not appear to be performing in accordance with expectations or may "adjust" a few data points to make the results look more convincing. Although such behaviour is obviously unacceptable, it almost certainly occurs at every level, from first-year undergraduate labs to major labs that are supported by millions of dollars in grant funds every year.

The purpose of discussing such unethical behaviour is not to disillusion you but to start you thinking about what is right and wrong when you are doing research or writing in psychology or in any other academic endeavour. Before we go further, let's take a look at what constitutes ethical scientific research and reporting.

Ethical Issues in the Conduct of Research

In the 1930s, a developmental psychologist interested in the role of experience in human development (Dennis, 1935; 1938) took over the care of a set of fraternal twins a few weeks after their birth. Dennis (1935) explained that he did so "because the father failed to provide for them" and that "the mother understood that we offered temporary care of the twins in return for the privilege of studying them" (p. 18). The purpose of the study was to determine how engagement in motor behaviours, such as walking or reaching, at an early age affected the development of these behaviours. The babies were kept lying on their backs in their cribs and were picked up only for feeding and changing. They were given no toys until they were 14 months old and were hand-fed so that they could not practise reaching. In addition, Dennis "kept a straight face in the babies' presence, neither smiling nor frowning, and he never played with them, petted them, tickled them, etc." (p. 19).

When we consider the research from today's perspective, we are horrified. Certainly such a study carried out now would lead to charges of child abuse. Remember, though, that the study was done long before anyone was aware of the effects of social deprivation on young children, and there is no doubt Dennis believed that what he was doing was in the children's best interests. But consider another major difference between then and now: when he was doing his work, there were no ethical review committees to consider the implications of such experiments. Individuals made their own decisions about what experiments to do. Nowadays, there is much greater scrutiny of experimental proposals.

When psychology students are first asked to carry out independent projects, they might propose to study the effects of, say, drugs, alcohol, or exposure to sexually explicit materials, on some aspect of behaviour. Although nothing is intrinsically wrong with such studies, they do require that the researcher observe a strict code of conduct. Whenever any experiment is carried out using human participants, **two requirements must be fulfilled**: first, there must be a good justification for doing the study; and second, the participants must be thoroughly informed about what they are committing to.

Ethical research guidelines

Because of the importance of ensuring that research is not conducted frivolously and that the participants in any kind of research study are treated appropriately, complex systems have been developed to monitor the conduct and activities of researchers. In Canada, most research conducted at educational institutions and hospitals is funded by one of the three federal granting councils: the Social Sciences and Humanities Research Council of Canada (SSHRC); the Natural Sciences and Engineering Research Council of Canada (NSERC); and the Canadian Institutes of Health Research (CIHR). Depending on their area of interest, psychology researchers may be funded by any one of these agencies.

In 2001, the three granting councils established the Interagency Advisory Panel on Research Ethics (PRE) to promote ethical conduct in research involving humans. PRE is responsible for developing and supporting a joint ethics policy known as the *Tri-Council Policy Statement: Ethical Conduct for Research Involving Humans* (TCPS), a document that governs all research in Canada that uses human participants. The TCPS guides the activities of research ethics boards, which oversee research within each institution and are responsible for approving every research project before it begins. So any research you do as a student that involves human participants must have been approved either as an individual project or as part of your supervisor's approval for a group of similar studies.

If your research involves the use of animals, then it will fall under the auspices of the Canadian Council on Animal Care (CCAC). This independent organization is funded primarily through CIHR and NSERC, and it is responsible for overseeing the care and use of experimental animals. This group carries out periodic inspections of all animal care facilities and has the power to shut down all animal research in an institution if they find that animals are not being treated in accordance with the CCAC standards. Again, all animal research proposals in Canada must be reviewed and approved by a research ethics board before the studies can begin.

If you are an undergraduate student, most of this activity will be invisible to you, but following ethical guidelines is nonetheless a vital part of the research process and is taken very seriously. Instructors may sometimes turn down student research proposals if they do not meet the necessary ethical standards. The fundamental ethical concern in any kind of research is a respect for human dignity and privacy. With this in mind, research ethics boards evaluate the impact research proposals may have on these basic human rights. For the vast majority of projects this is not an issue at all, but if the investigator plans to deceive the participant in some way, or if he or she might wish to ask for very personal information, then that study will receive greater scrutiny. In general, an ethics review committee will raise questions about the justification for a study, in terms of its overall costs and benefits, and will want to be sure that participants have given their informed consent. If the research is on animals, it is obviously impossible to ask for informed consent, so the justification must be even stronger.

Tri-Council policies

At this stage in your career, you do not need to understand every detail of the Tri-Council ethical policies, but if you do go on to be a full-time researcher in psychology, then it will be very important for you to be aware of the implications of your research and what limits there are on the kinds of research you can do. If you would like to know a little more about this, the Interagency Advisory Panel on Research Ethics has an online introductory tutorial for the *Tri-Council Policy Statement* (http://www.tcps2core.ca/welcome).

If you are doing animal research, you must follow different sets of guidelines, and different committees within an institution must approve any project using animals. These committees have stringent reporting requirements for keeping track of all animals and all procedures used in any study. More information about animal care guidelines can be found on the Canadian Council on Animal Care website (http://www.ccac.ca/en_/standards/guidelines).

Justification of studies

Sometimes you'll read an article in a newspaper that is reporting some unusual scientific finding that will leave you wondering "So what?" In other words, you are questioning whether that research was worth doing. Although some research is driven by simple curiosity, most studies also have either a theoretical or a practical rationale. This may not be obvious if you look at the title of an article out of context, but most studies are designed to answer questions that have been raised by earlier research—that is, the research that would be reviewed in an *Introduction* section. Beginning with the question "I wonder what would happen if . . ." is usually not enough to justify a study. For one thing, most journals will not publish a paper that does not offer a good rationale. In addition, when you try to write up a study of this kind, you will find it difficult to say anything useful in either your *Introduction* or your *Discussion*.

In general, the more invasive a study is, the stronger its justification must be. For example, a study to find out whether ingesting a hallucinogenic drug improves a person's perception of colours would be less likely to gain approval than a study of the effects of minor sleep deprivation on the detection of visual stimuli in a driving simulation test. In addition, most institutions take the position that undergraduate projects must not have any potential to cause harm to the participants.

Informed consent and feedback

In addition to ensuring that your study is carried out carefully, you must always make certain that your participants have a clear idea of what the study is about and an understanding that they have the right to refuse to participate—or even to drop out midway through the experiment if they wish. In almost all cases, the researcher does this by preparing an *informed consent form* that describes the essential aspects of the study. The participants read and sign the form to indicate that they understand and accept the terms under which they will participate.

Sometimes, you may want to exclude certain individuals from participating in a study, but the exclusion criteria may require your potential participants to reveal personal or embarrassing information. For example, if you are running a study involving alcohol consumption, you do not want to test anyone who may be pregnant, or who has a drinking problem, or who has a disease that might be exacerbated by alcohol. Although you could ask questions on your informed consent forms, some people may feel embarrassed about checking off an item about their personal lives. A simple way to get around this problem is to provide a list of all possible conditions that would automatically exclude someone from the study and to ask that potential participants excuse themselves if any of these conditions apply to them. This will allow them to leave the study gracefully without revealing information about themselves unnecessarily.

Typically, you will not tell participants details of the experimental hypothesis at the beginning of the study in order to reduce the risk that this might influence the outcome. In some studies, it will even be necessary for you to prevent participants from knowing the main purpose of the experiment because this knowledge would certainly affect the outcome. In some cases, the real purpose of the study may be disguised by actively misleading the participants. One famous example is the Milgram "obedience" study (Milgram, 1963), in which participants were led to believe that they were in a study investigating "memory and learning." But Milgram was really interested in the extent to which participants would administer what they thought were increasingly severe electric shocks to another person, simply because the experimenter asked them to. Nowadays, such a study would not be approved, but, in general, the use of deception may be permitted if the investigator can justify the scientific value of the study and meet necessary ethical standards.

Whether a study involves deception or not, after the experiment is over you must give participants a detailed explanation of exactly what the study was about. As an experimenter who is asking others to donate their time to assist you with your research, you have an ethical obligation to inform your participants about the purpose of the study. This is usually done using a feedback sheet that describes the study and provides references for follow-up. The experimenter should also be prepared to provide participants with additional information if necessary.

Ethical Issues in Writing

When you carry out any piece of research, it is assumed that you will do the research carefully, with appropriate regard to all ethical guidelines. Similar ethical standards are required for any written work you submit.

If you look through most university calendars, you will find a section dealing with academic offences. These fall into three broad categories: cheating on examinations (which we will not discuss here), fabrication, and plagiarism. Penalties for academic dishonesty can be severe, ranging from a reprimand, through failure in the course, to expulsion from the university in the most serious cases. Despite these penalties, however, many students submit work that is not entirely their own.

Often, instructors can easily identify material that has been taken from elsewhere. First, the writing style of most students usually differs from that of the authors they are copying from. Second, instructors are usually so familiar with the sources used by students that they will recognize the source from which the material has been lifted. In other cases, even if the writing style is not distinctive, the quality of the logic and argument may be well above what the instructor expects from a particular student.

Fabrication

Fabrication occurs when a student inserts false information into a paper. You are fabricating information if you take any of the following actions:

1. invent data from an experiment you have not performed;
2. pad a reference list or bibliography with sources you did not use in preparing the paper; or
3. include information that did not come from the cited source.

In each of these cases, you are trying to gain credit for work you did not do. Submission of falsified data is treated as outright fraud. Even adding an extra reference compromises the integrity of your work and may be considered an academic offence.

Plagiarism

Plagiarism occurs when you present someone else's words, ideas, or data as your own. You may think plagiarizing only means using direct quotations without attributing them to their source. But it is also plagiarism if you follow the structure and organization of someone else's work—that is, copying a theme, paragraph by paragraph, from someone else even if your words are different. You should also be aware that if you follow a source too closely, even if you acknowledge it as your source, you may still be regarded as having copied from that person. Your work must be a product of your own thought processes, not just a minor modification of something you have read.

Examples of plagiarism range from paraphrasing a sentence or two without appropriate acknowledgement of the source, to submitting a paper that has been lifted wholesale from somewhere else. Discussions with students who have been accused of plagiarism reveal that many do not realize that what they have done is inappropriate. This results in what could be termed "inadvertent" plagiarism. Inadvertent plagiarism is commonly caused by the failure to record adequate information about your source materials when taking notes. For example, you might have jotted down a series of direct quotes from a variety of sources while researching your topic but failed to place them in quotation marks. Later, when writing up your essay, you may string together sentences and phrases from your notes, forgetting that they are direct quotes. Even though you may not have intended to do anything dishonest, this is still plagiarism. At this stage of your academic career, ignorance is not a valid excuse: it is up to you to know the difference between original research and copying someone else's words and ideas.

Students may also commit unintentional plagiarism when they have been assigned a project that requires the work to be done as a group but the final write-ups to be submitted independently. In such cases, students may copy directly from each other and submit reports that contain identical passages; or, they may do the final write-ups separately but from an outline they have prepared together. The resulting papers will be written in different words but will have identical organization and structure. This too is considered plagiarism. When you are asked to write a paper independently, all the creative aspects—not just the actual words—must be your own.

To give you a clear idea of what might be considered plagiarism, here are several examples, all based on the same original source, with some comments on why the student version is inappropriate.

Original source material:

Why would scientists want to study the brains of other animal species, if their ultimate goal is to learn about human thought and behavior? Scientists interested in how the nervous system controls behavior study other kinds of animals for three main reasons (Bullock, 1984). First, they do so to understand the evolutionary history, or phylogenetic roots, of the human brain. They trace what is old and what is new in the human brain—what evolution has brought about.

Second, they try to discover general rules or principles of brain function. Scientists who take this approach ask two different kinds of questions: (1) What in the nervous system correlates with known behavioral differences among animals? For example, if one species is aggressive and another is passive, what differences in their brains account for the difference? (2) What kinds of behavior correlate with known differences in the brains of animals? For example, if a certain brain structure is present in humans but not in other primates, or if a brain structure is larger in one species than another, how do these differences relate to behavior?

Third, scientists study the nervous systems of other animals to obtain information that is impossible to obtain from humans. Many studies that, for technical or ethical reasons, cannot be carried out in humans can be conducted in other animals. Animals provide scientists with "model systems" in which to address questions about how the human nervous system works because the nervous systems of humans and other animals are so much alike. . . .

(From Spear, Penrod, & Baker, 1988, pp. 29–30.
Reprinted with permission of John Wiley & Sons, Inc.)

Incorrect direct quotation:

Why would researchers study the brains of lower animals, if their ultimate goal is to learn about human thought and behavior? Scientists interested in how the nervous system controls behavior study other kinds of animals for three main reasons (Bullock, 1984). First, they do so to understand the evolutionary history of the human brain, tracing what is old and what is new in the human brain. Second, they try to discover general rules or principles of brain function. Third, they study the nervous systems of other animals to obtain information that is impossible to obtain from humans. Many studies that cannot be carried out in other animals, for technical or ethical reasons, can be conducted in animals.

This is a clear example of plagiarism, in which the student has copied the source material almost verbatim, without any acknowledgement. The few minor changes in wording, and the omission of several phrases and sentences from the original, may have been intended to disguise the fact that this material was stolen.

Moreover, even if this passage were a paraphrase rather than a direct quote, the reference to Bullock (1984) would be inappropriate because the student has evidently not drawn directly from this source but has taken it from Spear et al. (1988). Rather than rely on secondary sources in this way, it is best to go to the original sources. The second-best solution would be to acknowledge the source as follows: (Bullock, 1984, as cited in Spear, Penrod, & Baker, 1988).

Incorrect paraphrase:

> In my view, there are three main reasons why scientists might study the brains of lower animals in order to learn about human brain function. First, by comparing the brains of animals at various levels of evolutionary development with those of humans, one can examine the evolutionary history of the human brain. Second, general rules or principles of brain function can be ascertained by examining ways in which behavioural differences between species are correlated with differences in their brain structures. Third, using lower animals for research allows scientists to conduct experiments that might be unethical if done on humans.

Even though the wording here is quite different from the source material, it still follows the train of thought of the original exactly. In failing to cite the source of these ideas, the student is making a false claim that they are his own. This dishonesty is compounded by beginning the paragraph with "In my view," which leads the reader to believe that the ideas are original.

Incorrect partial paraphrase:

> Why would scientists want to study the brains of other animal species, if they ultimately wish to learn about human thought and behaviour? As Spear, Penrod, and Baker (1988) have pointed out, there are three main reasons for studying lower animals. First, scientists do so "to understand the evolutionary history, or phylogenetic roots, of the human brain." Second, this type of research allows for an examination of the general rules and principles of brain function, by examining ways in which behavioural differences between species are correlated with differences in their brain structures. Third, using lower animals for research allows scientists to conduct experiments that might be unethical if done on humans.

Here the student does cite the source of the material. However, she still does not adequately acknowledge the extent of her debt. Although part of one sentence is placed in quotation marks, several other sentences and phrases that directly quote the original have not been placed in quotation marks. A paraphrase must be entirely the words of the writer; any borrowed words or phrases must be placed in quotation marks. In addition, the student has failed to point out that Spear et al. drew from Bullock in making these points.

We hope these examples will cause you to think about how you use your sources. Obviously, no one expects you to come up with something that is entirely original and completely removed from what other people have said. The trick is to acknowledge the ideas of others correctly and to use the information they provide as the basis for your own comments. Generally, you don't need to give credit for anything that's common knowledge. For example, you would not need to cite the original papers that first described the receptive fields of neurons in order to make a general reference to the term *receptive fields*. However, if you were discussing specific characteristics of receptive fields, then you would need to refer to your sources. Always document any fact or claim that is unfamiliar or open to question.

Don't be afraid that your work will seem weaker if you acknowledge the ideas of others. On the contrary, it will be all the more convincing; serious academic treatises are almost always built on the work of preceding scholars. If you are unsure whether you are relying too much on your sources, check with your instructor *before* you write your paper.

Submitting work that is not your own

There used to be many stories about fraternities and sororities that kept databases of term papers, which members could draw from when they were given assignments. Today, some students use the Internet in the same way. The Internet is now the major source of work submitted by students that is not their own. Some students will just lift text directly from websites such as *Wikipedia* or other sites that provide information about a certain topic. Others go to greater lengths and will order pre-written essays directly from online sources. Simply typing "custom term papers" in Google will bring up a long list of commercial essay-writing factories that provide a full paper for a price. In some cases, these may be drawn from a list of papers that have already been written. At some of the more sophisticated sites, students can ask for a custom-written essay on a particular topic. These essays may be written by other students who are paid for this work.

However, there are also now a number of online companies that can check suspicious papers. For a fee, universities and colleges can subscribe to a service, such as Turnitin (http://www.turnitin.com), that will take a paper and compare it with material on hundreds of different websites. Many universities now have regulations requiring students to submit their work in electronic format so that it can be checked in this fashion.

Since Turnitin is a way for instructors to find evidence of plagiarism, students sometimes worry that while they have been conscientious, they may have plagiarized inadvertently. Now students can access a service called WriteCheck (http://www.en.writecheck.com), which uses the same databases as Turnitin, to check their work before they submit their papers to their instructor. This program will identify and highlight all textual passages that match sources in the WriteCheck databases, regardless of whether the student has provided a citation. Students can then check these highlighted passages to make sure sources are documented appropriately.

Computerized evaluation is also being used more often to look for cheating in multiple-choice and similar kinds of exams. Such software analyzes the patterns of right and wrong answers and calculates the level of similarity between exam papers. Obviously there will be some overlap in the way people answer questions, but noticeable similarities in right *and* wrong answers suggests it is less likely that these test results occurred by chance. Such coincidental patterns of responses do not prove that cheating has occurred. However, if further investigation shows that two individuals were sitting very close together during the exam, for example, or that they happen to be roommates, an instructor may want to consider the possibility that an academic offence has been committed.

Summary

We have discussed ethical issues both in research and in writing. Although they may seem like different areas at first, both are concerned with someone who misrepresents what he or she has done in order to obtain undeserved credit. For professional scientists, this is one of the most serious transgressions a person can commit, and a number of formal mechanisms exist to prevent and punish unethical and fraudulent activity. For students, the rules may be more informal, but the impact on a student's career may be just as profound. In the most serious cases, students may be expelled and have a permanent notation on their academic transcripts, which could effectively end their aspirations to move on to a graduate or professional program. We cannot stress enough the importance of maintaining your academic integrity throughout your time at university. If you do not, you debase the value of your education.

References

Broad, W., & Wade, N. (1982). *Betrayers of the truth*. New York, NY: Simon & Schuster.

Cooper, H. (2010). *Reporting research in psychology: How to meet journal article reporting standards*. Washington, DC: American Psychological Association.

Deer, B. (2011). Secrets of the MMR scare: How the case against the MMR vaccine was fixed. *BMJ: British Medical Journal, 342*(c5347). doi: http://dx.doi.org/10.1136/bmj.c5347

Dennis, W. (1935). The effect of restricted practice upon the reaching, sitting, and standing of two infants. *Journal of Genetic Psychology, 47*, 17–32.

Dennis, W. (1938). Infant development under conditions of restricted practice and of minimal social stimulation: A preliminary report. *Journal of Genetic Psychology, 53*, 149–158.

Milgram, S. (1963). Behavioral study of obedience. *Journal of Abnormal and Social Psychology, 67*(4), 371–378.

Mnookin, S. (2011). *The panic virus: A true story of medicine, science, and fear*. New York, NY: Simon & Schuster.

Offit, P. A. (2010). *Deadly choices: How the anti-vaccine movement threatens us all*. New York, NY: Basic Books.

Spear, P. D., Penrod, S. D., & Baker, T. B. (1988). *Psychology: Perspectives on behavior*. New York, NY: Wiley.

Wakefield, A. J., Murch, S. H., Anthony, A., Linnell, J., Casson, D. M., Malik, M., . . . Walker-Smith, J. A. (1998). Ileal-lymphoid-nodular hyperplasia, non-specific colitis, and pervasive developmental disorder in children. *Lancet, 351*, 637–641.

Writing a Lab Report

6

> **Objectives**
> - determining your purpose and reader
> - understanding scientific objectivity
> - understanding the structure of a lab report

Introduction

If you are studying psychology, much of your writing will be in the form of lab reports—that is, formal descriptions of experiments you have done. Lab exercises have several purposes, but the most important one is to give you a "hands-on" introduction to experimentation. In most lab courses, you will receive a lab manual that outlines the projects you will be working on in the course. You should always look through it to see how the course is structured. Knowing what is ahead will help you to organize your assignments, so reading the required material before you go to the lab is very important. Although the lab work itself may not be difficult, there are always lots of details for you to grasp, especially if you are not familiar with routine lab procedures. In psychology, this will almost certainly be the case, and because you are likely to be dealing with human participants, you will need to be extra careful to ensure things run smoothly. You will also need to keep track of all of the experimental details in preparation for your write-up.

You will learn some very important lessons from a lab course when you begin to write your lab report. When you read a description of a study in a journal, especially if it is well written, you are presented with an eloquent account of what appears to have been a flawless procedure. In reality, experiments rarely go exactly according to plan. A researcher may begin by doing one thing and end up doing something quite different. However, these complications with and departures from the original plan are seldom apparent in the published paper. As a psychology student, you will have to learn how to distinguish the relevant aspects of your lab work from the snags and false starts that are not informative to the reader—that is, what should be included and what should be omitted.

Writing a lab report is different from writing an essay in the arts and humanities. Scientists are interested in the orderly presentation of factual evidence to support hypotheses or theories, so the structure of reports in the sciences will tend to be more formal than in non-science disciplines. This means you must be objective in the way you report your data. Although you may wish to make a case for a particular hypothesis, it is essential to separate the data from your own speculations about them. You must present your information so that anyone who reads your report can understand exactly what you've done in your experiment. On the basis of the evidence you present, the reader should be able to draw his or her own conclusions; if you've done a good job, they will reach the same conclusions as your own.

Purpose and Reader

Whether you are writing for a prestigious journal or for a graduate-student lab instructor, your goal is to present scientific information. As an undergraduate, you will be writing lab reports to describe an experiment you have carried out and to demonstrate that you understand a particular phenomenon or theory. You can assume that the reader—your instructor or, later on in your career, a colleague or a peer—is familiar with basic scientific terms, so it isn't necessary to define or explain them. However, you cannot assume that your reader is all-knowing. He or she will be frustrated to read, "The participant's settings were read from the dial on the back of the apparatus" if this is the first time that a dial has been mentioned. Be sure that you have introduced procedures and described pieces of equipment before you start making references to them. You can also assume that your reader will be on the lookout for any weaknesses in methodology or analysis and any places where you have missed important data.

Objectivity

Objectivity is essential in lab work. You should never let your preconceived opinions or expectations interfere with the way you collect or represent your data. If you do, you run the risk of distorting your results, perhaps even unwittingly (see Chapter 5 for more discussion on the ethics of research). Be aware that if there is some ambiguity about a piece of data, your decision to accept or reject it may be influenced by the way you think the results *should* turn out. You should conduct your experiment as objectively as possible and then present the results in such a way that anyone who reads your lab report will be likely to reach the same conclusions that you did. Although we always think that we can be objective, our wishes and ambitions can sometimes get in the way. In her novel *Intuition*, Allegra Goodman (2006) addresses scientific fraud by giving a fascinating and credible account of how pressure to gain recognition and grant funding can have serious effects on the judgment of otherwise honest scientists. As we mentioned in Chapter 5, outright fraud is rare, but narrow thinking and unwillingness to accept evidence that does not conform to one's own thinking are not uncommon.

The Structure of a Lab Report

Although the general format of lab reports is similar for all disciplines, formal style requirements vary considerably. In psychology, the gold standard for format and style is the *Publication Manual of the American Psychological Association* (American Psychological Association, 2010). Some instructors will require that you follow the APA guidelines very closely and others will give you more leeway in the details. The essential components will be the same, however, no matter which course you are taking (in Chapter 10, we will introduce you to the details of APA style).

Because the information in scientific reports must be easy for the reader to find, it should be organized into separate sections, each with its own heading. By convention, most lab reports follow a standard order:

1. Title page
2. *Abstract*
3. *Introduction*
4. *Method*—this may include some or all of the following subsections:
   - *Participants* (or *Subjects* if they are non-human)
   - *Materials* (or *Apparatus*)
   - *Experimental Design*
   - *Procedure*
5. *Results*—including figures and tables
6. *Discussion*
7. *References*
8. Footnotes

The order of these sections is always the same, although some sections may be combined or given slightly different names, depending on how much information you have in each one. Rules may vary somewhat from discipline to discipline, but the following discussion will give you an overview of what should go into each section of your psychology lab report. To give you a better sense of what a lab report should look like, we have provided a sample report for a simple experiment, with some additional information on the format, at the end of this chapter.

Title page

The first page of your report is always the title page. It should include the title of the paper, your name and student number, the name and number of the course, the instructor's name, and the date of submission. Your title should be brief—no more than 10 or 12 words—but informative, and it should clearly describe the topic and scope of your study. Use words in the title that you might use as keywords if you were doing a literature search for studies on your topic. Avoid meaningless phrases, such as "A Study of . . ." or "Observations on . . ." Simply state what you are studying: for example, *Effects of Gamma Rays on Growth Rate of Man-in-the-Moon Marigolds*. Sometimes, you may want to emphasize the result you obtained: for example, *Brief Exposure to Gamma Rays Increases Growth Rate of Man-in-the-Moon Marigolds*.

Abstract

The *Abstract*, a brief but comprehensive summary of your report, appears on a separate page following the title page. Your *Abstract* should be able to stand alone; that is, someone should be able to read it and know exactly what the experiment was about, what the results were, and how you interpreted them. Normally, it should be no more than 150–250 words. For a professional researcher, the *Abstract* is arguably the most important section of a paper because it is the first point of access in a literature search, after the title. If the *Abstract* does not attract the reader's interest, the whole report is likely to be ignored. For this reason, the *Abstract* section should include all the major points of your study, while excluding anything that is not in the report itself. In the space available, it should describe the purpose of the experiment, the participants, the experimental apparatus or materials, the procedure, the main results (including statistical significance levels), and the conclusions. Because the *Abstract* is so short, you don't have room to be vague. Avoid wordy phrases. Don't say, "The reason for conducting the experiments in this study of X was to examine . . ." when you can be more concise: "I studied X to examine . . ." At the end of the *Abstract*, avoid stating the obvious—for example,

"The study produced some very interesting results from which we can draw several conclusions . . ." Instead, state directly what your conclusions are: "The results show . . ." or "I conclude that . . ."

Introduction

In the *Introduction* section, you describe the problem you are studying, the reasons for studying it, and the research strategy you used to obtain the relevant data. You also present your experimental hypothesis and a statement of what you expected to find, or you describe the research question you want to answer. Not all experiments contain explicit predictions; some are intended to answer a question the researcher is interested in. For example, if you wanted to learn about the social development of infants, you might ask about the age of a baby's first smile and how the frequency of social smiling changes with age. If you don't make a specific prediction, you should state your research question clearly, so that your reader knows exactly what the purpose of your study is.

You should also explain the background of your topic in the form of a brief review of the relevant literature. This should not be an exhaustive discussion but rather an overview that recognizes the prior work of others and shows how your own study relates to the work that has come before. You don't need to summarize all the aspects of the studies you cite, only those points that are relevant to your own study, including, if appropriate, the theory underlying your experiment. If, as is often the case, the purpose of your study is to test a hypothesis about a specific problem, you should state clearly both the nature of the problem and what you expect to find.

The final paragraphs of your *Introduction* section should summarize what you did in your experiment. This includes providing a description of the variables you manipulated, a formal statement of your experimental hypothesis (if appropriate), and a brief explanation of the reasons why you expected to get a particular pattern of results.

Method

The *Method* section is usually made up of several labelled subsections. These describe your participants or subjects, your experimental apparatus and materials, your experimental design, and your procedure.

Participants (or subjects)

In a study that uses humans, this section will refer to the people in the study as *participants*. If a study uses non-human species, then the experimental animals will be referred to as *subjects*. Regardless of the species you are testing, you need to provide all of the information about your test participants or subjects that is relevant to the experiment. Including this information in your report is important because the extent to which you can generalize your results depends on how representative your sample is of a population. For example, if you were studying people's judgments of the meanings of certain kinds of words, it would be important to mention whether all the participants were native speakers of English. Typically, you would also give the status of each of the participants and the average age of the group (e.g., "university undergraduates" or "three-year-old children registered in a preschool program"). Whenever you're in doubt about whether to include certain information, ask yourself the following: "Is the information relevant to the purpose of the study?" or "Would it make any difference to the reader's understanding of the study if I left this information out?" This is a good way to make sure you stick to the essential details. When your experiment involves non-human subjects, you should mention the species or strain, the sex (if appropriate), and any special characteristics they might possess. For example, there are specific strains of rat that have been bred to have a strong preference for alcohol. If you were conducting an alcohol study, you would need to indicate what kind of rats you were using.

Materials (or Apparatus)

Depending on the discipline and on the kind of experiment you are doing, this section may be entitled either *Materials* or *Apparatus*. In studies where you present visual targets or sounds, you may also include a section on *Stimuli*. Always consult with your instructor to find out the rules that apply to your own experiment.

In this section, you should describe the components of any major pieces of equipment you used and how they were set up. If you used different arrangements of the equipment for different parts of the experiment, give a full list of the equipment in the *Materials* or *Apparatus* section, and then explain each separate arrangement before describing the procedure it was used for in the *Procedure* section.

If the equipment is a standard, commercially available item, it is customary to give the manufacturer's name and the model number. For example, if you did an experiment that involved administering alcohol to your participants and then measuring their breath alcohol levels, you might say that you measured the breath alcohol levels using a Dräger 6510 Alcotest breathalyzer. If you administered a psychological test, then you should give the information about the publisher if it is a commercially based test, or you should provide a citation to the test if it is one that has been described in a journal article.

Today, most experiments involve computers, so you should indicate the type of computer that was used in your experiment (e.g., a Mac or a Windows-based PC). If your computer needs were more specialized, then you must provide additional information about these components—for instance, if you used the computer to generate visual stimuli, you would include the name and model number of the monitor, or if you had a special kind of sound card to generate a particular combination of sounds, you would include a description of that sound card.

Experimental design

Sometimes, it is helpful to include a brief, formal description of your experimental design, especially if that design is complex. In general terms, *design* refers to the way in which you will run your experiment—what experimental conditions you will use, how many participants you will include in each group, and so on. But *design* also refers to the statistical model you will apply to your experiment. In this section of your lab report, you should describe that statistical model in relation to your experiment. Let's say that you want to run an experiment to study the effects of ambient temperature on the ability to perform three different tasks. You might choose to run two groups of participants, one working in a high temperature, the other in a low temperature; each group would perform the same three tasks. Such an experiment is referred to as a *between-within* design, because in your analysis you would compare the overall difference in performance *between* the two groups and you would look at whether performance on individual tasks differed *within* each temperature condition. These data would then be analyzed using a particular kind of analysis of variance. You would need to select your experimental conditions to fit the requirements of this design and describe these in your *Experimental Design* section.

The *Experimental Design* section should include descriptions of the following:

- the independent and dependent variables, indicating which are *between-subject* variables and which are *within-subject* variables;
- the composition of your experimental and control groups, and how the subjects were assigned to the groups; and
- the statistical model: for example, a *two-way factorial* or a *repeated measures* design.

Procedure

This section is a step-by-step description of how you carried out the experiment. If your experiment consisted of a number of tests, you should begin this section with a short summary statement listing the tests so that the reader will be prepared for the series. To avoid confusion when you describe the tests later on in this section, discuss them in the same order that you first listed them.

The *Procedure* section must be written with enough detail that others would have no difficulty repeating the experiment. However, you should avoid any information that is not directly relevant to the study. For example, if you were running an experiment on students' attitudes towards health promotion videos, it might be relevant to report whether the students were regular smokers; this would not be relevant if you were running a study on students' memory of the shapes and colours of objects.

As a general rule, if you are following instructions in a lab manual, you should not copy them out word for word because this might be considered plagiarism. If you want to be absolutely clear on this issue, ask your lab instructor what the policy is about using wording from your lab manual in your report.

When describing experiments, it is standard practice to use the past tense. However, there has been some debate among scientists about the use of active voice versus passive voice (e.g., "*I placed* the rat in the water maze" versus "*the rat was placed* in the water maze"). Traditionally, only the passive voice was used for scientific writing because the more formal, detached quality was considered appropriate for a scientific report. More recently, there has been a tendency to emphasize the active voice because it is clearer and less likely to produce awkward or convoluted sentences. The *Publication Manual of the American Psychological Association* (2010) advocates the use of the active voice to describe an action (e.g., "I placed five cards in front of each participant"); however, if you want to emphasize the recipient of the action, then the passive voice may be better (e.g., "the cards were arranged in a circle in front of the participant"). When deciding which voice you should use, imagine that you are talking to someone and telling them about what you did in the experiment. Then, write as if you were talking. It sounds natural to say, "I gave each participant several questionnaires to fill out," in contrast to the awkwardness of saying, "Several questionnaires were required to be filled out by the participants."

Results

When professional scientists come across a new paper, they read the *Abstract* first. After that, they may only glance at the *Introduction* and skim the *Method* section before focusing their attention on the *Results*. In a sense, all the other sections of a lab report are subordinate to the *Results*; readers will find the most important information here. They may have questions about the methodology, or they may disagree with the interpretation presented in the *Discussion*, but they should be able to make their own evaluation of the findings based on a *Results* section that presents the data unambiguously. For this reason, you should spend some time thinking about the best way to present your results.

The *Results* section should contain a summary of all the data you collected, with sufficient detail to justify your conclusions. You might use figures and tables to help display your results. Typically, you will provide statistical summaries for your overall results rather than data on individual subjects. It is important that you present all of your data, whether or not it supports your hypothesis. Although the *Results* section is not the place to discuss the implications of your data, it is appropriate to guide your reader through the findings. So, for example, you might describe the results as follows:

> This study asked whether listening to loud music on a personal stereo impaired performance in a word-search task. To answer this question, I measured the average time taken to complete the task for three different player volume levels. The results are presented . . . [*here you would give a description of your data and statistical analyses*]. These results are consistent with the experimental hypothesis.

Without discussing why the results turned out the way they did (which you will turn to in your *Discussion* section), you have provided the reader with a context for the data you describe. This kind of context is much easier to read than a dry listing of means and statistical tests without any explanation.

Because the *Results* section is so important, Chapter 7 of this book is devoted to the more technical aspects of presenting your data, including the preparation of tables and figures.

Discussion

This part of the lab report allows you the greatest freedom because it is here that you examine and interpret your results and comment on their significance.

You want to show how the experiment produced its outcome—whether expected or unexpected—and to discuss those elements that influenced the results.

Before beginning your actual discussion, you should give a brief overview of the purpose and the major findings of your study. For example, your overview might resemble the following:

> The goal of this study was to determine the effect of post-lecture activities on student recall of lecture material. The results demonstrated that university students could remember the details of lectures much better than control participants if they spent fifteen minutes organizing and expanding their lecture notes at the end of each class.

The rest of the discussion would deal with the reasons why these results might be so.

To help you decide what to include in the *Discussion* section, you might try to answer the following questions:

- Do the results reflect the objectives of the experiment?
- Do these results agree with previous findings, as reported in the literature on the subject? If not, how can you account for the discrepancy between your own data and those of other students and scientists?
- What, if anything, may have gone wrong during your experiment and why? What was the source of any error?
- Could the results have another explanation?
- Did the procedures you used help you to accomplish the purpose of the experiment? Does your experience in this experiment suggest a better way for next time?

The order of topics should be the same in both your *Results* and *Discussion* sections. Discuss each of your findings in turn. If you have a result that you can't explain, say so; never ignore an inconvenient finding in the hope that your instructor might not notice. A good *Discussion* section may not be able to tie up all the loose ends but it must acknowledge that these loose ends exist.

You should always end with a statement of the conclusions that may be drawn from the experiment. Sometimes the conclusions are put in a separate section, but typically they form the final paragraph of the *Discussion* section. You might end your discussion on the fictitious study above by stating the following: "The findings of the present study suggest that if students took a little extra time going over their notes at the end of each class, it is likely that they would improve their grades."

Sometimes, especially if the discussion is going to be straightforward, you can combine the *Results* and *Discussion* sections. In this case, the best strategy is to present each result, followed by a brief discussion. At the end of this section, you should try to pull the study together in a concluding paragraph.

References

We discussed plagiarism in detail in Chapter 5. To summarize, avoid any suspicion of plagiarism by supporting every non-original statement with a reference citation. Always refer to your sources, unless the information you are providing is considered common knowledge. Each time you refer to a book or an article, cite the reference within the text of your report; then at the end of the paper make a list of all the sources you have cited. The format for the citations and your reference list are described in great detail in the *Publication Manual of the American Psychological Association*, including the correct way to refer to online sources. We provide you with an overview of APA style in Chapter 10.

Footnotes

You should use footnotes as little as possible. If they are unavoidable, indicate where each one should go in the text by placing a superscript reference number at the point of insertion. At the end of the paper, after the references, list the footnotes in order, numbering them so that they correspond to the numbers you have used in the text.

Checklist

You can use the following checklist to make sure you have effectively addressed all of the sections in your lab report. Please refer to the sample lab report included at the end of this chapter to see how to employ the points we've made.

- ☐ Is my title informative? Does it allow the reader to understand what the paper is about?
- ☐ Does my *Abstract* contain a concise description of the purpose, method, and results of the experiment?
- ☐ Have I reviewed the *relevant* literature in the *Introduction* section?
- ☐ Have I made a logical argument that leads to my experimental hypothesis?
- ☐ Have I presented my experimental hypothesis in the *Introduction*?

☐ Is my *Method* section clear enough that someone could replicate all of the essential aspects of the experiment?

☐ Does my *Results* section progress from an initial description of the data through to the statistical analyses that will show if the results are significant?

☐ Are my figures and tables clear? Have I described them adequately in a figure caption or table note?

☐ Does my *Discussion* section begin with a statement of the purpose of the experiment and a summary of the data?

☐ Have I followed the same sequence of topics in the *Discussion* that I did in the *Introduction*?

☐ Does my *Discussion* section actually *discuss* the data or is it just another description?

☐ Do all of the references in the *References* section match up with the citations in the text?

☐ Have I used proper APA format throughout?

Summary

As a psychology student, even in your first or second year, you should have a basic knowledge of how to write a lab report. In this chapter, we have tried to go beyond the basics to give you a sense of the most effective way to construct a lab report. Although the *Publication Manual of the American Psychological Association* gives you the structural rules for presenting your report, two individuals using those rules and writing about exactly the same experiment can produce very different papers. The successful student is the one who starts from the assumption that the reader is familiar with the general area of the research but does not know about it in detail. Never write specifically for your TA by assuming that she or he knows all about the experiment. If you do that, you will leave out crucial details. Also, your writing does not have to be boring just because the format is constrained. Try to think of your experiment as a product that you are selling: you want to make it seem as attractive as possible to the reader. If you follow these guidelines, you will write a much better paper.

References

American Psychological Association. (2010). *Publication manual of the American Psychological Association* (6th ed.). Washington, DC: Author.

Goodman, A. (2006). *Intuition*. New York, NY: The Dial Press.

Oblique Effect and Myopia   1

Number pages consecutively, beginning with the title page. Include a brief *running head* with a truncated title.

The Influence of Myopia on the Magnitude
of the Oblique Effect

Denise Pitre
(Student #; email, or other contact information)

Psychology 2972
Laboratory in Sensation and Perception
Instructor: Prof. Phineas Gage

(Date of Submission)

Use a 12-point font, typically Times New Roman or similar.

Too much detail for an abstract.

Not clear, because there is not enough space to provide adequate detail. It is better to be generic in describing procedure.

Abstract

The Oblique Effect is a behavioural phenomenon that represents a lesser ability to perceive oblique patterns compared to cardinal patterns. It has been demonstrated under a wide variety of different conditions and even among different species. Although its origin is currently unknown, it has been found that East Asian populations display a smaller magnitude of the Oblique Effect than people of other ethnic backgrounds. We hypothesized that myopia, a visual impairment highly prevalent in East Asian populations, influences the development of a smaller Oblique Effect. After obtaining refractive error data from our participants, we measured their visual acuity for patterns of fine stripes. By using a computer-generated staircase procedure, we altered the width of the patterns to determine acuity for four orientations. An Oblique Effect was demonstrated, as finer stripes could be seen better when they were horizontal or vertical than when they were oblique. Using the index of anisotropy, we performed a correlational analysis between the magnitude of the Oblique Effect and refractive error and a significant correlation. The presence of the Oblique Effect was confirmed but there was no correlation between the index of anisotropy and refractive error.

The Abstract summarizes the purpose of the report, how the experiment was conducted, the major results, and how the data were interpreted. Usually it should be between 150 and 250 words long.

Don't use "the" unless you've referred to the topic previously. Use "an" instead.

This sentence is redundant with the previous ones.

There is no conclusion.

Abstract is about the right length (150–250 words), but it doesn't present the information efficiently. It should only contain essential information to give the reader an understanding of what you did. The rest of the lab report is to expand on what you have written here. The following is a revised version.

2   Oblique Effect and Myopia

Abstract (Revised)

The Oblique Effect (OE) is a perceptual phenomenon in which the ability to process information about stimuli that are oriented horizontally and vertically is better than for obliques. Although its origin is unknown, it is smaller within East Asian populations where there is also a high incidence of myopia. I tested the hypothesis that the magnitude of the OE is related to degree of refractive error, regardless of ethnic origin. A total of 30 Caucasian participants with varying degrees of myopia were tested. Visual acuity for fine lines was measured at four different orientations, using a computer-based display system. The results showed the presence of an OE, regardless of the presence of myopia, and there was a significant correlation between the amount of myopia and the OE. These data suggest that the OE may be influenced by optical factors.

Leave a margin of at least 2.5 cm to allow your instructor to write comments.

For several hundred years there has been a discussion about the role of experience in determining the way in which our nervous systems develop. This debate was first started by philosophers such as John Locke and George Berkeley, but more recently the discussion has continued among psychologists, who are able to test hypotheses about the Nature vs. Nurture debate by doing experiments. Although most of the debate has been focused on how experience can influence personality and social behaviour, it is possible to ask whether even basic aspects of our abilities might not be pre-determined.

There is no reason not to reuse some of the material that you have already used in a research proposal (see Ch. 8).

No need for reference because you're not citing their works.

Oblique Effect and Myopia   3

The Oblique Effect

The Oblique Effect (OE) is a well-known visual phenomenon in which a person's ability to process information about stimuli that are horizontal tends to be better than it is for those oriented at 45°. This was first described over 100 years ago by Jastrow (1893) when he found that individuals who were asked to reproduce lines drawn at various angles did much better for horizontal and for vertical. Since then, there have been many studies, both in humans and in animals, showing that the OE can be found for a wide variety of tasks, including the ability to judge and discriminate orientations as well as the ability to detect the presence of stimuli set at different orientations. For example, a number of authors have shown that visual acuity—the finest detail that can be seen—is better for horizontal and vertical lines than for obliques (e.g. Berkley, Kitterle, & Watkins, 1975; Emsley, 1925).

Early speculation regarding the cause of the Oblique Effect was that it resulted from optical defects in the eye (Emsley, 1925), but later studies (Campbell, Kulikowski, & Levinson, 1966) that eliminated the possibility that optics could play a role demonstrated that the effect was a neural one. Recent studies on animals have confirmed that within the visual cortex, there are more cells that respond to horizontal and vertical

Alphabetical then chronological order for citations.

If there are three or more authors, subsequent citations would be "Berkley et al."

This section gives the background for your experiment. It provides a very brief review of work that has been done and then poses a problem.

If you provide an abbreviation after the first use of a term, you can use that abbreviation in subsequent references to the term.

4   Oblique Effect and Myopia

patterns than to the obliques (Baowang, Peterson, & Freeman,
2003). However, these studies were not able to shed any light on
the origin of the OE and why there should be more horizontal and
vertical detectors.

The Oblique Effect and Visual Experience

In 1973, Annis and Frost measured the OE for visual acuity in a
group of First Nations Cree living in northern Ontario and reported
that it was smaller than that for a group of Caucasian students
from southern Ontario. They concluded that this was because the
southern group lived in a much more carpentered environment
with lots of horizontal and vertical contours. However, Timney
and Muir (1976) compared a similar group of Caucasian students
with a group of Asian students, mostly from Hong Kong, which
is a very urban, carpentered environment. The Asian students
also showed a reduced OE, raising the possibility that the external
environment does not play a significant role in the Effect.

If external environment is not the main factor, then perhaps
there is something else that might distinguish the different groups.
One characteristic that has been well-documented to be extremely
prevalent in East Asian populations, but less so in Caucasians, is
myopia, or near-sightedness. (Cheng, Schmid, & Woo, 2007; Park
& Congdon, 2004; Tim, 2010). There are also reports of a high

This section sets up the context for your hypothesis by looking at possible origins of the effect.

No need to put the reference date in parentheses in this case.

This is an online blog reference. Consider whether it is really appropriate to use.

If you want to present a hypothesis, make sure that you spell out the logic behind it clearly.

Oblique Effect and Myopia   5

incidence of myopia in Inuit populations (Morgan, Speakman, & Grimshaw, 1975). Is it possible that myopia is the common factor in a reduced OE?

The fact that there is a reduced OE in a population where there is also a high incidence of short-sightedness does not prove that short-sightedness causes the OE, because a correlation does not imply causation. But if there is a correlation between the size of the OE and the degree of myopia, this could be taken as evidence for a causative relationship.

In the present study I measured the OE for acuity in individuals who had some degree of short-sightedness for which they had a prescription. My primary hypothesis was that individuals with myopia would have a reduced OE compared to those with normal vision. My secondary hypothesis was that there would be a negative correlation between the degree of myopia and the size of the OE. To avoid any confounding due to ethnicity, only Caucasian participants were tested.

Method

Participants

Thirty first-year students with myopia (15 women, 15 men; M_{age} = 18.2 years) at Western University participated for credit in their introductory psychology course. All participants had

Because this is a study you have completed, you should use the past tense.

Describe "Participants" if human, "Subjects" if non-human.

Define the sample in sufficient detail to allow someone else to repeat the experiment.

By stating your hypotheses in this way, you will be able to address each of them in turn when you write your *Results* section.

6   Oblique Effect and Myopia

a Caucasian background (i.e. they and their parents were born in North America and/or Europe). They were required to bring their prescriptions for their spectacle corrections and to wear their glasses or contact lenses. A control group of 30 individuals with normal vision was also included

Apparatus and Materials

All of the stimuli were generated by computer on a 48 cm Sony television screen placed 140 cm from the participants who sat with their chins cradled in a rest to prevent them from moving their heads toward the screen. A two-button box in front of the head rest allowed them to indicate their responses to the patterns that were generated on the screen.

The stimulus patterns consisted of high contrast (90%) black and white stripes (gratings) whose orientation could be adjusted under computer control. The gratings were displayed on the centre of the screen and filled a circular window 10 cm in diameter. The rest of the screen was a uniform grey and had a luminance of 30 cd/m^2.

Procedure

When a participant arrived at the lab, the experimenter took note of his or her prescription correction. All participants were introduced individually to the testing apparatus and shown the

---

In vision experiments it is important to provide information about light levels. In other kinds of study include all the information that would allow someone to repeat your experiment in all its essential aspects.

The issue of gender-specific pronouns is a difficult one. "His or her" is cumbersome if used repeatedly, but it is misleading to use only "his" or "her." There is no completely satisfactory solution, but one option is to try to use plurals to avoid having to designate one gender, but occasionally revert to the singular.

Be systematic as you describe the procedure. Give the details step by step and in sequence so that the reader can imagine exactly what was going on as the experiment proceeded.

APA style requires the use of SI units, so milliseconds would be expressed as ms and all units of measurement will be metric.

Oblique Effect and Myopia   7

patterns that would be presented. They were also shown how to respond using the button box. Once they were familiar with the procedures they were allowed a number of practice trials, in which stripes of different widths were presented and they responded by pushing one of the response buttons to indicate whether or not the stripes were visible. In the experiment proper, which followed immediately after the practice trials, a pattern of stripes was presented on the screen for 500 ms. The orientation of the stripes was chosen at random by the computer and could be at one of four different orientations (vertical, horizontal, oblique right or oblique left). The task of the participant was to indicate, by pressing one of the two buttons, whether or not he or she had seen the stripes, and then another pattern was presented. Initially, the stripes were quite wide and could be seen easily, but with each "yes" response, the width was reduced by 5% until the participant could no longer detect them. If the participant pressed the "no" button, the width of the stripes at that orientation would be increased by 5% next time they were shown. This procedure is referred to as a "staircase" and the change in response is referred to as a "reversal." The staircase was continued until the participant had made a total of 10 response reversals for each orientation. A full testing session took about 45 min to complete.

Although this is not part of the data collection, it allows the reader to know whether the participant might have been making mistakes because she wasn't sure of the task.

A Results section should always start with how the data were summarized.

The next portion of the Results should be a description of the summarized data. Usually, this would be in the form of a table or a graph.

8   Oblique Effect and Myopia

Results

For each participant, a threshold visual acuity, indicating the finest stripes that could be detected, was calculated for each orientation. This was done by calculating the average stripe width across all of the response reversals. These averaged thresholds were then plotted as a function of orientation for the myopic and the normal-vision participants separately, and are shown in Figure 1. It may be seen that participants in both groups were able to detect narrower stripes when they were horizontal or vertical, then when they were oblique. (Note that because stripe width is expressed in millimetres, better performance is shown as a lower value.) This difference is the typical pattern for an Oblique Effect. This figure also shows that the differences between horizontal and vertical seem less for the myopes and that their overall acuity is lower.

If your data are not intuitive, be sure to give a short explanation.

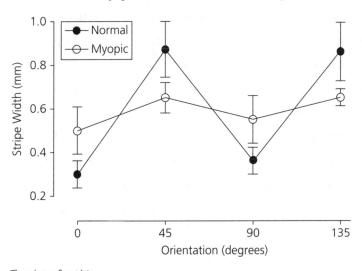

Note: The data for this section are not based on a real study.

Oblique Effect and Myopia   9

The third step is the statistical analysis. Once you have described the data, you can verify whether the differences you observed are statistically reliable.

To test the first hypothesis, that individuals with myopia would show a smaller OE, I carried out a 2 × 2 ANOVA with refractive status as a between-subjects factor and orientation as a within-subjects factor. This analysis showed that there was a main effect for orientation, $F(1, 174) = 4.55$, $p < .01$, confirming the presence of an overall OE, regardless of whether the individuals were myopic. There was also a main effect for group, $F(1, 52) = 5.03$, $p < .05$, that showed that the myopes overall had a reduced level of acuity. Finally there was a significant interaction, $F(3, 174) = 3.54$, $p < .05$, that indicated a smaller OE for the myopes.

My second hypothesis was that there should be a correlation between the magnitude of a person's short-sightedness and the size of the OE. To test this I needed a single measure of the OE, rather than four different orientation thresholds. I therefore constructed an index for each participant by dividing the average thresholds for the obliques by the horizontal/vertical (H/V) thresholds. This index was calculated so that a value of 1.00 represented equal detection of the H/V and oblique orientations. Any value above that indicated that an OE was present. It was then possible to create a scatterplot showing the size of the OE as expressed by the index plotted against the degree of myopia. For this analysis, I used only the data from the myopis group and the results are shown in Figure 2. They indicate that higher myopia is associated

10   Oblique Effect and Myopia

with a smaller OE. The Pearson product-moment correlation was significantly greater than zero ($r(28)$, p = .02).

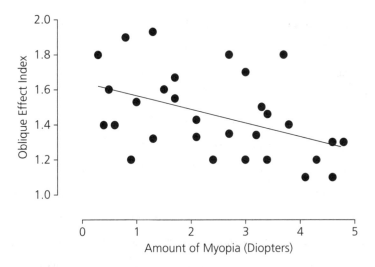

Discussion

The purpose of the present experiment was to determine whether a relationship existed between a refractive error, specifically shortsightedness, or myopia, and the Oblique Effect for visual acuity. I tested this hypothesis by measuring the OE in individuals with varying degrees of myopia and correlating the size of the OE with the amount of myopia. The results showed that, on average, the OE was present for all participants, regardless of whether or

Always begin the *Discussion* with an overview summarizing the purpose of the study, how it was conducted, and what the main finding was.

It is good practice to structure the *Discussion* to run parallel to the
Introduction and to talk about the same topics in the same order, if
possible.

Oblique Effect and Myopia   11

not they were myopic. However, the data also showed that there
was a moderate correlation between the degree of myopia and the
OE, confirming the hypothesis.

As mentioned in the Introduction, it was originally thought
that the OE was a consequence of optical aberrations in the eye
(Emsley, 1925), but that later research demonstrated unequivocally
that the OE was neurally based (Campbell et al., 1966). The
present results suggest that although the OE may occur because
of a differential distribution of orientation-selective neurons in
the visual cortex, there does seem to be a role for optical factors
in the development of the OE. It is not clear how myopia might
induce the OE in the first place, but it should be noted that myopia
itself typically occurs because the shape of the eye is different from
normal. The eye of a myope is longer than that of a person with
normal vision, so the light rays entering the eye come to a focus
in front of the retina. This means that without correction, most
images seen by an individual will be out of focus. This is corrected
by wearing spectacle lenses that allow the image to be pushed back
so that it focused accurately on the retinal surface.

The original study of Annis and Frost (1973) suggested
that the OE might be the result of visual experience, and there
are many studies in the literature to show that abnormal visual

Here, we've
gone back to
the question
of the role of
experience in
development.

A *Discussion* should not be simply a repeat of the
Introduction. It should start from the information
provided there and then proceed to try to explain
the results that were obtained.

12   Oblique Effect and Myopia

experience during early life can affect the development of
neurons in the visual cortex (Blakemore, 1977; Blakemore &
Cooper, 1970). The study by Timney and Muir (1976) suggested
that simply living in a carpentered environment did not seem to
have an effect on the OE. However, they did not consider that
other forms of abnormal experience might have occurred for the
individuals they were testing. Most children are not tested to see
whether they need glasses until they are several years old. This
means that if they are short-sighted from birth their experience
of the world could be quite blurry for quite some time, and this
in turn might affect the neurons in the brain that process visual
images. Perhaps the reduced quality of the images reduces the
disproportionate development of neurons that respond to the
cardinal orientation.

The present experiment does not allow us to test this
hypothesis any further, but it might be possible to determine if the
blurry images caused by myopia are having an effect by studying
the OE in individuals who were corrected at different ages. If
it is the case that poor image quality reduces the asymmetrical
development of orientation-selective neurons, then the earlier that
children had their vision corrected, the larger the OE might be.

It's not necessary to suggest further
studies, but if there is a clear next step, it
is worth suggesting it.

References

Annis, R. C., & Frost, B. J. (1973). Human visual ecology and orientation anisotropies in acuity. *Science, 182*, 729–731.

Appelle, S. (1972). Perception and discrimination as a function of stimulus orientation: The "oblique effect" in man and animals. *Psychological Bulletin, 78*(4), 266–278.

Baowang, L., Peterson, M. R., & Freeman, R. D. (2003) Oblique effect: a neural basis in the visual cortex. *Journal of Neurophysiology, 90*, 204–217.

Berkley, M. A., Kitterle, F. L., & Watkins, D. W. (1975). Grating visibility as a function of orientation and eccentricity. *Vision Research, 15*, 239–244.

Blakemore, C. (1977). Genetic instructions and developmental plasticity in the kitten's visual cortex. *Philosophical Transactions of the Royal Society of London, B. 278*, 425–434.

Blakemore, C., & Cooper, G. F. (1970). Development of the brain depends on the visual environment. *Nature, 228*, 477–478.

Campbell, F. W., Kulikowski, J. J., & Levinson, J. (1966). The effect of orientation on the visual resolution of gratings. *Journal of Physiology, 187*, 427–436.

Cheng, D., Schmid, K. L., & Woo, G. C. (2007). Myopia prevalence in Chinese-Canadian children in an optometric practice. *Optometry and Vision Science, 84*, 21–32.

14   Oblique Effect and Myopia

Emsley, H. H. (1925). Irregular astigmatism of the eye. *Transactions of the Optical Society, 27*, 28–41.

Jastrow, J. (1893). On the judgment of angles and positions of lines. *American Journal of Psychology, 5*, 214–248.

Morgan, R. W., Speakman, J. S., & Grimshaw, S. E. (1975). Inuit myopia: An environmentally induced epidemic? *Canadian Medical Association Journal, 112*, 575–577.

Park, D. J. J., & Congdon, N. G. (2004). Evidence for an "epidemic" of myopia. *Annals of the Academy of Medicine of Singapore. 33*, 21–26.

Tim. (2010). Chinese more likely to be nearsighted. Retrieved from http://www.8asians.com/2010/06/18/chinese-more-likely-to-be-nearsighted/

Timney, B., & Muir, D. W. (1976). Orientation anisotropy: Incidence and magnitude in Caucasian and Chinese subjects. *Science, 193*, 699–701.

Presentation of Data

Objectives

- organizing your results
- using data tables
- graphing your data
- preparing figures and graphs
- making your figures more informative
- presenting your statistical analyses

Introduction

The *Results* section is the heart of an experimental paper. Most readers will look first to the *Abstract* and then move to the *Results* to find out more about your data. No matter how well you write the rest of your paper, if your results are not presented clearly, the paper will have lost much of its value. It is frustrating to read about a study and not be able to understand exactly how it turned out. In some cases, authors do this deliberately to exaggerate or diminish their findings in support of a particular point of view. But often, ambiguous writing occurs simply because the authors don't think about the reader as they write their *Results* section.

The *Results* section really consists of two parts: what the reader is presented with and what the reader *doesn't* see. Before you actually begin to write your *Results* section, you will need to make a number of decisions about the many possible ways of organizing and presenting your results. Once you have gathered a set of data, you must first analyze them and then decide how to present them. You will likely have a number of options with respect to what analyses you do, and it is not unusual to carry out several different analyses, only one or two of which may end up in your paper. Similarly, if you are going to present tables or graphs, you may try several different approaches before selecting the ones that you think will most fairly represent your study. As well, you should always introduce your *Results* section with a description of your findings. Before you do that, however, you should ask yourself how you want to present your results. Your questions might include the following:

- Should I present individual participant data or group averages?
- Should I describe the results in words or using figures and/or tables?
- If I choose a figure, what type of graph or chart would be most effective?
- If it is a graph, how should I arrange the axes?
- What summary statistics should I include?

And this is just the beginning! With experience, the decisions will become much easier to make, but you should always put effort into designing your *Results* section. It is not just a matter of writing down your data; you are trying to sell your results to the reader so that she or he understands and accepts them.

Organizing Your *Results* Section

When you carry out an experiment, the raw data will be in the form of a set of scores, or responses, or settings for each individual participant. Obviously, there will be way too much information to present in your paper, even if you formatted it in an attractive way. Your first step will always be to reduce the data to a manageable level by taking averages and calculating measures of variability, among other things. Then, you will carry out your statistical analyses, and finally, you will consider what to include in the *Results* section. However, you should be aware that many journals, in the interest of preventing fraud, now encourage authors to submit their raw data along with their paper. These data are archived and made available so that other researchers can verify the analyses that have been done. So although you won't include all of your raw data in the *Results* section of your paper, you might be asked to provide this information separately.

A good *Results* section should begin with a summary of the data and then a report of the analyses. As with writing an essay (see Chapter 4), the essence of any strong research paper is its ability to tell a story, and the first part of a story involves setting the scene. Your data summary does just that; then, your analysis develops the plot. It is not unusual to see the *Results* section of a psychology report begin along these lines: "An analysis of variance was performed on the data and there was a significant main effect for *X*." This sentence is not very informative. The *Results* section is where you begin to try to convince the reader of the validity of your work. Although you should not interpret your data in this section, you should present them in such a way that your reader is directed towards the same conclusions that you plan to draw. In general, you should start by stating your experimental hypothesis or by outlining the question you were asking, followed by a brief summary of your main findings. Then, you should lead your reader through the data, one level of analysis at a time, providing enough information to justify the conclusions that you will make in the *Discussion* section. Deal with the main findings first, and then go on to the secondary results.

Summarizing your main findings

As we mentioned above, for most of your experiments you will not be able to present all of your raw data. When you are measuring behaviour, human or animal, there will almost always be variability across individuals or even within individuals over successive measurements. For this reason, many experimenters take repeated measurements of the same thing and determine an average. Typically, you would begin by reporting your group means, together with some measure of variability. For example, if you ran an experiment that examined the effect of cellphone use on driving errors in a driving simulator, you might summarize your results this way:

> Individuals who used a cellphone while driving made more driving errors ($M = 7.3$, $SD = 1.7$) than individuals who did not use a cellphone while driving ($M = 4.9$, $SD = 1.3$).

A brief summary like this is appropriate if you have only one or two variables to deal with. But what if your experiment had been more complex? Let's say that you still asked questions about driving and talking on the phone, but you also compared handset versus hands-free talking and tested males and females as separate categories. Now you have eight means to report rather than just two. At this point, you might want to consider using a data table or a figure.

Tables or graphs?

Using a table is one way to present your data, but you must always consider whether it is the most effective way of getting your point across. Tables have the advantage of providing precise numerical data, but graphs often give a more compelling impression of the overall pattern of results. Your decision to make a table versus a graph should be based on determining which one will convey the information most effectively. In general, a table is a good choice if you have several sets of numbers that might get buried if listed in the body of the report and if a graph would provide no additional information (such as the overall pattern of results). A graph should go beyond what you can provide in numerical or textual form. If you have collected data for a number of conditions that vary systematically, then a graphical representation is by far the best way to look for, or express, a functional relationship. Sometimes, however, the choice between a table and a graph comes down to personal style or preference.

Using Data Tables

If you can make your data summary clearer by using a table, by all means do so. However, it's essential that the tables themselves are well-organized and straightforward. Don't overload them with data, and be sure to plan the layout carefully. For the above example on cell-phone use and driving errors, you might create something along the lines of Table 7.1.

With a table like this, the reader can see the results at a glance. A good table should be self-explanatory. Nevertheless, it's important to refer to each table in the text and point out the most important aspects, without repeating everything it contains. For example, you might describe Table 7.1 as follows:

Table 7.1 shows that regardless of whether someone uses a handset or hands-free phone, the rate of driving errors increases. However, more errors occurred when individuals used a handset.

Table 7.1 Number of driving errors in a driving simulator

	Handset		Hands-free	
	Using phone M (SD)	No phone M (SD)	Using phone M (SD)	No phone M (SD)
Males	7.5[a] (1.6)	4.8* (1.6)	6.0 (1.9)	4.3* (2.1)
Females	7.3 (1.8)	5.0* (1.0)	6.5 (2.4)	4.9* (1.9)

Note: The means represent the number of driving errors during a 15-minute observation period. See text for details.

[a]One participant in this group did not complete the whole experiment and was dropped from the analysis.

*Phone/No phone comparison $p < 0.05$.

Preparing tables

Table 7.1 was prepared according to APA guidelines (APA, 2010). Remember to keep in mind these guidelines when preparing a table:

- Everything in the table should be double-spaced, including the headings and any notes at the bottom.
- Use as many decimal places as needed by the precision of measurement, and be consistent throughout.
- Each table should have a brief, informative title.
- Do not use any vertical lines in the table. If necessary, use extra spacing to make the table easier to read.
- Make sure that each column has a heading.
- Explain any abbreviations or special symbols in a note placed below the table.
- If you have made statistical comparisons between items in the table, be sure to identify them with asterisks and give the significance levels in a note.
- If you do use notes to clarify information in the paper, they should be listed in the following order: *general notes* that provide information relating to the table as a whole; *specific notes* that refer to individual cells in the table and are identified by superscript lower case letters (for example, mentioning that a subject dropped out from a group); and *probability notes* that indicate the significance levels used.

These technical requirements aside, you should also ask yourself several questions:

- Do the data in the tables complement—rather than duplicate—what is in the text? (You should avoid repetition as much as possible.)
- Are the tables numbered sequentially throughout the paper?
- Is the style of the tables consistent throughout?
- Have you referred to the tables in the body of the paper?

Graphing Your Data

The ability to represent data clearly in graphical form is a skill well worth learning. You should be aware of the major kinds of graphs that you might use in a research project and the advantages of each. When you are preparing a graph, think about style as well as content; the most successful figure is often the simplest.

Line graphs

Line graphs, in their simplest form, plot the value of a dependent variable (on the vertical or y-axis) against changes made in the independent variable (on the horizontal or x-axis). They are particularly well suited to those cases where you want to show a continuous change in the value of a variable under different experimental conditions, or to show a trend.

Scattergrams

Scattergrams are useful when you want to show a correlation between two variables. When you plot a scattergram, each data point represents a measurement or score made under two conditions. If you are trying to make predictions about one score on the basis of another, then you would use the x-axis to represent the independent (predictor) variable, and the y-axis for the dependent (predicted) variable. The scatter of the points on the graph will provide the reader with a sense of the *variability* of the data—in other words, the strength of the relationship. You can also quantify the trend by calculating the best-fitting regression line.

Bar graphs

Bar graphs consist of bars whose lengths are proportional to the value of the variables you are displaying. They are best suited to situations in which you want to compare the results of a limited number of experimental conditions— usually not more than two or three. If you include more than that, the graph becomes more difficult to interpret. Although you can plot bar graphs in several ways, always remember to place the conditions you most want to compare next to each other.

Histograms and area charts

Histograms and area charts are not used very much in psychology reports, but they are useful if you want to show how many participants received a particular score on a test or how many of the participants fell into each of a series of different categories. A conventional histogram has multiple bars, each representing a subset of the data you have collected. An area chart is a specific type of histogram that plots only the midpoints of the bars and therefore looks more like a line graph.

Pie charts

Pie charts graphically represent proportions of data like slices cut out of a whole pie on a plate. They are not often used in scientific papers, although they are very common in media presentations or reports directed to the general public. The results of survey research are sometimes displayed in pie charts.

Preparing Figures and Graphs

Many spreadsheet programs, such as Microsoft Excel, are capable of producing the kinds of graphs you will need for your term papers. However, because these programs were originally designed for preparing business presentations, their default graphs may not reflect what you will need for your paper. Nevertheless, with a little reorganization, you can produce graphs that match the format typically used in your discipline. A number of commercially available software packages are available that will allow you to create virtually any kind of graph you might need. If you are working on your thesis, it is likely that your advisor will have a program you can use. You should also check to see if your institution has a site licence for one of these programs. Two of the most popular are GraphPad Prism and SigmaPlot. If you don't have access to a computer graphics package, then you will need to draw your figures by hand. Whether you are preparing your graphs by hand or on a computer, the following APA guidelines (APA, 2010) will be helpful:

- Your figures should be as neat as possible.
- If you are drawing a figure by hand, use a ruler and black ink. You might consider drawing a rough version on graph paper and then tracing it onto plain paper.
- The independent variable (the one you have manipulated) should be on the horizontal axis, and the dependent variable (the one you measure) should be on the vertical axis.
- The vertical axis should be about 75 per cent of the length of the horizontal axis.
- Use large and distinctive symbols, with different symbols for each line on the graph. If you have multiple graphs with the same data categories, be consistent and use the same symbols for each category.
- Label the axes clearly. Start each main word with a capital and run the axis label parallel to the axis. Always include the unit of measurement on the axis label.

- Show only essential detail. A cluttered graph is difficult to read.
- Include a caption describing the figure. If the figure includes lines or symbols that convey information, include a legend that indicates what the different symbols represent.

Presenting Data: Some Examples

Let's reconsider the data in Table 7.1. You could present these data very easily in the form of a bar graph, as shown in Figure 7.1. In this figure, we have chosen to make two separate bar graphs, one for handset use and one for hands-free

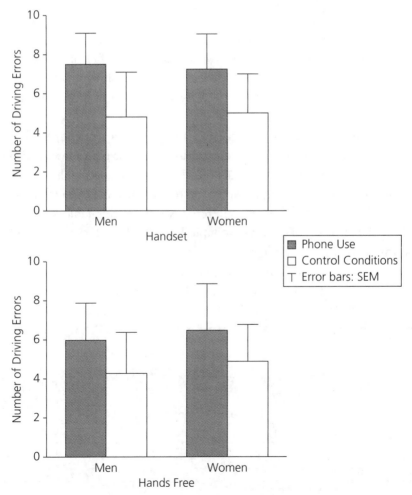

Figure 7.1   Mean number of driving errors during phone use

use, although we could also have created a single graph with four sets of columns. We have also chosen to juxtapose the control (non-phone) condition with the phone condition to emphasize that comparison. If the emphasis of the study had been on differences in male and female performance, we might have put the *Men* and *Women* columns next to each other for each of the conditions. You must decide the best way to arrange your graph depending on what aspects of your data you want to emphasize.

In this example, there is no strong reason for choosing a graph over a table or vice versa. However, if you have a lot of data and the points the data make are unclear even with a large table, then a graph is your best choice. As with tables, be sure to refer to each graph in the body of your report and mention the major points that each graph illustrates.

Now, let's suppose you had done an experiment where you studied the extent to which children exposed to cartoon violence showed signs of aggressive behaviour. In this experiment, you varied the number of violent acts in a film in order to see whether the amount of violence shown had an effect on aggressive behaviour. One way of reporting such data is in the form of a table, as shown in Table 7.2.

The numbers in Table 7.2 suggest that boys have a tendency to show increasing aggression with increasing exposure, whereas girls show an increase followed by a decrease. A data table of this sort is an acceptable way of presenting your results, although if you tried to include a measure of variability, the table would start to become cluttered. Contrast this table with a graph showing the same set of data, as shown in Figure 7.2—you can see at a glance how differently the two groups react.

The actual numbers are probably less important than the pattern of results shown in the graph. You could take this analysis further and look at the strength of the relationship between exposure to violence and aggressive behaviour by creating a scattergram, as shown in Figure 7.3, which shows the

Table 7.2 Number of aggressive acts by children following exposure to TV violence

	Number of violent scenes in cartoon							
	0	1	2	3	4	5	6	7
Boys	0.3	1.4	2.3	2.6	3.3	5.6	5.8	5.7
Girls	0.2	1.1	2.5	3.8	4.1	3.2	2.4	1.2

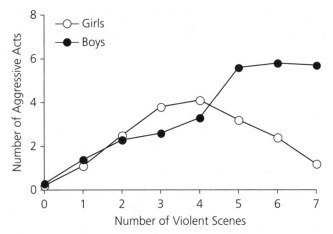

Figure 7.2 Number of aggressive behaviours following exposure to violent cartoon scenes

This figure shows the data from Table 7.2 in the form of a line graph. Filled symbols represent the boys, and open symbols represent the girls. Note how much easier it is to see how the number of violent acts by the girls increases then decreases.

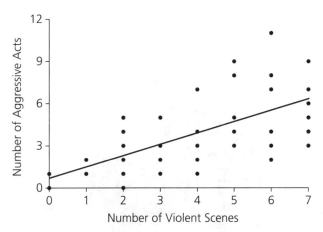

Figure 7.3 Relationship between violent incidents on TV and aggressive behaviours

The data in Table 7.2 and Figure 7.2 represent means. Figure 7.3 shows how you could represent the data from individual participants as a scattergram. For each of the experimental conditions, the number of violent acts for six boys is shown. Because several boys had the same score, the points overlap. The connecting line represents the mean for each group. By using a scattergram, you can get a better sense of the degree of relationship between two variables. You could also go one step further and calculate a regression equation so that you could fit a regression line to the data.

results just for boys. By plotting all of the points for each individual subject, you can see if this is a very strong trend or just a weak relationship. You can also show the degree of relationship by carrying out a linear regression and plotting the best-fitting line, as we have done in this figure.

Scattergrams are effective when you want to show a correlation between two variables—such as violent TV scenes and aggressive acts—but they aren't suitable for illustrating data that fall into a number of categories. Suppose, for instance, that you wanted to find out how students *really* spent their time while they were "working." You provided a group of students with a diary to keep track of the amount of time they spent in various activities. You could represent your data in several different ways. Although a line graph would not be appropriate for these data, there are alternatives. You could make a table, listing the percentage of time students spent doing different things; or you could draw a bar graph to make the point more graphically. In this case, however, you could probably make the greatest impression by presenting a pie chart, as in Figure 7.4. Here it is easy to see that your sample of students actually spent only 60 per cent of their "work time" doing things that might be construed as work, such as reading or note-taking.

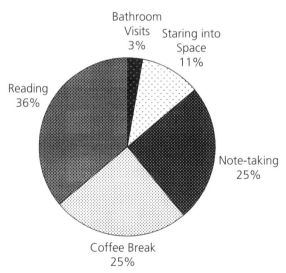

Figure 7.4 Percentage of time students spent in different activities during an evening when they were "working"

When you have data that can be broken into percentages or proportions, a pie chart gives the reader an intuitive sense of the distribution.

As you can see, there are many ways to present your data graphically. Figures that are informative and well-presented can make the difference between a mediocre grade and a good one.

Making Your Figures More Informative

The suggestions we have made above will give you the tools to prepare simple, informative graphs. You should also be aware that a graph can be modified in a variety of ways to provide much more information to the reader.

Curve-fitting

We have already mentioned the possibility of calculating a regression equation and plotting the best-fitting straight line onto your scattergram. If your data are more complex, then you may want to use more sophisticated curve-fitting programs that will allow you to fit and plot other functions onto your data. For instance, if the measurements increase and then decrease, you might need to calculate a non-linear regression equation, or you might find that your measurements are best described by an exponential function. In some cases, for example, when you are doing perception or cognition experiments, these functions will give you additional information about the underlying mechanisms that are responsible for the pattern of results you obtain.

Measures of variability

A more common addition to both bar and line graphs is some indication of the variability within the data. Depending on the kind of data you have and the point you are trying to illustrate, this variability might be the *standard deviation*, the *standard error of the mean*, or the *95 per cent confidence limits*. Figure 7.5 shows a line graph that contains standard error bars. Notice that when two lines are close together, as they are in this figure, the graph can be made neater by plotting the error bars for each variable in opposite directions.

Use of different scales

Sometimes you may have data that cover a very large range of values. This is not unusual if you are working in some areas of sensory psychology or neuroscience. If you plot these data on a regular graph, any differences that exist at low values might become invisible on a linear scale. One way to get around

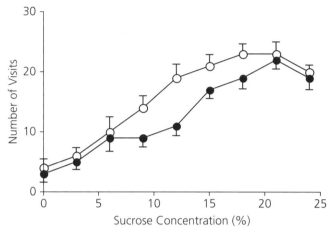

Figure 7.5 Feeding behaviour of hummingbirds based on sucrose concentration

This figure shows a set of fictitious data on the feeding behaviour of hummingbirds. The graph shows the mean number of visits to a bird feeder, plotted as a function of the concentration of sucrose in the feeding solution. The open symbols represent birds that were nesting, while the filled symbols represent birds that were not nesting. The error bars represent one standard error of the mean. Standard error bars are a useful way to indicate the amount of variability in the data. The standard error is an estimate, based on the standard deviation, of the amount of variability within a whole population, rather than just the sample you tested. It forms the basis for some statistical tests.

this problem is to use a *logarithmic scale*. When you create a log scale, you are converting your data values into their logarithms and plotting these on your graph. This expands the low end of the scale and compresses the high end. Figure 7.6 (on pages 143–144) shows you the same set of data plotted on both linear and log *x*-axes. Once the values are converted to logarithms, it is much easier to see how the sensitivity changes.

Presenting Your Statistical Analyses

For the most part, your figures and tables are descriptive: they show what the results are and serve as accompaniments to the text. The next step is to give an account of the statistical tests you have done.

If the analysis is straightforward, you can report it directly in the text, giving enough information for the reader to confirm that the analysis has been done correctly. The exact information will vary with each test, but it may include the value of the test statistic, the degrees of freedom, and the level of statistical significance.

If your analysis is a complicated one—for example, a multifactorial analysis of variance, or an analysis involving a series of correlations—you might consider using a statistical table showing all the details of your analysis. As you become more experienced at presenting data, it will become easier to decide what to include in the text or in tables. Initially, though, you should refer to the *Publication Manual of the American Psychological Association* or ask your instructor what is required.

The goal of most of your experiments will be to test a specific hypothesis. Even if you are asking a question for which you do not have a specific prediction, you may set your experiment up formally as a test of a statistical

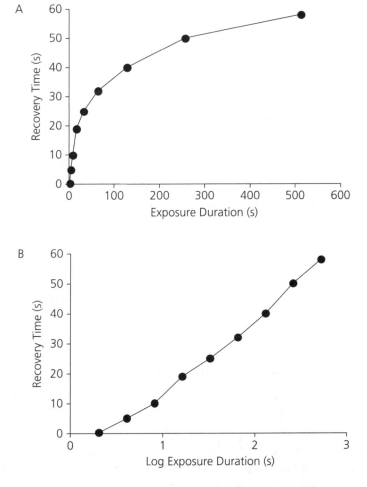

Figure 7.6 Visual sensitivity following exposure to bright light stimulus

continued

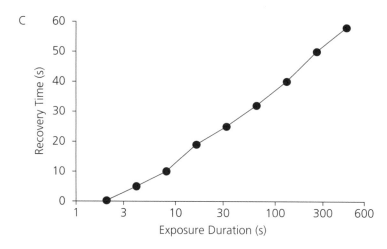

Figure 7.6 (continued)

This figure shows a set of fictitious data on the recovery of visual sensitivity following exposure to a very bright light. The same data are plotted in two different ways. In Panel A, standard linear axes are used, and they indicate that recovery is very fast following brief exposure but is much slower after long exposures. The same data are plotted in Panel B, but this time the exposure durations, plotted along the x-axis, have been converted to base-10 logarithms. An alternative way to plot the x-axis would be to keep the logarithmic scale but to use the original (antilog) numbers, as shown in Panel C (at the top of page 144).

hypothesis. For example, the question "What is the effect of different drugs on the rate of learning in rats?" could be rephrased as a statement: "Drug *A* produces significantly better learning than drug *B*." You could then test that hypothesis using the appropriate statistical tests.

In your analysis, you should present the actual statistical values followed by a brief statement of what they mean. Although you may know exactly what your *F*-ratios imply, your reader may not. For example, in the experiment testing the effect of different drugs on the rate of learning in rats, you might have evaluated your data using an analysis of variance. You could describe the results of this analysis by writing the following:

> The analysis of variance showed a significant difference in the effectiveness of the two drugs $F(1, 15) = 14.5$, $p < .01$. The rats that were given drug *A* took fewer trials to learn the task than those that received drug *B*.

Finally, if you have performed several different analyses on your data, you should start by reporting the overall analysis and then move on to the secondary analyses. Remember, you are leading the reader through your paper, and the better your organization, the clearer it will be.

Summary

The proper presentation of data is a skill that even some professional scientists have not fully grasped. It is almost certain that you, as a student, have struggled through a *Results* section without really "getting" it. Although it's tempting to think that this occurs because you don't have enough background to understand what the researcher did, quite often it's actually because the researcher did not consider his or her audience. In presenting a case, it is crucial to show all the steps you took to get from *A* to *F*. If you skip over some of the interim elements, the reader is left to fill in the blanks. So when you are presenting your data, always keep your reader in mind and keep asking whether you would understand what you had written if you were reading it for the first time.

Reference

American Psychological Association. (2010). *Publication manual of the American Psychological Association.* (6th ed.). Washington, DC: Author.

Research Proposals and Honours Theses

8

Objectives

- understanding the differences between research proposals and honours theses
- preparing a research proposal
- researching and writing an honours thesis

Introduction

Learning to write lab reports teaches you many skills. In particular, writing lab reports in your early years at university will prepare you for a much more extensive project in your senior years. At some institutions, you may be expected to do an honours thesis involving an independent research project; elsewhere, you may be required to prepare a formal research proposal without actually carrying out the study itself. You can apply some of the guidelines we've provided for writing lab reports and research papers to preparing research proposals and theses, but these larger projects will require more planning and independent thought on your part. They will have a somewhat different organization from a simple lab report or essay, so we will discuss how to organize a research proposal and thesis later in this chapter.

Research Proposals

One of the requirements for your thesis course may be that you submit a research proposal for your project. Certainly, this would be a requirement once you are in a graduate program. If you go on to be a professional scientist, you will need to write a research proposal whenever you complete an application for a grant. Because grant funds are the lifeblood of any research scientist, the application is a crucial document. The earlier you learn the skills involved in applying for grants, the more likely it is that your future applications will be successful.

Writing a research proposal serves a number of purposes:

- it allows you to do a focused literature search within a specific research area;
- it gives you an opportunity to think through all aspects of a research problem before you begin the project; and
- it gives you an opportunity to convince your reader that the project is worthwhile.

You can think of the proposal as a strategic plan for a research project. As such, it should have three statements:

1. what the problem you intend to study is;
2. why studying this problem is important; and
3. how you will carry out your study.

The research proposal combines elements of both an essay and a lab report. The introductory or background section presents a critical review of a body of literature with the addition of a statement of your experimental hypotheses. The rest may resemble a lab report written in the future tense.

As with a lab report or an essay, your proposal will have a number of parts. Although the order of the parts we describe below is typical, you may prefer to rearrange the order for the proposal you write, depending on your particular needs.

Introduction

Your introduction should include sections such as the following:

- **Context of the research project.** The first thing you need to do is to set the stage. After you have introduced your topic, you should describe briefly the current thinking in that area.
- **Review of the literature.** You need to establish the relationship between your proposed work and the existing literature in the field. Here, you are moving from the current thinking in the general area to the opinions and evidence presented in the specialized literature that are directly relevant to your own project. This review does not have to be exhaustive; rather, it is intended to show the reader that you are familiar with the research literature in the area.

- **Statement of the problem.** Once you have established a context, you will need to introduce your own study. Indicate what you plan to study and what your rationale is. If you have any underlying assumptions, you should state them here. Finally, you should state your experimental hypotheses or describe the questions you hope to answer.

Methodology

This section should include information on research design and data analysis. This is where you should talk about the kinds of data you will collect, the methods you will use to gather the data, and the rationale for using these particular methods. Although the amount of detail you provide here will depend on the space limitations of the proposal, you should always include enough information to show that you know what you are doing.

You should also describe the formal experimental design you will be using. You can avoid a lot of problems if you know exactly how you will analyze your data *before* you run your study. So, if each participant will be tested under both experimental and control conditions, you should be using a within-subjects design. Other experiments might require a multifactorial analysis of variance design or multiple correlations. You should also be thinking of how you will collate and organize your data as you collect it so that it will be simple to carry out the analysis. This information may not actually appear in the text of your proposal itself, but it will make your analysis much easier to do.

Anticipated results

This section is similar to the *Discussion* section of a lab report but is written in the future tense. For the proposal, you do not need to place the results in the context of the literature. Instead, you should draw out the implications or the significance of your results if they turn out according to your predictions. For example, suppose you are proposing to study whether jet lag is more severe when travelling east than when travelling west. You propose to measure this by surveying frequent fliers who travel between Toronto and London, England. Your hypothesis is that because the easterly flights tend to be overnight and the westbound ones are during the day, eastbound passengers often go to bed soon after arriving, thereby sleeping during the day and disrupting their circadian clock. In your proposal, while you would of course describe your hypothesis, you could also go further by saying, "If it is the case that the increased jet lag is a result of sleeping immediately after arriving, then travellers should be advised to stay up during their first day and go to bed at their normal time."

Thinking about your anticipated results also allows you to consider how you might organize them in a *Results* section. It is often very helpful to create hypothetical figures of what your results might look like if they were to confirm your predictions. Doing so will help you be more prepared when it comes time to actually write up your *Results* section.

Limitations

Few studies are perfect. When you work on an undergraduate thesis, you will not have all the resources that a fully funded research professor might have. As a result, you may not be able to carry out your study exactly as you would like, and the results you obtain might not be perfect. Such flaws and limitations will not be held against you, but you must indicate to your reader that you are aware of them. You might also have to concede that there may be alternative explanations for the data you will gather. Acknowledging the potential problems with your study will not weaken your proposal, as long as you can defend everything you plan to do.

If you have aspirations to be a professional scientist, then learning how to write a proper research proposal may be one of the most important skills you acquire as an undergraduate. When you apply for a grant as a new investigator, the adjudication committees have little to go on other than what you have written in your proposal. If you can develop a convincing style and combine it with logical thinking, you will be well on your way to being a successful, and well-funded, scientist.

Honours Theses

In a typical lab course, you will be assigned several experiments to carry out and write up. And in those courses, most of the time you will be working under close supervision. As you progress through your university career, however, you will be required to do more independent work; this will sometimes include writing an honours thesis. In their final form, lab reports and theses are quite similar, and many of the rules we described in Chapter 6 apply also to theses. However, the thesis is a much larger project, and it requires much more preparation.

The primary purpose of this book is to help you express yourself well in writing, and what you write is largely a product of the preparation you've done first. You will spend a whole academic year preparing to write your honours thesis, so it is all the more important that you think carefully about how you'll proceed. Some students do not have a clear idea of what is required for an honours thesis until they have actually begun work on it, and in some cases, not until they have been working on it for quite a while. Knowing what is expected of you from the beginning will make it much easier to write a final paper that will earn you a good mark. This section will give you a brief overview of what is required to prepare for an honours thesis involving an empirical research project.

What is an honours thesis?

An honours thesis is a piece of empirical research that gives you an opportunity to demonstrate your ability to carry out independent scientific work (albeit with some guidance from your advisor) and present it in the form of a paper. It is equally important to be aware of what a thesis is not.

An honours thesis is not primarily intended to be an original and significant contribution to the literature of your discipline. Although many theses are excellent pieces of work, and some of the best are good enough to get published, publication is not the reason for doing the work. You must not assume that you have to create a masterpiece that solves a "big" problem in your discipline. Many students get bogged down after designing complicated experiments involving dozens of subjects; as a result, they run out of time and cannot do a good job on their data analysis or write-up. Research is time-consuming, and it often involves several false starts. When you are doing a thesis over the course of a single year, you don't have the flexibility to go back and start again if things don't work out. For this reason it's essential to set reasonable goals and choose a project that will be manageable. You can demonstrate your research skills just as well, and sometimes better, with a simple project as you can with a complicated one.

Be aware that the specific topic area in which you choose to do your thesis is less important than you might think. For example, many psychology students who aspire to go on to graduate programs in clinical psychology naturally want to do their theses in this area. However, clinical psychology is one of the most difficult areas in which to do meaningful research in a short period of time. Several obstacles can slow down this kind of research: it may be difficult to get ethics clearance; the potential participants may not be readily available; and the rules of confidentiality may prevent a student from gathering important data. It is possible (with the right advisor and a carefully chosen project) to produce an excellent thesis in an area such as clinical psychology, but you may have to work a lot harder than if you were doing a cognitive psychology thesis. Similarly, students who do animal research often find they have to commit themselves to many hours of testing, often over weekends and holidays.

The important thing is to choose a feasible project that you will find interesting. If you keep this in mind, the tasks of selecting a topic and running the study will be much easier.

Differences between a lab report and an honours thesis

The main differences between a lab report and an honours thesis are the amount of background that you will be expected to provide in your *Introduction*, the scale of your study, and the extent of your *Discussion* section. Otherwise, the final write-up of a thesis should follow a format similar to the one used for a lab report. One advantage to writing a thesis is that you should have the chance to submit preliminary drafts to your advisor for comments before you write the final version. Remember, though, that to get feedback you have to submit the drafts in time for someone to read them. Don't leave everything until the last minute!

Depending on your advisor, you may be assigned a topic—perhaps a general topic area in which to work or a specific topic—or you may be told to start reading the literature and come up with your own topic independently. The more freedom you are given, the more important it becomes to organize your time. Think about all the steps you have to take, and think about your own strengths and limitations. Plan accordingly. For instance, if you know that statistics is not your forte, plan to spend more time on data analysis. Whatever you do, *do not procrastinate*. No matter how well organized you are, you will almost certainly be rushed at the end. Don't let a whole year's work get graded down just because you didn't give yourself enough time to write a polished final draft.

Start by making a schedule that outlines when different aspects of your project should be completed. Consult with your advisor, because he or she will know which parts of your project are most likely to slow you down. Although the specifics of your schedule will depend on your project, we discuss below the major stages you will have to complete for your thesis.

Background reading

Whether your topic has been assigned or you have chosen it yourself, you will need to do some background reading before you are ready to prepare a research proposal. Your advisor will probably start you off with some papers, but then you will have to do a proper literature search and spend time going through what you find. Although you will be reviewing some of the relevant literature in the field, just as you would do for a review essay, your approach to the readings will be somewhat different when you are preparing a thesis.

There may be a very large body of literature in your general area, but your task will be to seek out only those studies that are directly relevant to your topic. Although most of the references you will include in your thesis will focus on questions similar to the ones you are asking, you should begin by reading broadly to get better acquainted with the kinds of research being conducted. For the thesis itself, you won't be doing an exhaustive review of everything that has been written on the subject of your study, but you should still be familiar with the broad issues.

A thesis *Introduction* section differs from a regular research essay in that it is much more narrowly focused. Some students find it difficult to be selective and to decide what to include and what to exclude. It is not at all unusual to see a thesis *Introduction* section that refers to a large number of papers, only a few of which are directly relevant to the specific aspect of a student's research. One way to help you decide what to include is to consider that the papers that you describe in detail in your *Introduction* section should be the same ones you refer back to in the *Discussion* section. Let's say you wanted to do a study of the possible relationship between the ways students use social media and their academic performance at university. A number of studies have already looked at this relationship in a variety of different ways and for several different kinds of social media: Facebook, Twitter, blogs, and so on. If you decided that your study would be on the use of Twitter, you should devote most of your attention to examining that social network. You would refer to studies on Facebook, but you would talk about them in much less detail than the studies on Twitter.

Formulating a project and preparing a research proposal

Although your advisor may not ask for a formal proposal, writing one is to your advantage. You may be able to use your proposal later on as part of your *Introduction* section, and it will also serve as a guide as you proceed. You can follow the suggestions made earlier in this chapter about preparing research proposals.

Getting ethics approval

If you are running a full experimental study, you will be introduced to the practical side of research ethics. We discussed ethical issues in general in Chapter 5, but today's regulations governing research are thorough and strict. Every university has a local research ethics board, and sometimes several boards, to oversee work that involves animals or that has human medical implications. Every research project has to follow ethical guidelines and must be approved by these boards. In the case of an honours thesis, it is likely that your faculty advisor has already been granted approval for the general type of research you want to do, so you will only need to make a simple request for an extension. That said, it is very useful for you to practise filling out ethics forms so that you can get a sense of how important ethical conduct during research is. The rules are extremely strict for projects that involve testing on animals.

Because of the ethics approval requirement, advisors may strongly discourage students from taking on any project involving the collection of individuals' personal data, involving the presentation of potentially offensive materials such as pornography, or involving drugs. Unless that kind of research is an integral part of your advisor's research program, you should not even consider those kinds of studies.

Part of the ethics process involves getting informed consent from your participants. The process of setting up your experiment will include developing consent forms that participants must agree to before the experiment begins and preparing debriefing forms that explain the purpose of the study to the participants after the experiment is completed.

Setting up the experiment

Your proposal should contain the formal experimental design for your study. This stage involves working out what materials and apparatuses you will need to run the experiment. For example, do you need to build an experimental apparatus? Is there new software that you need to become familiar with? Are the tests or questionnaires you plan to administer readily available?

There will also be other questions about your experiment to consider at this stage. For instance, how will you recruit the participants for the study? How should you arrange your data sheets for ease of entry? How long will an experimental session last? These are only some of the issues you will need to consider before you begin your experiment. You must work through them all so that you will be prepared once the study begins.

Defining the experimental protocol

The final step before you begin to run your study is to work out exactly the procedure you will follow, starting from the moment the participant walks into the lab. It is worth writing down precisely what you will be doing for two main reasons. First, this preparation will give you confidence once you begin to run your study. Second, when it comes time to do your final write-up, you will have your own detailed account to work from. See Chapter 2 for more on the importance of organizing your research materials and keeping track of your experiment both before and during the data collection phase.

Surprisingly, few students bother to make a summary of what they intend to do before beginning an experiment. Instead, they try to *recall* the procedure when the time comes to do the write-up. If you're writing a thesis or an article for publication, there might be quite a delay between the time you run the experiment and the time you do the final write-up. Sometimes, if the apparatus has been dismantled since you completed your study, you may have no way of gathering missing information. For this reason, it makes sense to put all this information together as you set up your experiment. Prepare a binder that contains essential information about the experiment before you bring your first participant into the lab. You might include the following kinds of information:

1. **A one-paragraph statement of the purpose of the study.** This will remind anyone looking at your data what the study is all about. You should also include a statement of your main experimental hypotheses.

2. **An outline of your research design.** This should include a description of the experimental and control conditions and of the experimental design you plan to use.

3. **A description of the main pieces of equipment or other materials to be used in the experiment.** This should include the brand names and model numbers of commercial equipment or a description of any custom-built equipment. For example, if you were using blocks of different colours to test counting ability in young children, you would describe the number of blocks, their shapes, and their sizes, as well as their colours. If you are using commercially available questionnaires, you should give their names and publication information.

4. **A description of your experimental stimulus conditions.** These might include levels of light or sound intensity, concentrations of liquids, weight of reward pellets in an animal study, and so on. This should also include a description of the experimental procedures that you plan to use, including the number of trials you plan to run.

5. **A description of the experimental protocol.** Think of this as a script that you will follow when your participant arrives. You can even create a checklist that you can work through step by step. In some cases, you will be giving standardized instructions to your participants. If you are doing that, you should write the instructions down so that

you can be consistent when you give them to the participants. Often, you will be testing first-year students who participate in research studies as part of their course requirements. They will expect to be treated professionally when they are in the lab, and if they meet a confident experimenter who knows what she is doing, they will feel more comfortable in the laboratory environment.

6. **Your proposed data analysis.** Here, you would indicate how you plan to analyze your data, including the statistical tests you plan to use. If you want to be really conscientious, you might also note how you would expect these analyses to turn out if your hypothesis was correct.

7. **Any additional information that is specific to your experiment.** For example, if you were going to have to travel to different places to gather your data, you might want to set up a schedule of your visits and estimate what your trip might cost.

Data tabulation

In any experiment you run, it is critical that you keep an accurate record of the data you collect. When you are working on an honours thesis, it is not likely that you will be analyzing and writing up your experimental results until several weeks after you've actually gathered the data, so you need to be sure you can keep track of all the data. In a typical lab course, most of the experiments you do are "canned," meaning the information you need, including data tabulation sheets, has been included in your laboratory handbook. For your thesis, however, this will all be your responsibility; you will be expected to set up your own data tabulation sheets. These are where you will keep all the information on the testing of each subject, as well as all of your raw data, so they are crucially important. Whatever you do, don't just scribble numbers down on a piece of paper with the intention of transcribing everything neatly later. Your data sheets should be planned and made up before you start any of your testing, so that all you have to do is fill in the appropriate blanks. Depending on the circumstances of the particular experiment, and if the data you gather are numerical, it may even be possible to set up a series of spreadsheets for your different conditions and simply enter the data directly.

Keep two things in mind when you design your data sheet. First, you should set it up in such a way that entering the data you collect is easy; that is, you should not have to search for the right spot to enter your results, which might increase your chance of making an error. Second, you should consider how you will then enter your data into your chosen analysis or graphing program.

It is very frustrating when you are trying to enter a series of data points into your analysis package to have to look on separate pages for successive numbers on a list. Try to keep the numbers you will be entering in sequence on the same data sheet. Also, keep in mind that for every experiment, you should ensure that you have a list of all the conditions relevant to the data, which will be included on each data sheet. There should be a notation identifying individual participants and the order in which they were tested.

Your data sheet should contain at least the following:

- the date;
- the title of the experiment;
- the experimental condition(s);
- participant identification (including the computer file name if applicable); and
- a simple grid arrangement to allow you to enter the data easily.

If you have prepared your data sheet properly, you should be able to return to it six months later and know exactly what the data represent.

Running the experiment

You might find it a little daunting when you see your first participant walk through the door. You want everything to run smoothly, and so it should if you are well prepared. You will probably have done some pilot testing before you run the main part of the study, but it is always worthwhile to conduct a full dry run of your experiment with a friend or someone else in the lab to make sure there are no procedural glitches and to correct any that do come up. This will also help you estimate how long it will take to test each participant. Each day before you start testing, you should make sure that all your equipment is in working order and that you have all your experimental materials, your consent and debriefing forms, and your data sheets ready to use. If you have organized everything well beforehand, then you have nothing to worry about.

Data analysis

Once you have collected your data, you will need to analyze it. At one time, this would have been a complicated and time-consuming procedure. These days, as long as you have planned your experiment carefully, it should be very straightforward: all you need to do is plug your numbers into an analysis program and see how it turns out. However, be aware that even though it is now easy to use commercially available software to analyze your data, you are still responsible for knowing what these programs are doing so that you can explain the analysis to a reader or to the members of an oral examination committee. Your findings will not be as convincing if you cannot explain how the software processed your data to generate the results it did.

For some studies, you can summarize your data in the form of tables. For others, you may need to draw graphs. Prepare draft copies of your tables and graphs based on the kind of data you expect to get, even before you begin to run your study. Doing this will help you think through your experiment before you start to collect your data. It will also allow you to consider exactly how to fine-tune your experimental conditions to show off the results in the best possible light.

Writing up the thesis

Logically, writing the thesis is the final stage of your research project. However, if you are well organized, you will have drafted a significant part of the final paper over the course of the year. The background reading you do in the early part of the year will form the basis for your *Introduction* section. You should start working on your *Introduction* as soon as possible. Similarly, you could write a draft version of your *Method* section once you have worked out how the experiment will be run. Finally, you should consider preparing a draft outline of your *Results* section. This could simply be a list of each piece of data and each analysis result, including templates of the data tables and figures you might use. If you can project what kinds of data and analysis should be in your *Results* section, then you can check to see if you have designed your experiment so that all of that information will be available. It is also useful to make up hypothetical data figures based on your experimental predictions; this will make it easier to interpret your results when you get them. Sometimes, even though you thought you had designed an experiment properly, you may realize when you come to plot the data that you can't interpret them in the way you had hoped.

Of course, you will be making changes to your paper as you proceed. You will have to read more; you may need to modify your procedure; and you will not be able to write your *Discussion* section until you have collected and analyzed all of your data. But if you start preparing drafts as you work on the study, you won't have to panic at the end. Perhaps more important, you will be able to give a draft copy of your thesis to your advisor for comments before you prepare the final draft. For further illustration, we have included a sample research proposal at the end of this chapter for you to peruse.

Summary

In this chapter, we have introduced the two kinds of projects you may be assigned in your upper years. If you are planning to continue on to graduate school, then the kind of experience you gain from writing research proposals and a major research paper like an honours thesis will be invaluable. Although all the rules for writing that we have discussed elsewhere still apply, the way in which you organize these kinds of assignments is crucial. In some respects, the preparation is more important than the actual write-up because you have to be sure that your study will be done properly, and you can't do that without thinking it through before you start.

Denise Pitre   1

Research Proposal
Psychology 2081

The Effect of Myopia on the Oblique Effect
Denise Pitre
(Date of Submission)

General Background ◄─────────────

For several hundred years, there has been a discussion
about the role of experience in determining the way in which
our nervous systems develop. This debate was first started
by philosophers, such as John Locke and George Berkeley,
but more recently the discussion has continued among
psychologists, who are able to test hypotheses about the nature
vs. nurture debate by doing experiments. Although most of
the debate has been focused on how experience can influence
personality and social behaviour, it is possible to ask whether
even basic aspects of our abilities might not be predetermined.
For this project I would like to study how certain aspects of
visual experience might influence the way in which people see.

The Oblique Effect ◄─────────────

The oblique effect is a well-known visual phenomenon in
which a person's ability to process information about stimuli that

Try to set a broad context for the proposal so that the reader can see how it fits within the discipline.

A research proposal for a student project is often quite short, so you should give only a brief overview of your topic without doing a full review.

2   Denise Pitre

are horizontal tends to be better than it is for stimuli oriented at

45°. This was first described over 100 years ago by Jastrow (1893)

when he found that individuals who were asked to reproduce

lines drawn at various angles did much better for horizontal and

for vertical. Since then, there have been many studies, both in

humans and in animals, showing that the oblique effect can be

found for a wide variety of tasks, including the ability to judge

and discriminate orientations as well as the ability to detect

the presence of stimuli set at different orientations. The earlier

studies have been reviewed by Appelle (1972). For my proposed

experiment, the most relevant studies are those that have shown

that visual acuity—the finest detail that can be seen—is better for

horizontal and vertical lines than for obliques (e.g., Emsley, 1925;

Berkley, Kitterle, & Watkins, 1975).

   Proper visual acuity requires an ability to recognize contours

of different orientations. More often than not, humans experience

anisotropies in their visual perception. The oblique effect is an

example of such an occurrence. This phenomenon represents a

lesser ability to perceive oblique patterns compared to horizontal

and vertical, or cardinal, patterns (Appelle, 1972). Early speculation

regarding the cause of the oblique effect was that it could be a

result of aberrations affecting the optical lens system. This was

not found to be the case, since direct stimulation of the retina,

Referencing a review paper
is a useful way to provide
information to your reader.

Denise Pitre   3

which bypassed the eye optics, maintained orientation preferences
(Campbell, 1966). Electroretinogram recordings also did not
detect any change in the evoked potential amplitude when stimulus
orientations changed (Maffei, 1970, p. 90). In addition, the
oblique effect does not occur when viewing gratings of large width
and high contrast, as it should if the effect were optically based
(Campbell, 1966, p. 81). In fact, only at high spatial frequency is
there a significant oblique effect, which increases in prominence as
the stimulus contrast decreases (Li, 2003, p. 35).

The Oblique Effect and Visual Experience ◄——— This section
                                                  sets up the
In 1973, Annis and Frost measured the oblique effect for   context
visual acuity in a group of First Nations Cree living in northern   for your
Ontario and reported that it was smaller than that for a group   hypothesis.
of Caucasian students from southern Ontario. They concluded
that this was because the southern group lived in a much more
carpentered environment with lots of horizontal and vertical
contours. However, Timney and Muir (1976) compared a similar
group of Caucasian students with a group of Asian students,
mostly from Hong Kong, which is a very urban, carpentered
environment. The Asian students also showed a reduced oblique
effect, raising the possibility that the external environment does
not play a significant role in the effect.

4   Denise Pitre

Hypothesis: Myopia and the Oblique Effect ◀───────────

If external environment is not the main factor, then perhaps
there is something else that might distinguish the different
groups. One characteristic that has been well-documented to
be extremely prevalent in East Asian populations, but less so in
Caucasians, is myopia, or near-sightedness. (Cheng, Schmid,
& Woo, 2007; Park & Congdon, 2004; Tim, 2010). There are
also reports of a high incidence of myopia in Inuit populations
(Morgan, Speakman, & Grimshaw, 1975). Is it possible that
myopia is the common factor in a reduced oblique effect?

I propose to carry out a study in which I will measure the
oblique effect for acuity in groups of individuals who have
completely normal vision or who are moderately short-sighted.
I will test only Caucasian participants to eliminate ethnicity as a
factor. My hypothesis is that individuals with myopia will have
a reduced oblique effect compared to those with normal vision
and that there will be a negative correlation between the degree of
myopia and the size of the oblique effect.

────▶ Proposed Method

I will use the equipment that is available in my supervisor's
lab that allows me to measure visual acuity. It is a computer-based
system that allows me to present patterns of stripes on a display

This is not the place to present   Note that not all studies will require
a full *Method* section. Only give   a hypothesis. Sometimes you may
enough information to let your ───   simply be gathering data about a topic ─┘
reader know that you have a   so that you can better understand a
particular method.   process.

Denise Pitre   5

screen in a way that I can adjust their thickness. I will then use
one of the standard psychophysical methods (to be discussed
with my supervisor) to allow me to measure visual acuity for line
patterns at four different orientations: horizontal, vertical, and left
and right oblique. I plan to test 10 participants who have normal
uncorrected vision and 10 with varying amounts of myopia. I will
obtain the spectacle corrections for all the myopic participants so
that I can examine the relationship between the size of the oblique
effect and the degree of myopia.

Proposed Data Analysis

I will calculate the average acuity for each of the line
orientations and plot them on a graph showing acuity as a
function of orientation. I will also create an index of the oblique
effect (OEI) using the average of the horizontal and vertical
thresholds divided by the average of the obliques. A number
greater than 1.0 means that the H/V acuity is higher. I will plot
these data as a scattergram showing the relationship between the
degree of myopia (from the participants' prescriptions) and the
OEI. I will then calculate the Pearson product-moment correlation
and test to see if the relationship is statistically significant.

Quite often you will have to write a proposal before you have time to do all of the background work, so it is acceptable to refer to areas where your experiment is not fully designed.

The student has missed the fact that she is also comparing the myopes with the non-myopes. Always remember to — refer to each of the aspects of your experiment.

For a proposal at your level, the instructor needs to know that you have an idea of how — you might analyze your data, but there's no need to go into great detail.

6   Denise Pitre

References ◄——————————

Annis, R. C., & Frost, B. J. (1973). Human visual ecology and
    orientation anisotropies in acuity. *Science*, 729–731.
Appelle, S. (1972). Perception and discrimination as a function of
    stimulus orientation: The "oblique effect" in man and animals.
    Psychological Bulletin, 78(4), 266–278.
Berkley, M. A., Kitterle, F. L., & Watkins, D. W. (1975).
    Grating visibility as a function of orientation and eccentricity.
    Vision Research, 15, 239–244.
Cheng, D., Schmid, K. L., & Woo, G. C. (2007). Myopia prevalence
    in Chinese-Canadian children in an optometric practice.
    Optometry and Vision Science, 84, 21–32.
Emsley, H. H. (1925). Irregular astigmatism of the eye.
    Transactions of the Optical Society, 27, 28–41.
Jastrow, J. (1893). On the judgment of angles and positions of
    lines. *American Journal of Psychology, 5*, 214–248.
Morgan, R. W., Speakman, J. S., & Grimshaw, S. E. (1975).
    Inuit myopia: An environmentally induced epidemic?
    Canadian Medical Association Journal, 112, 575–577.
Park, D. J. J. & Congdon, N. G. (2004). Evidence for an "epi-
    demic" of myopia. *Annals of the Academy of Medicine of
    Singapore, 33*, 21–26.
Tim. (2010). Chinese more likely to be nearsighted. Retrieved from
    http://www.8asians.com/2010/06/18/chinese-more-likely-to-be-
    nearsighted/
Timney, B., & Muir, D. W. (1976). Orientation anisotropy:
    Incidence and magnitude in Caucasian and Chinese subjects.
    Science, 193, 699–701.

Make
sure your
Reference
section
is in APA
format.

9

Giving a Seminar or Oral Presentation

Objectives

- preparing yourself for your talk
- giving your talk
- preparing visual aids
- making posters

Introduction

For some students, the prospect of standing in front of a class to give a seminar can be terrifying. The reason some students dread speaking to a group is almost always that they are afraid of appearing foolish by not knowing what to say or how to answer questions. But there is no reason you can't give a good presentation even if your knees are knocking when you begin—you just have to be prepared. Think about all the bad seminars you've heard in class. You'll probably find that you couldn't follow what was going on because the speaker jumped from topic to topic, or left out crucial segments of an argument, or took for granted that the audience possessed information that was not provided in the talk. The good seminars you have heard were more likely well organized and systematic, and led you in a logical manner through the material being discussed. Some individuals are naturally more comfortable in front of an audience than others, and these students do have a slight advantage. However, you will find that even if public speaking is not one of your natural talents, you can still achieve decent grades by following a few simple rules. The two most important of these are *be prepared* and *be organized*.

Making Preparations

Know your topic

For the purposes of an in-class seminar, you are the expert and will almost certainly know more about your topic than any of the other students present. You need to show your audience that your grasp of the subject matter goes beyond what you include in your talk. If you know no more than what you present, you will not be able to answer questions. The more background reading you do, the more you will have to fall back on when someone asks you a question. This can be a confidence booster.

Consider your audience

It is a mistake to prepare a seminar based on what you know about your topic. In fact, you should approach the talk from precisely the opposite direction: put yourself in the mind of your audience. If *you* were sitting in class instead of standing up at the front, what would you expect of the speaker? How much will the typical audience member know about this topic? What will the typical audience member find most interesting? What can you take for granted as common knowledge in the context of the course? If you combine these with your own question—*What do I want my audience to know?*—then you have the basis for setting up your talk.

Plan your presentation

Giving a presentation involves much more than writing an essay and then reading it out to the class. Remember that talking to people requires a very different style of presentation. By the time you are asked to give an in-class presentation, it is likely that you have sat through dozens of lectures. Think about the ones you enjoyed most and what it was about them that made them interesting. If you do that, you will realize that your best lecturers were the ones who seemed the most prepared, who spoke without reading directly from their notes, who used a range of visual aids, and who seemed animated and interested in what they were talking about. You can be just as interesting by following some of these suggestions:

- **Don't write out everything you plan to say.** You should not write out your whole talk. Unless you are a skilled reader, the presentation will sound awkward and monotonous. Instead, draw up an outline that will serve as a guide as you move through your talk. This will help keep you on track. You should also prepare notes—perhaps on index cards—for each of the points that you are planning to discuss. Because you can't read rough notes to your audience, you will be forced to use your own words and, likely, a more natural speaking style. If you are worried that you may freeze when you first begin, then you could write out the first paragraph of what you want to say, just to get you started.

- **Consider preparing an outline for your audience.** Having a copy of your outline will give your audience something to follow along with as you talk. Typically, you would base this outline on the one you use to organize your talk, but you may want to include additional detail and a bibliography for your audience.
- **Use visual aids.** Having visual aids serves several purposes. First, visual aids can attract and focus the audience's attention. If you think you will be self-conscious when standing in front of a group, you will be more at ease when all eyes are on your visual aids and not on you. Second, visual aids provide another form of lecture notes to remind you what you need to say. Most instructors will allow, or even encourage, the use of PowerPoint for your presentation. This will give you much more flexibility in the way that you present your information. Perhaps more important, if you prepare your PowerPoint presentation carefully, it will serve as an outline for your talk.
- **Rehearse.** The better you know what you are going to say by rehearsing your talk in advance, the smoother your presentation will be once you deliver it to your audience. A couple of practice runs will show you where the weak points in your seminar are and will also let you know if you are running over or under time.

Giving Your Talk

Dress comfortably

Dressing comfortably means not overdressing but also not dressing down for the occasion. If you generally come to class in jeans and a T-shirt, it may look odd if you give your presentation in a suit. On the other hand, don't go too far the other way: ripped jeans and an old T-shirt may be too informal for giving a seminar. Something that's clean, comfortable, and casual sets the right tone.

Give yourself time at the beginning

If you have equipment to set up or other preparations to make, be sure to do this before the class begins if you can. If everything is ready, you won't get flustered trying to get your props set up with your classmates looking on. Sometimes, particularly if students need to plug in their own laptops for their talks, there may be problems getting the right connections. Try to connect your own computer before the class begins so that you can be sure that it's working. Also, be sure to bring along a separate copy of your presentation on a USB drive. If, for whatever reason, your computer connection fails, you'll have a backup of your presentation.

Begin with an overview

If the audience knows how the talk will flow, they will be able to understand what you are doing as you move from one point to the next. Introduce your topic, and then give a brief statement of the main areas that you will discuss. The best way to do this is to begin with a title slide that shows what your talk is about, and then provide an outline of your presentation on the second slide. You should walk the audience through this slide, describing very briefly how you will present your talk. This can be very helpful to your listeners because it gives them a map of where the talk is going to go.

Don't go too fast

One of the most common failings in a student presentation is speaking too quickly. It's easy to do this when you're nervous, so you must make a conscious effort to slow down. If you listen to a professional newsreader, you might notice two aspects of the delivery. First, the speaking rate in words per minute is slower than that for normal conversation. Second, and this is probably less evident, the pauses between sentences are typically much longer. This gives the listener time to process what has just been said. When you speak, try to take note of how fast you are talking and slow down. Prepare yourself before you open your mouth; take a few deep breaths and then make a conscious effort to speak slowly. If you feel as though you are talking just a little too slowly, then that will be about right. To the listener, this is likely to be a comfortable rate.

Beyond the speed at which you talk, be aware that a good talk is one in which the delivery of content is well-paced. If you're discussing background information that everyone is familiar with, you can go over it a little faster; if you're describing something complex or less familiar, go slowly. It often helps to explain a complicated point a couple of times in slightly different ways.

Don't be afraid to ask your audience if they understand. Almost certainly, someone will speak up if there is a problem.

Project your voice

A nervous presenter will also sometimes speak too softly. When you speak, be sure you're loud enough that everyone in the classroom can hear you, and try to put some feeling into what you say. It is difficult to remain attentive to even the most interesting presentation delivered in a monotone. By projecting your voice, you create a "presence" that holds your listener's attention.

Don't be apologetic

The worst way to start a talk is by saying: "I'm sorry, I'm really nervous about this," or "I hope this projector is going to work properly." Even if you are nervous, try to create an air of confidence. Remember, you know more about the topic than anyone in the class, with the possible exception of your instructor.

Maintain eye contact with your audience

Look around the room as you speak. When you look at individuals, you involve them in what you are saying. Also, as you scan the faces in front of you, you can monitor for signs of boredom or incomprehension and can adjust your talk accordingly.

Work with your visual aids

If you have visual aids, then take advantage of them; but remember that the visual material should only enhance your talk, not deliver it on its own. Later in this chapter, we will give you some guidance on how to prepare visual materials to make the strongest impression, but for now here are some pointers on how to present the slides to your audience:

- As each slide comes up, describe what is on it; do *not* read from it word for word. One of the worst errors that speakers make when using PowerPoint is to treat the slides as reading notes. Keep the text to a minimum and *expand* on it.
- Give your audience enough time to read through each slide. It is frustrating to see overheads or slides flash by before you've had a chance to take them in.
- Explain your figures. If it's a graph, describe what the *x*- and *y*-axes represent, and then explain what the graph shows. If it's a diagram,

take the audience through it step by step; you may be familiar with the material, but your audience might not be.

- Don't feel like you're "dumbing down" the talk by explaining everything in simple terms. People like to understand, and they will appreciate it if you walk them through a set of complex concepts.

Monitor your time allotment

As well as pacing your delivery, you should try to ensure that you aren't going to finish too soon, or worse, go over your allotted time. If you've rehearsed your talk, you should know roughly how long it will take. Remember to take into account that people might ask questions as you are talking. Ideally, you should plan to make your talk a little shorter than the amount of time you have available so that you have some leeway to answer questions.

Make your ending strong

Don't let your talk fade away at the end. You should finish by summarizing the main points you have made and drawing some conclusions. These conclusions should be available on your visual material so they are available during the discussion. If you can raise some questions in your conclusions, this will set you (and the class) up for the question period to follow. If your audience doesn't know whether it's time to applaud, you will know that your ending isn't strong enough. Rather than saying something like: ". . . and that's about it," and trailing off, make your concluding statement, pause briefly, and then say "Thank you" to signal that the talk is over. You could also include a final "Thank You" slide.

Be prepared for questions

The question period is when you can really make a good impression. Use this time as an opportunity to demonstrate your thorough understanding of the topic and even to reinforce one or two points that you think may have been missed. If you know your material well, you should have no problem dealing with the content of the questions, but the manner in which you answer these questions is important too.

- It's a good idea to repeat a question if you are in a large room where everyone may not have heard it. That should also solidify the question in your mind.
- If you didn't hear or didn't understand a question, don't be afraid to ask the questioner to repeat it or to clarify what they meant.

- Keep your answers short and to the point. Rambling answers are not helpful to anyone. If you don't know an answer, say so. It's okay to admit that you don't know everything—as long as you don't do this for every question. And, certainly, it's better to admit that you don't know an answer than to guess or to make up a response that everyone will know is not correct.
- Try not to be defensive. When someone asks a question about why you did or did not do something, do not automatically assume that they are right. This was your project, and you should be able to justify what you did.

Preparing Visual Aids

Not so many years ago, the only ways to illustrate points in a talk were to use photographic slides (which were expensive and inconvenient to prepare) or to make overhead transparencies (which usually had to be handwritten). Today, with the availability of graphic presentation software, as well as laptops and video projectors, your ability to use visual aids in a presentation is limited only by your own ingenuity and your instructor's willingness to let you use the technology in class.

Developing a PowerPoint presentation that includes video clips and sound as well as animated diagrams is quite easy. If a data projector isn't available, or if your instructor does not allow you to use PowerPoint, you can still prepare your presentation using your software and print the slides onto transparencies. Then you can show them using an overhead projector.

Keep it simple

This is the cardinal rule and it applies to every aspect of your visual aids. It is much better to put too little material on a slide than too much.

- **Use a simple slide design.** If you're using PowerPoint to make your slides, choose a design that will not detract from the presentation. PowerPoint has lots of templates, and you can find many more online. If you select one containing a border pattern, be sure to leave yourself with enough room to enter your text without encroaching on the borders. Also, you should use a light-coloured, plain background. A patterned background, even a faint one, can be distracting for an academic presentation. Once you have chosen a design, you should use it for every slide. In Figure 9.1, we show you two examples. The slide on

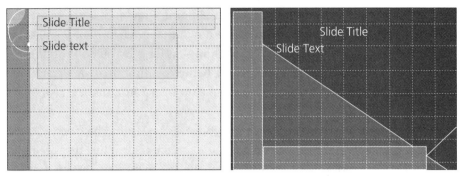

Figure 9.1   Examples of how to format PowerPoint slides

the left is much cleaner looking than the one on the right and it also has more space for your own material.

- **Use a plain font.** Any word-processing or graphics program will give you lots of font options. Unless you need a fancy one for a specific reason, stick with the simple ones. Most guides to preparing presentations suggest that you use a *sans serif* font, that is, one that does not have serifs, or ornamentation, on the ends of letters. Arial is a sans-serif font, whereas Times New Roman is a serif font. Your slides look cleaner with a sans serif font. If at all possible, avoid fonts that are too elaborate. A font like *Lucida Handwriting* or **Broadway** can get irritating after a few slides.

- **Choose an appropriate font size.** The last thing you want on your visual aids is writing that is too small to be seen. The regular 12-point font you use for your papers will almost certainly be too small when placed on an overhead projector. The minimum size you can use will depend on how far the projector is from the screen. You should try making a trial slide with fonts of different sizes; then you can check them out in the room where you'll be presenting your talk. Typically, font sizes between 18 points and 32 points will cover the different text sizes you will need, from the running text up to the slide title.

- **Don't overuse colour or other effects.** Unless you have a good reason for doing so, avoid multicoloured slides or other kinds of flashy effects.

- **Don't put too much information on one slide.** If you treat your slides as a script, then you'll be tempted to read directly from them. Instead, make your point briefly on the slide, then expand on the material as you talk. This will make your presentation sound much more natural and professional. If you have a diagram or graph, use the simplest version that you can.

- **Don't use too many slides.** The number of slides you use will depend to some degree on your topic and the kind of material you are presenting, but if you are trying to determine a reasonable number of slides to use during your presentation, a rule of thumb is to have no more than one slide for each minute of your talk. You'll go through some quickly, but you'll need to take more time with others.

- **Use simple transitions.** If you're using PowerPoint, you have the option of introducing text or images onto a slide in a variety of ways, even letter by letter if you wish. Stay away from such special effects as much as possible. Display everything that relates to a single point onto the screen at once. You might want to have two or three elements appear on a slide in sequence, for example if you want to show a series of graphs. But there's no need for a fancy transition. Occasionally, you may want to make an impression by having a picture or text emerge onto the screen. But if you do it for every slide, it gets annoying. It is also more work for you to ensure that the transitions occur at the appropriate time.

Keep it organized

The second fundamental rule of using visual aids is to make sure your material is well organized. If you use a consistent organizational scheme, the audience will become used to it and will be able to follow along more easily.

- **Begin with a title slide.** A title slide sets the tone and orients the audience to your topic. It should contain the title of your presentation, your name, and the name of the course.

- **Have an overview slide.** An overview slide should give an outline of your talk so that your audience knows what to expect.

- **Use headings and subheadings.** Most of your slides should be in point form, using numbers or bullets, with headings and subheadings. If you do this, the audience will be able to tell your main points from your subtopics or elaborations.

- **Consider section breaks.** If your talk falls naturally into several sections, you could start each one with a new title page. It is worth doing anything that allows the audience to see the structure of your talk.

- **End with a summary and/or conclusions slide.** If your topic is a review, you should summarize the main features of your talk at the end. If you are making an argument, then you should present your conclusions at the end.
- **Keep your overheads in order.** If you are using overhead transparencies, make sure that they are in the correct order—and in the correct orientation—before you start your presentation, and be sure to place your transparencies in an ordered pile as you use them. You may have to refer to one later, and you don't want to be shuffling through a disorganized pile in order to find the one you want.

Making Posters

The poster is a form of presentation that has become standard practice at scientific conferences as an alternative to the oral presentation. A poster is a self-contained display that uses a mix of text and graphics to describe a project from start to finish. The author typically stands by the poster for a period of time so that he or she can explain the details of the study and answer questions from other conference participants. This form of presentation is now being used in some senior university courses, particularly fourth-year honours thesis courses.

While this may seem simple, making an effective poster requires some skill and a lot of planning. A poster should not be just a condensed version of your paper printed in a slightly larger font. The ideal poster should be sufficiently eye-catching that someone walking by will be tempted to stop and look it over; it should be self-contained so that all of the essential aspects of your study can be understood, even if you are not there to explain them; and it should be laid out in a logical fashion so that the reader can follow the sequence easily.

The physical appearance

When poster sessions were first introduced at scientific conferences, many of the posters were no more than printed versions of oral presentations—just several typed sheets containing large amounts of text. Now, posters are much more sophisticated. Of course, the availability of graphics software has made preparations much easier, but you still have plenty of work to do.

Posters have their own structure, just like a talk. You can construct a poster in one of two ways: First, you can prepare each of the elements on separate sheets of paper mounted on some form of backing, which are then pinned individually to the poster board. Second, and much more popular, you can prepare your poster as a single, very large PowerPoint slide. This can be printed using a large format printer and mounted as a single unit. Most commercial printing establishments have the capability to print posters like this, and most campuses have print shops that can take care of printing large posters for you. If you want the poster to look even more professional, you can have it laminated.

The typical poster at a scientific conference will be about 1.5 metres wide by 1 metre high and will contain several separate sections. Some of these sections will contain limited amounts of text printed in a fairly large font; the rest will contain visual material, such as diagrams, photographs, figures containing data, or tables. Each section may be mounted on a sheet of poster board, or the whole poster may be generated onto a single laminated sheet. Figure 9.2 gives you an idea of what a typical poster looks like. The following are some guidelines for enhancing the appearance of your poster.

Choose the right font size

All of the text should be legible from a distance of up to two metres. This means that the minimum font size you should use is 18-point font. As with your slide presentation, use plain fonts. Do not use all capital letters, because they are much more difficult to read than combinations of upper-case and lower-case letters. Your title should be even larger so that it can be read from a distance of five metres or so.

Creating the poster

Using PowerPoint is the easiest way to prepare a poster. You can set the dimensions of individual slides in PowerPoint—a single slide can be as large as two metres by one metre. Your instructor should tell you how big the poster presentation board should be. Before you begin, double-check with your print shop to be sure your poster is within their printing size limits. Usually, you will be able to print something that is about one metre high and as long as you want it to be. Once you have the dimensions, you can insert text and figures, and then you can rearrange them to make the sequence of your study easy to follow. Then it is just a matter of sending the file to the printer.

If you don't have the resources to make a full poster in one piece, you can still make your presentation attractive. You can still use PowerPoint, but this time make the slides regular size and print them on regular paper. After you have done this, you can mount each element of your poster onto a piece of poster board—heavy cardboard similar to that used for mounting photographs. If this is not available, you can use bristol board, which is thinner. Whatever you do, don't use unmounted pieces of paper.

Title of a Typical Poster Presentation
A. Student and B. Professor. University of Southern Ontario, Fort Erie, Ontario, Canada

Introduction

Brief statement of the problem you will be investigating

Include hypotheses

Method

Only the essential details about the experimental conditions and the procedure

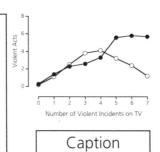

Caption

Apparatus

Only the essential details. A diagram or photograph may be helpful

Results

Use data figures to illustrate your main findings

Summary table if appropriate

Conclusions

Briefly state the main findings and your major conclusions

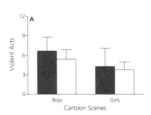

Caption

Caption

References
(Optional)

Figure 9.2 Layout of a poster presentation

Make an effort to attract people's attention
Judicious use of colours or pictures (as long as they are relevant) will make your poster stand out from others. But don't go too far by making the poster garish.

The essential elements
Title
Include the title of your poster, your name, and the name of your instructor or advisor. Capitalize the first letter of each word (but use lower-case letters for the rest, as in any normal document) and make them large enough to be legible from a distance of about three metres. The title should be mounted by itself on a separate sheet, usually at the top of your poster.

Headings
The poster should include the same essential elements as a journal article, in roughly the same order: *Introduction*; *Method*; *Results*; and *Discussion* or *Conclusions*. You might also include a very short reference list.

Visual content
For posters, it really is true that a picture is worth a thousand words—or at least a couple of hundred. Because you want to keep the text to a minimum, use illustrations, diagrams, and graphs wherever possible, and try to make them self-explanatory.

The format
Text
- **Be concise.** You should keep the amount of textual material on your poster to a minimum. The person reading the poster should be able to read through all of the text in just a couple of minutes. That means you should not have more than about 400 words of text in total. Keep asking yourself whether the text you have written is absolutely essential; if not, delete it.
- **Use point form.** Given the space limitations, you can save words by writing brief, declarative sentences, or by writing in point form.
- **Be clear.** If you have limited space, you won't be able to put in any qualifying statements; save those for when someone asks you about the project. Also, the typical poster reader will look at the title first, will look at the statement of the problem next, and will then read the conclusions. This initial overview is often used to determine whether the

poster is worth the additional effort of reading through the methods and the data. Therefore, you should have strong and clear statements in both the first and the last sections.

Graphics

- **Be relevant.** Include only illustrations and figures that relate to the main theme of your study; there is no room for extraneous information.
- **Keep it simple.** While maintaining clarity and accuracy, create the simplest figures possible. This is to the benefit of both your audience and you, because it will save you from having to explain very complicated diagrams.
- **Be logical.** Arrange your figures in a logical sequence so that the reader can follow your thinking with respect to the project.

Layout

- **Plan for the available space.** Before you begin to design your poster, find out the required dimensions; typically it will be in landscape format, 1.5 metres long by 1 metre high, but dimension requirements may differ. Once you know this, you can figure out where you will place the various components of the poster. Try using graph paper (cut proportionally to the dimensions of the poster board) to make a scale model of your poster, along with small pieces of paper representing your text and graphics to see how you might arrange them. Don't let the space become too cluttered. Try to arrange things so that you have space on the top and sides and between each section.
- **Arrange the elements logically.** You want to lead the reader through each element of the poster in the right sequence. Someone standing in front of your poster will likely start at the top left-hand corner and work down, then move over to the right and start again at the top. So, the best way to arrange your poster is in a series of columns. If it's possible, use the leftmost column for your *Introduction* and *Method* sections, the centre columns for your *Results* section and data, and the rightmost column for your *Conclusions* and *References*. If the board dimensions don't allow you to do this, consider using arrows or other pointers to lead the reader through your poster material.
- **Label your illustrations.** Although your illustrations should be self-explanatory, a label or a brief description will help to orient the reader.

- **Be neat.** Try to arrange the various elements so that they are balanced, with equal amounts of space surrounding them. Make small but easily visible labels to go above each section (or include them on the mounting board containing that section). When you paste your text and graphics onto the mounting board, you should leave a narrow border around the outside to contrast the paper with the background.
- **Do a final run-through.** Before you actually put your poster up, lay it out on the floor to see if everything fits. Mark out the actual dimensions of the poster board on the floor, and then put each piece in its proper place. You can fine-tune the arrangement and see if there's anything you should alter to make it easier to follow the sequence.

Summary

In this chapter, we have talked about giving seminar presentations and presenting posters. Although these may seem quite different, they share an underlying principle: you are trying to sell a product to your audience. In this case, the product is your intellectual competence and your knowledge. For a psychology student, standing in front of a class reading from a script is not an acceptable way to give a presentation. The wide availability of presentation software packages means that you are limited only by your own creativity, although we often see students who create wonderful PowerPoint slides but who lose marks because they don't deliver their presentations well. To make an overall positive impression on those who are listening to you, you must be confident, you must be organized, and you must be logical. Keeping things simple can sometimes be difficult when you know a great deal about a topic, but you should always remember that your audience does not need to know all the details, just the ones that are directly relevant to the story you are telling. You need to know the background or the fine details of an experiment, but you can keep that knowledge for questions that might come afterwards.

10

APA Editorial Style and Documentation

Introduction

Chapters 4 through 8 offered you guidelines for written assignments. The main goal of those chapters was to help you organize your thoughts and your writing so you could present your story clearly. Now it's time to think about the style of your papers. In this context, the term *style* has two different meanings. The first refers to the manner in which you express your ideas: the words you choose, the length of your sentences, and so on; this expressive style is discussed in Chapter 11. The second kind of style is editorial and concerns the physical arrangement of the words on the paper. For anyone working in psychology, the definitive style guide is the *Publication Manual of the American Psychological Association*. First published as a seven-page guide in 1929, the *Publication Manual*, now in its sixth edition (American Psychological Association, 2010a), has grown to over 270 pages. There are also a number of companion volumes, such as the condensed *Concise Rules of APA Style* (APA, 2010b). If you want to learn about practical uses of APA style, you might look at *Mastering APA Style: Student's Workbook and Training Guide* (APA, 2010c), which includes exercises and practice tests on various aspects of APA style. This book also covers both essay papers and research reports. You can find online tutorials and other information on the APA's official website (http://www.apa.org).

In this chapter, we will cover two aspects of APA style. The first deals with the rules of presentation—how to organize the structure of your paper and how to format the text on the page. The second deals with the rules for documenting your sources. If you have any questions about style or documentation that are not answered here or elsewhere in this book, you can consult the *Publication Manual* (APA, 2010a), which offers much more detailed guidelines, or check out the APA Style website (http://www.apastyle.org).

Rules of Presentation

In our previous chapters on writing, we described the various sections you should include for papers and lab reports and what they should contain. We have also discussed the presentation of data and figures. In all cases, we have used the *Publication Manual* as the basis for our advice. In this section, we will deal with the mechanics of APA style, that is, how you should physically arrange your paper.

Format of a written paper

The following guidelines apply to how the individual pages of your report or essay should appear:

- Use a single side of each page and double-space all the text lines, including the references. The preferred typeface for APA-formatted documents is 12-point Times New Roman.
- Number each page, including the first, with Arabic numerals in the top right-hand corner. It's also good practice to use a *page header*—a short version of the title—at the top of each page; that way, if a page gets separated, it will be easy to identify. The header should be set in upper-case letters, and it should appear in the top left-hand corner of the page.
- Always leave generous margins—at least an inch (2.54 cm) on all sides—so that your instructor can add comments. You should not right-justify the text or hyphenate words at the ends of lines. Your word processor will likely do all of this by default.
- Indent the first line of every paragraph five to seven spaces (1 cm) using the Tab key. The default setting on most word processors will do this for you.
- In a paper submitted for publication, you must always place tables and figures at the end of the manuscript; however, for a student paper you

may incorporate the tables and figures into the text, unless your instructor tells you otherwise. Depending on the size of the tables and figures, and on your instructor's preferences, you may choose to do this in one of two ways: by placing these elements on a separate sheet immediately following the page where they are first referenced; or by inserting them into the main text, immediately following the paragraph in which they are referenced.

- Depending on the size and complexity of a given figure, and on your instructor's preferences, you may place the figure caption either under the figure itself or on a separate page, facing the figure. The figure legend, which explains the meaning of any lines or symbols used in the figure, should appear on the same page as the figure, preferably within the figure itself. Always ask your instructor.

Headings and subheadings

When you are writing a research paper, you will often break it down into several sections, particularly if you have organized your paper using an outline, as discussed in Chapter 4. When you are writing a lab report, headings and subheadings are essential. Using different levels of heading helps establish a hierarchy of importance for the different sections of your paper. The most recent edition of the *Publication Manual* (APA, 2010a) describes five levels of heading, as shown in Table 10.1.

By breaking down your headings into different levels, you can distinguish the main from the subordinate topics. You may not need to use all the heading levels for every section, but you should be consistent in how you use them. Always begin at the highest level and work down. In a lab report, for example,

Table 10.1 Visual representation of APA-style headings

Level of heading	Format
1	Centred, Boldface, Upper case and Lower case[a]
2	Flush Left, Boldface, Upper case and Lower case
3	Indented, boldface, upper case only for first word; end with a period.
4	*Indented, boldface, italicized, upper case only for first word; end with a period.*
5	*Indented, italicized, upper case only for first word; end with a period.*

[a]This type of capitalization is also referred to as *title case*.

the headings *Method, Results,* and *Discussion* would all be set at Level 1; the most important headings within each of these sections would be set at Level 2; the most important headings within a Level 2 section would be set at Level 3, and so on. An example is shown in Table 10.2.

In this example, the number of levels varies, but the ordering remains the same. Note that the same heading may be at a different level depending on the structure of a particular section. Also note that the *Discussion* section does not always have any sub-sections, so there may be no need for subsequent headings in this section.

Table 10.2   Examples of APA-style headings

Method (Level 1)
Participants (Level 2)
Twenty participants . . .
Materials (Level 2)
The materials . . .
Cognitive tests. (Level 3) We used a number of tests . . .[a]
Colour vision tests. (Level 3) The colour vision tests . . .
Ishihara test. (Level 4) For the Ishihara test . . .
Farnsworth-Munsell test. (Level 4) The Farnsworth-Munsell test . . .
Results (Level 1)
Cognitive Tests (Level 2)
The results of the cognitive tests . . .
Stroop test. (Level 3) The data from the Stroop test . . .
Corsi block task. (Level 3) The outcome of the Corsi block task . . .
Colour Vision Tests (Level 2)
The results of the colour vision test . . .
Discussion (Level 1)
The main finding of this experiment . . .

[a]Note that Level 3, 4, and 5 headings are run into the paragraph they precede.

Numbers

In general, when using numbers in your writing you should spell out the numbers one through nine, and use numerals to express all numbers greater than nine (10 and above). One notable exception to this rule is that you should never start a sentence, a title, or a heading with a numeral. If you find that you have written a sentence that begins with a number, try to recast the sentence so it does not start with a number. If you must start your sentence with a number, spell it out.

In addition, the following items should always be expressed in numerals:

- numbers relating to statistical and mathematical functions and measurements;
- numbers that indicate precise times, dates, and ages;
- numbers that represent exact sums of money;
- numbers that represent scores or points on a scale;
- numbers that describe part of a numbered series; and
- numbers that appear in tables and figures.

In most other circumstances—for example, when expressing common fractions or approximate measures of time (e.g., roughly seven hours)—you should use words. When in doubt, go with the form that makes your statement easiest to read.

Units of measurement

All documents in APA format use the metric system for measurements. In most cases, this system is consistent with the International System of Units (SI). If you did not make your original measurements in metric units, you should report the metric equivalents for your original measurements. For clarity, you may want to report both, for example: "The platform was placed 15 in. (38 cm) above the landing surface." You should also be sure to use the appropriate SI abbreviations for the units.

Statistical references in text

When you report the results of your statistical analyses in the text of your paper, you need to provide enough information for the reader to understand exactly what you did. When discussing your analysis of variance, for example, you might report that your analysis was based on a repeated measures design rather than a randomized groups design. If you have a large number of descriptive statistical data, you might want to include the information in a table or a figure. If you present your data in a table or a figure, then you do not need to repeat the information in the text. Simply refer to the table or the figure.

For statistical terms, use standard symbols such as *M* for *mean* and *N* for the *total number of cases*. Table 10.3 shows a few of the most common symbols

Table 10.3 Standard symbols for statistical terms

Abbreviation/Symbol	Definition
English character set	
ANOVA	Analysis of variance
CI	Confidence interval
d'	Discriminability, a measure of sensitivity in signal detection theory
df	Degrees of freedom
f	Frequency
f_e	Expected frequency
f_o	Observed frequency
F	F distribution, Fisher's F ratio
$F(v_1, v_2)$	F with v_1 and v_2 degrees of freedom
H_0	Null hypothesis
H_1 (or H_a)	Alternative hypothesis
LSD	Least significant difference
M (or $\bar{X}$)	Sample mean, arithmetic average
Mdn	Median
MS	Mean square
MSE	Mean square error
n	Number of cases (generally in a subsample)
N	Total number of cases
ns	Not statistically significant
p	Probability; probability of a success in a binary trial
r	Estimate of the Pearson product–moment correlation coefficient
r^2	Coefficient of determination; measure of strength of relationship; estimate of the Pearson product–moment correlation squared
SD	Standard deviation
SE	Standard error
SEM	Standard error of measurement; standard error of the mean
SS	Sum of squares
t	Student's t distribution; a statistical test based on the Student's t distribution; the sample value of the t-test statistic
z	A standardized score; the value of a statistic divided by its standard error

(*continued*)

Table 10.3 *(continued)*

Abbreviation/Symbol	Definition
Greek character set	
α	In statistical hypothesis testing, the probability of making a Type I error; Cronbach's index of internal consistency (a form of reliability)
β	In statistical hypothesis testing, the probability of making a Type II error ($1 - \beta$ denotes statistical power); population values of regression coefficients (with appropriate subscripts as needed)
$\triangle$	Increment of change (delta)
μ	Population mean; expected value
ν	Degrees of freedom
σ	Population standard deviation
σ^2	Population variance
χ^2	The chi-squared distribution; a statistical test based on the chi-squared distribution; the sample value of the chi-square test statistic

that you are likely to use. Use English characters to represent *statistical sample values* and Greek symbols to represent *population values.*

If you are using a statistical term in the running text, you should use the term itself, not the symbol or abbreviation. For example,

The mean, median, and standard deviation were . . .

not

The *M, Mdn,* and *SD* were . . .

Quotations

In Chapter 5 we stressed the importance of acknowledging any quotations you use. You should also be aware of how to present the quotations in your text.

- **Short quotations.** If the quotation contains fewer than 40 words, enclose it in double quotation marks (". . .") and include it as part of the main body of the text. Provide the citation, including the page number, in parentheses immediately following the quotation.

- **Long quotations.** If the quotation contains 40 or more words, set it off from the main body of the text by indenting the whole quotation five to seven spaces from the left margin (same as for the first line of a paragraph). Do not indent on the right side. The quotation should not begin with a paragraph indent, but the first lines of second and subsequent paragraphs within the block quotation should be indented from the new left margin. You do not need to place quotation marks around this kind of quotation. You should provide the citation, including the page number, in parentheses immediately following the quotation's final punctuation mark.

- **Quotations within quotations.** If the passage you are quoting includes material already in quotation marks, make the pre-existing quotation marks single ('. . .') if the main quotation is in the running text and double (". . .") if it is set off as a block quotation. For more information on using quotation marks, see Chapter 13.

- **Quoting online sources.** If an electronic source does not have page numbers, you should refer to your reference in an accessible way, to ensure the reader can find the quotation within the source. You could do this by citing the paragraph using the abbreviation *para.*—for example: According to Kingsmills (2010) "blogs should not be considered as a form of academic research" (para. 3). If the source contains headings, refer to the heading that precedes the quoted material and add a paragraph number by counting the paragraphs after that heading, starting with one—for example: (Shelly, 2013, Results section, para. 1) or (Nordqvist, 2014, "Studying the Mind," para. 3).

- **Modifying quotations.** If you change any words within a quotation—for instance, to maintain grammatical sense—the non-original words should be enclosed in brackets ([ ]). To create emphasis, apply italics to the word or words you want to emphasize and insert "[italics added]" immediately after this change. When you omit part of a quotation, indicate the missing section with an *ellipsis*—three spaced periods (. . .). If the omission is between sentences, include the original period (without a preceding space) before the ellipsis. For more information on brackets and ellipses, see Chapter 13.

Documenting Your Sources Using APA Format

When lawyers present their arguments in a courtroom, they back them up with references to the relevant case law. When you are writing a paper in psychology, you are also making arguments and citing evidence. You have to be sure to provide citations for your sources and to make a list of those references at the end of your paper. If you look at different scientific journals, you will see a huge amount of variation in accepted formats for referencing sources. Even within the same discipline, different journals have different rules about how to cite a source in the text of an article and how to format the reference in the *References* section. The most prestigious science journals, *Science* and *Nature*, have their own idiosyncratic style requirements, regardless of the discipline you are writing for. Psychology is fortunate because all of the journals that are published by the APA use a common format. In addition, the majority of all psychology journals that are not affiliated with the APA have also adopted APA-style conventions. If you are a psychology student, you will almost certainly be asked to use APA style when you write a paper for a course. Some instructors are strict about citation practices, so it is absolutely necessary to have a good understanding of APA format.

There are two aspects to the documentation of sources. The first is the in-text citation, which identifies the source; the second is the reference list at the end of the paper, which contains publication information. We will describe these separately.

Citations

The citation format used by the APA is an author-date system; that is, each time you refer to a source, you put the surname of the author and the year of publication in parentheses immediately following the reference. The *References* section at the end of the paper then lists all the publication details for each of the sources you have cited; entries in the *References* section are arranged alphabetically by the authors' surnames. This style contrasts with *numerical* citations, where each citation is followed simply by a number and the references are listed numerically at the end. Numerical citation is not very common in the psychology literature, but you will find it in a number of medical and life science journals.

If your source was written by a single author, it is very simple to make a citation, but if your source has multiple authors, or if you are citing multiple works by the same author, or if different authors have the same surname, the citation becomes more complicated. Below are the guidelines for the most common types of sources you will encounter:

Sources with a single author

A parenthetical citation that lists the author's surname and the year of publication is inserted into the text at the most appropriate point, often at the end of the sentence in which you refer to the work:

> A recent study of the personality characteristics of computer hackers has found that most hackers prefer to work independently, rather than in groups (Salander, 2014).

If reference to the author has already been made within the text, it can be omitted from the parentheses:

> Salander (2014) studied the . . .

or the parentheses may be omitted entirely:

> In 2014, Salander reported . . .

If you are citing several sources written by the same author, list the surname once with the dates following chronologically and separated by commas:

> (Larsson, 2008, 2009, 2010)

Several sources published by the same author in the same year are distinguished with lower-case letters (*a*, *b*, *c*, etc.). Always include the year and be sure to use the same letter codes in the list of references at the end of your work:

> (Monture, 2005a, 2005b)
>
> Monture (2005a) found that . . . In another study, Monture (2005b) discovered that . . .

If two authors have the same surname, use initials to distinguish them, even if the year of publication is different:

> (B. G. Roy, 1999; P. E. Roy, 2009)

If the author is an organization that is easily recognized by an abbreviated form of its name, use the organization's full name in the first citation, but use the abbreviation in subsequent citations:

> The most recent edition of the *Publication Manual* (American Psychological Association, 2010) . . .

> The *Publication Manual* (APA, 2010) . . .

If the organization is less familiar, use its full name each time.

Sources with multiple authors

If there are two authors, include both authors' surnames every time you cite the source in the text. Use an ampersand (&) when the names are in parentheses, but use *and* in the running text:

> An early report suggested that neonates did not differentiate between small frequency differences between tones (Leventhal & Lipsitt, 1964). However, a later study by Morrongiello and Clifton (1984) showed that . . .

If there are three, four, or five authors, APA style lists the surnames of all the authors when the source is first cited; in second and subsequent citations, it lists only the first author's surname, followed by *et al.* For six or more authors, the text citation should contain only the surname of the first author, followed by *et al.*:

> Pola, Wyatt, and Lustgarten (2011) studied eye movements . . .

> Pola et al. (2011) found that subjects suppressed eye movements . . .

Note that the year should be included the first time a work is cited in a paragraph but not in subsequent citations within the same paragraph (unless you mention more than one work by the same author).

Specific references

Typically, when you are referring to an entire source, all you need to include in the citation is the author's surname and the year of publication. If, however, you are referring to a particular part of a source, you must give the specific location. In most cases, you will indicate the location by providing a page number. Always give the page number if you quote a source directly. Note that APA format uses *p.* (with a period) for a single page number and *pp.* for several page numbers:

(Cormack, Stevenson, & Schor, 1994, pp. 2601–2602)

(Schmidt, 2005, Figure 2)

(Choudhry, 2007, Table 3.1)

(Li & Knowles, 2011, Chapter 8)

For a description of how to make specific references to an online source that lacks page numbers, see the discussion above, under the heading *Quotations*.

Multiple works in the same citation

Several works by different authors can be included in the same citation, separated by semicolons. These works are cited in alphabetical order according to the authors' surnames, in the same order as they will appear in the reference list. If you have two or more works by the same author(s), put in the surname(s) followed by the successive dates of publication:

(Aaron, 2007; Diaz & Quan, 2013; Hicks et al., 2002, 2004; Schiller, 1980; Zuk, 1932, 1934)

Sources with no author

If the work you are referencing has no known or declared author, as is the case with an anonymously written newspaper article, cite the first few words of the reference list entry (usually the work's title):

("Substance Abuse Becoming a Problem," 1999)

In this case, the full title of the article might be "Substance Abuse Becoming a Problem Among Seniors, Study Shows."

Websites and online documents

If you are citing an entire website, you can simply cite the URL in parentheses. You do not need to include the reference in the reference list:

Ronald Rensink has provided a number of examples of change blindness (http://www.psych.ubc.ca/~rensink/flicker/download) . . .

If you want to cite a specific document on a website or a specific post on a blog or on a social media site such as Facebook or Twitter, you should give a regular author–date citation in the text and include the website information in the *References* section.

Secondary sources

Sometimes, if you are unable to locate an original work, you may have to rely on a description in a secondary source. In this case, you should cite the secondary source that you have read and include only that work in the *References* section:

> According to Wilcox and Wolf (as cited in Symons & Pearson, 2003, p. 16) . . .

Personal communications

Sometimes you will want to refer to a source that is not published. For example, you may want to reference your notes on material that has been presented in a lecture, or you may want to reference an email from an instructor or a thesis advisor. In these cases, where the reader would not have access to the information, you should cite the source as a personal communication in the text only. You should include the initials and surname of the source person and as exact a date as possible:

> J. Smith (personal communication, June 23, 2009)

> (M. L. Atkinson, lecture notes, Psychology 1000, March 14, 2014)

Do not list personal communications in the *References* section.

Format of the Reference List

The reference list is a crucial element of your paper. It should contain every published work that you have cited in the text—and none that you have not cited. (To include uncited references in your *References* section is considered academic fraud.) The *Publication Manual* gives both general guidelines on the overall format of the reference list and specific instructions for a wide variety of sources, including electronic sources. We describe the general guidelines below and then give you some examples.

General guidelines

The following guidelines apply to the treatment of entries in the *References* section:

1. List the references alphabetically using the first author's surname, then initials.
2. When citing more than one work by the same first author but with different subsequent authors, list the references alphabetically by surnames of the subsequent authors.
3. List more than one work by the same author (or by the exact same combination of authors) chronologically.
4. Alphabetize *Mac* and *Mc* prefixes letter by letter, so *MacDonald* precedes *McDonald*.
5. When citing a work with multiple authors, list up to seven authors. If there are more than eight authors, list the first six, followed by an ellipsis (. . .) and then the last author's name.
6. For works published in the same year by the same author (or by the identical combination of authors), add a letter suffix (*2014a, 2014b*, etc.), as you did in the text.
7. Capitalize only proper nouns and the first word of the title (and, if there is one, the subtitle). An exception to this rule is that you should capitalize all major words in the titles of journals.
8. Format each entry with a hanging indent, and double-space the entire reference list.

Figure 10.1 shows the standard format for an entry for a journal article. Figures 10.2 and 10.3 show the standard format for entries for an authored book and an edited book, respectively.

Abbreviations

Although the names of journals and books should be written out in full, APA style does use a number of abbreviations for describing certain parts of a publication. Table 10.4 gives a list of abbreviations that are acceptable in the reference list.

Electronic sources and the DOI system

Perhaps the greatest change to the citation and referencing process is due to the enormous growth in electronic sources. These include not only websites

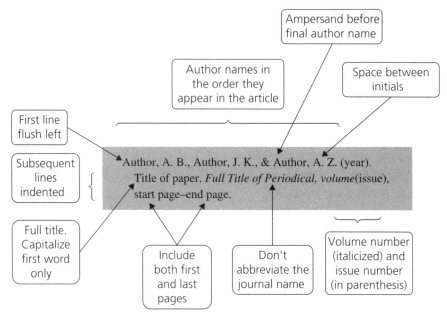

Figure 10.1 APA referencing: journal article

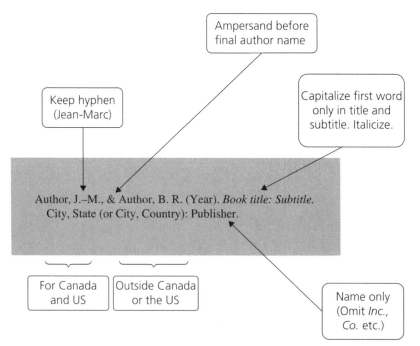

Figure 10.2 APA referencing: book

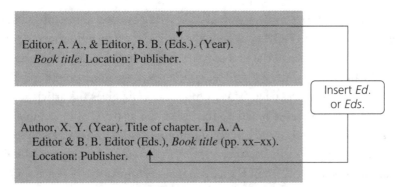

Figure 10.3 APA referencing: edited book (top), chapter in an edited book (bottom)

Table 10.4 Abbreviations used in the reference list

Abbreviation	Publication element
ed.	Edition
Rev. ed.	Revised edition
2nd ed.	Second edition
Ed. (Eds.)	Editor (Editors)
Trans.	Translator(s)
n.d.	no date
p. (pp.)	page (pages)
Vol. (Vols.)	Volume (Volumes)
No.	Number
Pt.	Part
Suppl.	Supplement

but also electronic journal articles, books, newspaper articles, and magazine articles. A number of journals and other publications that are available online also provide supplementary material containing additional data or video clips that cannot be found elsewhere.

The proliferation of online publications raises a number of issues when you want to direct your reader to one of these sources. One difficulty occurs when several versions of a source appear online. This difficulty often arises in relation to journal articles. For example, some journals allow for a "pre-publication" version to appear, which may be slightly different from the final copy. Or corrections to a paper may be made through an update. Thus, it is important to try to find and cite the *version of record*, that is, the official version of a paper.

Fortunately, there is now a way of identifying versions of record using the *digital object identifier* (DOI) system that was developed by publishers to provide a unique identifier for material that appears online. If you look at any recent article in any scholarly journal, you will see a DOI reference number either at the top or the bottom of the first page. This number not only gives the article a unique identifier, it also directs the reader to the paper and also any of the supplemental material associated with it, including questionnaires that might have been used in the study, or copies of the raw data. If the article you are citing has a DOI, the *Publication Manual* recommends that you include it in your reference list.

Sample Entries

The following examples of APA references cover the most common kinds of sources you will have to refer to. To cite other kinds of sources, check the detailed instructions in the *Publication Manual* or on the APA Style website (http://www.apastyle.org). Note that although you must always include the volume number for a journal article, you should include the issue number (in parentheses following the volume number) only if each issue of the journal begins at page one. Most magazines use this kind of numbering.

Articles
Journal article by one author (with DOI)

Bobocel, D. R. (2013). Coping with unfair events constructively or destructively: The effects of overall justice and self–other orientation. *Journal of Applied Psychology, 98*, 720–731. doi: 10.1037/a0032857

Journal article by two or more authors (without DOI)

Koo, M., & Fishbach, A. (2010). Climbing the goal ladder: How upcoming actions increase level of aspiration. *Journal of Personality and Social Psychology, 99*, 1–13.

If you retrieved the article online but the article was not assigned a DOI, include the uniform resource locator (URL) for the home page of the journal in which the article appears, preceded by the descriptive phrase *Retrieved from*:

Ross, A. S., Anderson, R., & Gaulton, R. (1987). Methods of teaching introductory psychology: A Canadian survey. *Canadian Psychology, 28*, 266–273. Retrieved from http://www.apa.org/pubs/journals/cap

If you must break a URL at the end of a line, do so *before* a punctuation mark. Never add a hyphen to break a URL.

Magazine article

If you are referring to an article in a magazine, you should also include the month of publication (for monthlies such as *Scientific American*) or the month and day of publication (for weeklies):

> Lilienfeld, S. O., Lynn, S. J., Ruscio, J., & Beyerstein, B. L. (2010, March). Busting big myths in popular psychology. *Scientific American, 21*(1), 42–49.

If you have accessed the article online, also provide the URL for the home page of the magazine:

> Kluger, J. (2014, October). The narcissist in all of us. *Psychology Today, 47*(5), 78–85. Retrieved from http://www.psychologytoday.com

Newspaper article (signed and unsigned)

> Abraham, C. (2010, August 5). Probing deep for an Alzheimer's solution. *The Globe and Mail*, p. A4.

> Scientists shed light on firefly flickering. (2010, June 29). *National Post*, p. 7.

If you have accessed the article online, also provide the URL for the home page of the newspaper:

> Knapton, S. (2014, February 18). Depression saliva test may reveal those at risk of lifelong mental illness, revolutionize treatment, researchers say. *National Post*. Retrieved from http://www.nationalpost.com

Article on a website (organization as author)

> Canadian Food Inspection Agency. (2013, October 4). Pre-submission consultation procedures for novel foods, novel feeds, and plants with novel traits. Retrieved from http://www.inspection.gc.ca/plants/plants-with-novel-traits/ applicants/pre-submission-consultation/eng/1368394145255/1368394206548

Books

For books published in Canada or the United States, give the city and province or state of publication as well as the publisher; use standard two-letter postal abbreviations for the province or state of publication. For books published elsewhere, give the city and country of publication. In publishers' names, omit unnecessary words such as *Publishers*, *Co.*, and *Inc.*, but retain the words *Books* and *Press*.

> Heine, S. J. (2008). *Cultural psychology*. New York, NY: W. W. Norton.

Book with two or more authors

> Passer, M. W., Smith, R. E., Atkinson, M. L., Mitchell, J. B., & Muir, D. W. (2011). *Psychology: Frontiers and applications* (4th Canadian ed.). Toronto, ON: McGraw-Hill Ryerson.

Book with an organization as author

> National Advisory Committee on Immunization. (2002). *Canadian immunization guide*. Ottawa, ON: Canadian Medical Association.

Book with an edition number

If the reference is to a second or subsequent edition, be sure to include the edition number immediately following the title:

> Myers, D. G. (2011). *Psychology* (10th ed.). New York, NY: Worth.

Book with a volume number

> Zanna, M. (Ed.). (2009). *Advances in experimental social psychology* (Vol. 41). San Diego, CA: Academic Press.

Book with an editor or editors

> Albarracin, D., Johnson, B. T., & Zanna, M. P. (Eds.). (2005). *The handbook of attitudes*. Mahwah, NJ: Lawrence Erlbaum Associates.

Chapter in an edited book

In the text, you should cite the author(s) of the chapter you have read, and then give both the chapter title and the full book reference in the *References* section:

> Rogers, A. G. (1998). Understanding changes in girls' relationships and in ego development: Three studies in adolescent girls.

In A. Westenberg, A. Blasi, & L. D. Cohen (Eds.), *Personality development: Theoretical, empirical, and clinical investigations of Loevinger's conception of ego development* (pp. 145–162). Mahwah, NJ: Lawrence Erlbaum Associates.

Additional online sources

Online government document

Many government documents that used to be available in print versions are now available online. Treat the titles of such documents as you would treat the title of a printed equivalent. If the document has been assigned an official catalogue or publication number, include this information in parenthesis after the title. Conclude with the URL that will direct your reader to the document:

Health Canada. (2014). *Health Canada's 2014–15 departmental sustainable development strategy* (Catalogue No. H126-3/ 2014E-PDF). Retrieved from http://www.hc-sc.gc.ca/ahc-asc/ pubs/sd-dd/2011-2015-strateg-performance-2014-15-eng.php

Social media sites

The guidelines for citing material posted on social media sites are still evolving, so you should check the APA Style website (http://www.apastyle.org) to see if these have changed since the publication of this book. In general, however, you should include a short description of the material in brackets after the title. If the material does not have a clear title, include the first few words (to a maximum of 40 words) of the post. If you know the author's real name, provide it first, followed by her or his screen name or full first name in square brackets. If you don't know the author's real name, provide only her or his screen name (not in square brackets):

Kauffman, L. [ChildPsych]. (2014, October 17). Longitudinal study: Teen girls at greater risk of depression due to relationship stress 1.usa.gov/ZyjL59: @medlineplus [Tweet]. Retrieved from https:// twitter.com/ChildPsych

Hadley, T. [Timothy]. (2010, August 3). Yes, but why is there a comma after the year? [Facebook comment]. Retrieved from http://www .facebook.com/APAStyle/posts/140121156019989

Blog post

> Dean, J. (2014, July 27). Poor sleep can lead to false memories [Web log post]. Retrieved from http://www.spring.org.uk/2014/07/poor-sleep-can-create-false-memories.php

Summary

Anyone who does research and writes in psychology will use APA format. It is also the standard in many other disciplines in science and the social sciences, so it is well worth your while to spend some time learning the basics of APA style. The examples in this chapter should cover the types of material that you are likely to cite in an undergraduate paper. If you need to reference a less common kind of source, consult the *Publication Manual* or the APA Style website (http://www.apastyle.org). In addition, your college or university department may have its own website with information on how to document sources. It's a good idea to check to see whether there are particular conventions or a particular style preferred by your own department.

References

American Psychological Association. (2010a). *Publication manual of the American Psychological Association* (6th ed.). Washington, DC: Author.

American Psychological Association. (2010b). *Concise rules of APA style*. Washington, DC: Author.

American Psychological Association. (2010c). *Mastering APA style: Student's workbook and training guide*. Washington, DC: Author.

Writing with Style

11

Objectives

- setting the tone
- being clear
- being concise
- developing a forceful style
- being aware of neutral language

Introduction

The main goal when writing in any scientific discipline, including psychology, is to communicate ideas in a clear and straightforward way. However, this does not mean that you should forget about your writing style. If you've had a chance to read many articles in psychology journals, you've almost certainly been struck by how dull they can be, even though the scientific content may be very interesting. But you may also have come across papers that are a pleasure to read because they convey the sense of excitement that the author was feeling when she or he wrote the paper. That is the essence of writing with style.

As we've said before, writing is all about telling a story and bringing the reader along with you. It's true that scientific writing does not usually call for evocative words and extravagant turns of phrase, but just because you're writing about research, you don't need to be boring. One of the most important scientific papers of the twentieth century—the article by James Watson and Francis Crick (1953) that first described the structure of the DNA molecule, thereby transforming the whole science of biology—begins with the following words:

> We wish to suggest a structure for the salt of the deoxyribose nucleic acid (D.N.A.). This structure has novel features which are of considerable biological interest. (p. 737)

Of course, Watson and Crick knew that their finding was monumental. Watson describes how in February 1953, before their paper was published, they went to a pub for lunch and Francis Crick "winged into the Eagle to tell everyone in hearing distance that we had found the secret of life" (Watson, 1968, p. 126). But beginning the paper in this low-key way has a much greater impact on the reader. Writers who are known for their style typically are those who have projected something of their own personality into their writing: we can hear a distinctive voice in what they write. You may not have such aspirations for a lab report, but in addition to being clear and concise, think about how you will present your work. Throughout this chapter, we will give you a variety of suggestions for writing effectively.

Set the Tone

Scientific writing is expository writing; that is, its purpose is to describe and explain the author's topic to the reader. This means that your writing should be clear and logical. You should avoid any kind of writing style that interferes with these two goals. Even if you have been asked to write an opinion paper, you should adopt a fairly formal tone. Formal does not mean stilted, and sometimes you may want to relax the rules a little, but there are some stylistic elements that are definitely not appropriate for scientific writing.

Use of colloquial expressions

There aren't many times when the use of a colloquial word or phrase is appropriate in a scientific paper. If you describe a rat moving quickly down one arm of a maze as "going like a bat out of hell," you convey a lack of seriousness to the reader, even if the phrase does indicate that the animal was moving quickly. Sometimes, though, the use of a colloquial expression is not only inappropriate but also confusing to the reader because the meaning is ambiguous and may signify different things to different people. Just think of how widely the meaning of the terms *hot*, *cool*, and *sick* can vary, depending on the context.

Frequent use of contractions

Contractions such as *can't* and *isn't* are not usually suitable for scientific writing, although they may be fine when writing emails or when you are trying to create a conversational tone, as we do in this book. This is not to say that you should avoid using contractions altogether: even the most serious academic writing can sound stilted or unnatural without any contractions at all. If you do use contractions in a paper, be sure to use them sparingly; excessive use of contractions makes formal writing sound too chatty and unofficial.

Use of first-person pronouns

There has long been a tradition in scientific writing of taking the author out of the text. This has meant avoiding the use of *I* and *we* and using passive constructions to avoid having to identify who was carrying out the actions. A typical sentence from a *Method* section might have read, "The participants were given the questionnaire" or "the IQ test was administered to each child individually by the experimenter." The *Publication Manual of the American Psychological Association* (APA, 2010) now discourages the overuse of the passive voice. If you are the one carrying out the action, then you should say so directly: "I gave the questionnaire to the participants." However, you can break this rule if you want to draw attention to the objects that were acted upon. So, you might say, "the stimuli were coloured disks presented on a computer screen."

Be Clear

Choose clear words

The key to good writing is using words that clearly and accurately convey your intended meaning. Two tools that will prove indispensable in this regard are a dictionary and a thesaurus. Most word-processing software has these tools built in, so you have no excuse for not using them. Microsoft Word, for example, has a Research task pane that allows you to easily search online dictionaries, thesauruses, and encyclopedias.

A dictionary is a wise investment, although there is now ample opportunity to access dictionaries online. A good dictionary will help you understand unfamiliar, archaic, or technical words or senses. A dictionary can also help you with spelling and with questions of usage: if you are uncertain whether a particular word is too informal for your writing or if you have concerns that a certain word might be offensive, a good dictionary will give you this information. It can also help you use these words properly by offering example sentences that show how certain words are typically used.

You should be aware that Canadian usage and spelling may follow either British or American practices, but usually combines aspects of both; check before you buy a dictionary to be sure that it gives these variants. The *Oxford English Dictionary*, widely recognized as one of the most comprehensive

English-language dictionaries, is now available online and almost every university library will have a subscription to it. Oxford University Press also offers a free online dictionary of modern English through the Oxford Dictionaries website (http://www.oxforddictionaries.com).

A thesaurus lists words that are closely related in meaning. It can help when you want to avoid repeating yourself or when you are fumbling for a word that is on the tip of your tongue. Be careful, though: make sure you remember the difference between *denotative* and *connotative* meanings. A word's denotation is its primary, or "dictionary," meaning. Its connotations are any associations that it may suggest. They may not be as exact as the denotations, but they are part of the impression the word conveys. If you examine a list of synonyms in a thesaurus, you will see that even words with similar meanings can have dramatically different connotations. For example, alongside the word *indifferent*, your thesaurus may give the following: *neutral, unconcerned, careless, easy-going, unambitious*, and *half-hearted*. Imagine the different impressions you would create if you chose one or the other of these words to complete this sentence: "When questioned about the project's chance of success, he was _____ in his response." In order to write clearly, you must remember that a reader may react to the suggestive meaning of a word as much as to its "dictionary" meaning.

These tools can help you avoid unclear, awkward, and repetitive writing. Be sure to make good use of a dictionary and thesaurus, and you will be surprised by how much better your writing will sound.

Avoid unnecessary jargon and use plain English

All academic subjects have their own specialized terminology, or *jargon*. It may be unfamiliar to outsiders, but it helps specialists explain things to each other. Precise disciplinary jargon may be suitable for informed audiences, such as your instructor. The trouble is that people sometimes use this sort of special technical language unnecessarily, thinking it will make them seem more sophisticated. "Never use a short word if a longer, more esoteric one will do," seems to be a general rule for many writers in scientific disciplines. Too often, the result is not clarity but confusion. Even when the meaning is clear, most scientists tend to default to longer words. Think about how often you see *utilize* when *use* serves just as well.

The guideline is easy: use specialized terminology only when it's a kind of shorthand that will help you explain something more precisely and efficiently to a knowledgeable audience. If your writing seems stiff or pompous, you may be relying too much on jargon, high-flown phrases, long words, or passive constructions. Although sometimes you must use specialized terms to avoid long and complex explanations, the rest of your paper can be written in simple English. At first glance it may not appear so impressive, but it will certainly be a lot easier to understand.

The following passage appeared in a Ph.D. thesis that was submitted just a few years ago:

> By ameliorating schizophrenic proclivity toward inefficiently deploying their attentional capacity, it is not beyond the realm of possibility that this population could become closer to healthy individuals in terms of cognitive and behavioural functioning.

Roughly translated, this means, "If individuals with schizophrenia were able to direct their attention more efficiently, they might function more like healthy individuals." Without lapsing into writing that is too informal, it is possible to produce a clear statement just by eliminating the excess words.

Plain words are almost always more forceful than fancy ones. If you aren't sure what plain English is, think of the way you talk to your friends (apart from swearing and slang). Many of our most common words—the ones that sound most natural and direct—are short. A good number of them are also among the oldest words in the English language. By contrast, most of the words that English has derived from other languages are longer and more complicated; even those that have been used for centuries can sound artificial. For this reason, you should beware of words loaded with prefixes (*pre-*, *post-*, *anti-*, *pro-*, *sub-*, *maxi-*, etc.) and suffixes (*-ate*, *-ize*, *-tion*, etc.). These can make individual words more precise and efficient, but putting a lot of them together will make your writing seem dense and hard to understand. In many cases, you can substitute a plain word for a fancy one:

Fancy	*Plain*
accomplish	do
cognizant	aware
commence	begin, start
conclusion	end
determinant	cause
fabricate	build
finalize	finish, complete
firstly	first
infuriate	anger

maximization	increase
modification	change
numerous	many
obviate	prevent
prioritize	rank
proceed	go
remuneration	pay
requisite	needed
sanitize	clean
subsequently	later
systematize	order
terminate	end
transpire	happen
utilize, utilization	use

Suggesting that you write in plain English does not mean that you should never pick an unfamiliar, long, or foreign word; sometimes these words are the only ones that will convey precisely what you mean. Inserting an unusual expression into a passage of plain writing can also be an effective means of catching the reader's attention—as long as you don't do it too often. And, of course, writing clearly does not mean that you should avoid all specialized scientific terms. Just remember that when you use technical language, your instructors will not be impressed by the mere presence of these words: appropriate disciplinary terminology must be used correctly.

Be precise

Always be as precise as you can. Avoid all-purpose adjectives like *major*, *significant*, and *important* and vague verbs such as *involve*, *entail*, and *exist* when you can be more specific:

orig. Catalysts <u>are involved in</u> many biochemical reactions.

rev. Catalysts <u>speed up</u> many biochemical reactions.

Here's another example:

orig. The discovery of genetic engineering techniques was a <u>significant</u> contribution to biological science.

rev. The discovery of genetic engineering techniques was a <u>dangerous</u> contribution to biological science.

(or)

> *rev.*   The discovery of genetic engineering techniques was a <u>beneficial</u> contribution to biological science.

Avoid unnecessary qualifiers

Qualifiers such as *very*, *rather*, and *extremely* are overused. Saying that something is *very elegant* may have less impact than saying simply that it is *elegant*. For example, compare these sentences:

> They devised an <u>extremely elegant</u> hypothesis to explain their data.

> They devised an <u>elegant</u> hypothesis to explain their data.

Which has a greater impact? When you think that an adjective needs qualifying—and sometimes it will—first see if it's possible to change either the adjective or the phrasing. Instead of writing

> Multinational Drugs made a <u>very big</u> profit last year,

write a precise statement:

> Multinational Drugs made an <u>unprecedented</u> profit last year,

or (if you aren't sure whether or not the profit actually set a record)

> Multinational Drugs had a profit <u>increase of 40 per cent</u> last year.

In some cases, qualifiers not only weaken your writing but are redundant because the adjectives themselves are absolutes. To say that something is *very unique* makes as little sense as saying that someone is *slightly pregnant* or *extremely dead*.

Create clear paragraphs

Paragraphs come in so many sizes and patterns that no single formula could possibly cover them all. The two basic principles to remember are these:

1. a paragraph is a way to develop and frame an idea or impression; and
2. the divisions between paragraphs are important—paragraphs are the building blocks of your paper, with each division signalling a shift in focus.

With these principles in mind, you should try to include three elements in each paragraph:

1. a topic sentence, to introduce the subject of the paragraph to the reader;
2. a supporting sentence or sentences, to provide evidence or develop the argument; and
3. a conclusion, to tell the reader that the paragraph is complete.

Keep these points in mind as you write. The following sections offer additional advice on creating clear paragraphs.

Develop your ideas

Most writers don't think in terms of paragraphs when they start to write; they tend to think in terms of the ideas they want to present. Paragraphs are a way to organize your thoughts and to set them out in a logical sequence—what comes first is the idea you intend to develop. The structure of the paragraph should flow from the idea itself and the way you want to discuss or expand it.

You may take one or several paragraphs to develop an idea fully. For a definition alone, you could write 1 paragraph or 10, depending on the complexity of the subject and the nature of the assignment. Just remember that ideas need development, and that each new paragraph signals a change in idea.

Consider the topic sentence

Skilled skim-readers know that they can get the general drift of a book simply by reading the first sentence of each paragraph. The reason is that most paragraphs begin by telling the reader what the paragraph is about by stating the main idea or point to be developed.

Like the thesis statement for the paper as a whole, the topic sentence is not obligatory: in some paragraphs, the controlling idea is not stated until the middle or even the end, and in others, it is not stated at all but merely implied. Nevertheless, it's a good idea to think out a topic sentence for every paragraph. That way you'll be sure that each one has a definite point and is clearly connected to what comes before and after. When revising your initial draft, check to see that each paragraph is held together by a topic sentence, in which the central idea of the paragraph is either stated or implied. If you find that you can't formulate one, it could be that you are uncertain about the point you are trying to make; in this case, it may be best to rework the whole paragraph.

Maintain focus

A clear paragraph should contain only those details that are in some way related to the central idea. It must also be structured so that the details are easily *seen* to be related. One way of showing these relations is to keep the same grammatical subject in most of the sentences that make up the paragraph. When the grammatical subject is shifting all the time, a paragraph loses focus, as in the following example (based on Cluett & Ahlborn, 1965, p. 51):

> *orig.* Students at our school play a variety of sports these days. In the fall, football still attracts the most, although an increasing number now play soccer. For some, basketball is the favourite when the fall season is over, but you will find that swimming and gymnastics are also popular. Cold winter temperatures may allow the school to have an outdoor rink, and then hockey becomes a source of enjoyment for many. In spring though, the rinks begin melting, and so there is less opportunity to play. Then some students take up soccer again, while track and field also attracts many participants.

Here the grammatical subject (underlined) changes from sentence to sentence. Notice how much stronger the focus becomes when all the sentences have the same grammatical subject—either the same noun, a synonym, or a related pronoun:

> *rev.* Students play a variety of sports these days. In the fall, most still choose football, although an increasing number now play soccer. When the fall season is over, some turn to basketball; others prefer swimming or gymnastics. If cold winter temperatures permit an outdoor rink, many students enjoy hockey. Once the ice begins to melt in spring, though, they can play less often. Then some take up soccer again, while others choose track and field.

Naturally, it's not always possible to retain the same grammatical subject throughout a paragraph. If you were comparing the athletic pursuits of boys and girls, for example, you would have to switch back and forth between boys and girls as your grammatical subject. In the same way, you will have to shift subjects when you are discussing examples of an idea or exceptions to it.

Avoid monotony

If most or all of the sentences in your paragraph have the same grammatical subject, how do you avoid boring your reader? There are two easy ways:

1. **Use stand-in words.** Pronouns, either personal (*I, we, you, he, she, it, they*) or demonstrative (*this, that, those*), can stand in for the subject, as can synonyms (words or phrases that mean the same thing). The revised paragraph on school sports, for example, uses the pronouns *some, most,* and *they* as substitutes for *students.* Most well-written paragraphs have a liberal sprinkling of these stand-in words.

2. **"Bury" the subject by putting something in front of it.** When the subject is placed in the middle of the sentence rather than at the beginning, it's less obvious to the reader. If you take another look at the revised paragraph, you'll see that in several sentences there is a word or phrase in front of the subject. Even a single word, such as *first, then, lately,* or *moreover,* will do the trick. (Incidentally, this is a useful technique to remember when you are writing a letter of application and want to avoid starting every sentence with *I.*)

Link your ideas

To create coherent paragraphs, you need to link your ideas clearly. Linking words are those connectors—conjunctions and conjunctive adverbs—that show the relations between one sentence, or part of a sentence, and another; they're also known as transition words because they bridge the transition from one thought to another. Make a habit of using linking words when you shift from one grammatical subject or idea to another, whether the shift occurs within a single paragraph or as you move from one paragraph to the next. The following are some of the most common connectors and the logical relations they indicate:

Linking word	*Logical relation*

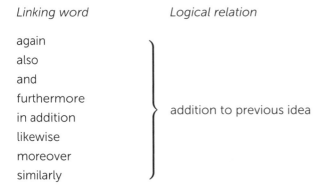

again	
also	
and	
furthermore	
in addition	addition to previous idea
likewise	
moreover	
similarly	

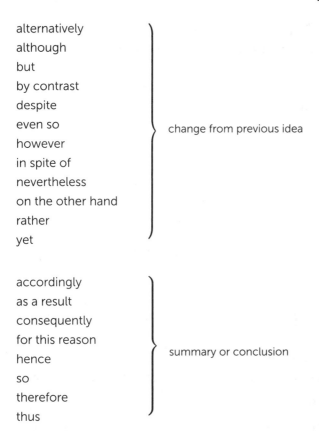

alternatively
although
but
by contrast
despite
even so
however
in spite of
nevertheless
on the other hand
rather
yet

⎱ change from previous idea

accordingly
as a result
consequently
for this reason
hence
so
therefore
thus

⎱ summary or conclusion

Numerical terms such as *first*, *second*, and *third* also work well as links.

Vary the paragraph length, but avoid extremes

Ideally, academic writing will have a balance of long and short paragraphs. Avoid the extremes—especially the one-sentence paragraph, which can only state an idea without explaining or developing it. A series of very short paragraphs is usually a sign that you have not developed your ideas in enough detail or that you have started new paragraphs unnecessarily. On the other hand, a succession of long paragraphs can be tiring and difficult to read. In deciding when to start a new paragraph, always consider what is clearest and most helpful for the reader.

Be Concise

At one time or another, you will probably be tempted to pad your writing. Whatever the reason—because you need to write 2,000 or 3,000 words and have only enough to say for 1,000, or just because you believe that "length is strength" and hope to get a better mark for the extra words—padding is a mistake. You may occasionally fool some readers, but most will not be convinced by excessively wordy writing.

Strong writing is always concise. It leaves out anything that does not serve some communicative or stylistic purpose, and it says as much as possible in as few words as possible. Concise writing will help you do better on both your essays and your exams.

Avoid ambiguous pronouns

You will confuse the reader if you use a pronoun like *it* or *this* without having a clear connection to the noun the pronoun is referring to:

> As the light intensity was lowered, the mixture became viscous. It also turned blue.

Does *it* in this example refer to the colour of the light or to the colour of the mixture? Repeat the relevant noun if there is any possibility of confusion.

Avoid using too many abstract nouns

Whenever possible, choose a verb (or, in some cases, an adjective) rather than an abstract noun:

> *orig.*   Our combination and modification of the lists resulted in the partici-
> pants' confusion between the items.
>
> *rev.*   When we combined and modified the lists, the participants became
> confused about the items.

Avoid vague qualifiers

Scientific writing should be precise. In particular, you should avoid words such as *quite*, *very*, *fairly*, *some*, *many*, or *roughly* if you can use more exact terms:

> *orig.*   The survey revealed that a few of the participants experienced some
> side effects.
>
> *rev.*   The survey revealed that 6 per cent of the participants experienced
> mild headaches, dizziness, and nausea.

Use adverbs and adjectives sparingly

You should also avoid the scattergun approach to adverbs and adjectives: don't use combinations of modifiers unless you are sure they clarify your meaning. One well-chosen word is always better than a series of synonyms:

orig. As well as being <u>costly</u> and <u>financially extravagant</u>, the project is <u>reckless</u> and <u>foolhardy</u>.

rev. The venture is <u>costly</u> as well as <u>foolhardy</u>.

Avoid noun clusters

A recent trend in some writing is to use nouns as adjectives (as in the phrase "*noun* cluster"). This device can be effective occasionally, but frequent use can produce a monstrous pile-up of nouns. Breaking up noun clusters may not always result in fewer words, but it will make your writing easier to read:

orig. personal video recorder user manual

rev. manual for using a personal video recorder

orig. pollution investigation committee

rev. committee to investigate pollution

Certain nouns that are used routinely as adjectives—"*reaction* time," "*block* design," "*water* bottle," and so on—are quite acceptable. Again, use your judgment to decide what sounds best.

Avoid chains of relative clauses

Sentences full of clauses beginning with *which*, *that*, or *who* are usually wordier than necessary. Try reducing some of these clauses to phrases or single words:

orig. The solutions <u>that</u> were discussed last night have a practical benefit, <u>which</u> is easily grasped by people <u>who</u> have no technical training.

rev. The solutions discussed last night have a practical benefit, easily grasped by non-technical people.

Try reducing clauses to phrases or words

Independent clauses can often be reduced by subordination. Here are a few examples:

orig. The report was written in a clear and concise manner, and it was widely read.

rev. Written in a clear and concise manner, the report was widely read.

rev. Clear and concise, the report was widely read.

orig. His plan was of a radical nature and was a source of embarrassment to his employer.

rev. His radical plan embarrassed his employer.

Eliminate worn-out expressions and circumlocutions

Trite or roundabout phrases may flow from your pen without a thought, but they make for stale prose. Unnecessary words are deadwood; be prepared to hunt and chop ruthlessly to keep your writing lively:

Wordy	Revised
due to the fact that	because
at this point in time	now
consensus of opinion	consensus
in the near future	soon
when all is said and done	[omit]
in the eventuality that	if
in all likelihood	likely

Avoid *it is* and *there is* beginnings

Although it may not always be possible, try to avoid beginning your sentences with "It is . . ." or "There is (are) . . ." Your sentences will be crisper and more concise:

orig. There are only a few days in the year on which the phenomenon may be observed.

rev. The phenomenon may be observed on only a few days of the year.

orig. It is certain that pollution will increase.

rev. Pollution will certainly increase.

Be Forceful

Developing a forceful, vigorous style simply means learning some common tricks of the trade and practising them until they become habit.

Choose active over passive verbs

As we mentioned earlier, traditional science writing emphasized use of the passive voice rather than the active voice ("The rat was placed in the starting box of the maze," rather than "I placed the rat in the starting box"). It was widely thought that the impersonal quality of the passive voice helped to maintain the detached, impartial tone appropriate for a scientific report. Today, more and more scientists are using the active voice because it is clearer and less likely to lead to awkward sentences. Passive constructions tend to produce convoluted phrasing:

orig.   It <u>has been decided</u> that the utilization of small rivers in the province for purposes of generating hydroelectric power <u>should be studied</u> by our department and that a report to the deputy <u>should be made</u> by our director as soon as possible.

The passive verbs in this example make it hard to tell who is doing what. This passage is much clearer without the passive verbs:

rev.   The minister of natural resources <u>has decided</u> that our department <u>should study</u> the use of small rivers in the province to generate hydroelectric power and that our director <u>should make</u> a report to the deputy as soon as possible.

An active verb also creates more energy than a passive one does:

Passive   The data <u>were collected and analyzed</u> by the technician.

Active   The technician <u>collected and analyzed</u> the data.

Passive verbs are appropriate in four specific cases:

1. When the subject of the sentence is the passive recipient of some action:

   The politician <u>was heckled</u> by the angry crowd.

2. When you want to emphasize the object rather than the person acting:

   The anti-pollution devices in all three plants <u>will be improved</u>.

3. When you want to avoid an awkward shift from one subject to another in a sentence or paragraph:

   The guppies had adjusted to their new tank but <u>were eaten</u> by the larger fish a short time later.

4. When you want to avoid placing responsibility or blame:

   Several errors <u>were made</u> when graphing the data.

Use personal subjects

Most of us find it more interesting to learn about people than about things. Wherever possible, therefore, make the subjects of your sentences personal. This trick goes hand in hand with the use of active verbs. Almost any sentence becomes livelier with active verbs and a personal subject:

> *orig.* Publication of Darwin's work was delayed because the materialistic implications of his theory were recognized.

> *rev.* Darwin delayed publication of his work because he recognized the materialistic implications of his theory.

Here's another example:

> *orig.* It can be concluded that the reaction had been permitted to continue until it was completed because no sign was shown of any precipitate when the flask was examined.

> *rev.* We can conclude that the reaction had ended because we could not see any precipitate when we examined the flask.

Use concrete details

Concrete details are easier to understand—and to remember—than abstract theories. Whenever you are discussing abstract concepts, therefore, always provide specific examples and illustrations; if you have a choice between a concrete word and an abstract one, choose the concrete. Consider this sentence:

> Watson and Crick described the structure of DNA and discussed the replication of genetic material.

Now see how a few specific details can bring the facts to life:

> Watson and Crick discovered that the DNA molecule is arranged as a double helix and proposed that this three-dimensional structure could explain how genetic material is replicated.

Adding concrete details doesn't mean getting rid of all abstractions; it simply means balancing abstract concepts with accurate details. The example above is one instance where adding words, if they are concrete and correct, can improve your writing.

Make important ideas stand out

Experienced writers know how to manipulate sentences in order to emphasize certain points. The following are some of their techniques.

Place key words in strategic positions

The positions of emphasis in a sentence are the beginning and, above all, the end. If you want to bring your point home with force, don't put the key words in the middle of the sentence—save them for the end:

> *orig.* People are less afraid of losing wealth than of losing face in this image-conscious society.
>
> *rev.* In this image-conscious society, people are less afraid of losing wealth than of losing face.

Subordinate minor ideas

Small children connect incidents with a string of *and*s, as if everything were of equal importance:

> Our bus was delayed, and we were late for school, and we missed our class.

As they grow up, however, they learn to *subordinate*—that is, to make one part of a sentence less important in order to emphasize another point:

> Because the bus was delayed, we were late and missed our class.

Major ideas stand out more and connections become clearer when minor ideas are subordinated:

> *orig.* Spring arrived and we started preparing for the annual conference.
>
> *rev.* When spring arrived, we started preparing for the annual conference.

Make your most important idea the subject of the main clause, and try to put it at the end, where it will be most emphatic:

> *orig.* I was relieved when I saw my marks.
>
> *rev.* When I saw my marks, I was relieved.

Vary sentence structure

As with anything else, variety adds spice to writing. One way of adding variety, which will also make an important idea stand out, is to use a periodic rather than a simple sentence structure.

Most sentences follow the simple pattern of subject–verb–object (plus modifiers):

> The <u>dog</u> <u>bit</u> the <u>man</u> on the ankle.
>   S   V   O

A *simple sentence* such as this gives the main idea at the beginning and thus creates little tension. A *periodic sentence*, on the other hand, does not give the main clause until the end, following one or more subordinate clauses:

> Because the scientists had succeeded in gathering new data and in analyzing the results, in the following year the <u>study</u> <u>was published</u>.
>   S   V

The longer the periodic sentence is, the greater the suspense and the more emphatic the final part. Since this high-tension structure is more difficult to read than the simple sentence, your readers would be exhausted if you used it too often. Save it for those times when you want to make a compelling point.

Vary sentence length

A short sentence can add punch to an important point, especially when it comes as a surprise. This technique can be particularly useful for conclusions. Don't overdo it, though—a string of long sentences may be monotonous, but a string of short ones can make your writing sound like a children's book.

Use contrast

Just as a jeweller will highlight a diamond by displaying it against dark velvet, you can highlight an idea by placing it against a contrasting background:

> *orig.*   Most psychology students do not enrol in animal laboratory courses.
>
> *rev.*   <u>Unlike physiology students</u>, most psychology students do not enrol in animal laboratory courses.

Using parallel phrasing will increase the effect of the contrast:

> Although <u>she often gave</u> informal talks and seminars, <u>she seldom gave</u> formal presentations at conferences.

Use a well-placed adverb or correlative construction
Adding an adverb or two can sometimes help you to dramatize a concept:

> *orig.*   After finishing the experiment, he realized he had made a mistake.

> *rev.*   After <u>hastily</u> finishing the experiment, he <u>quickly</u> realized he had made a mistake.

Correlatives such as *both . . . and* or *not only . . . but also* can be used to emphasize combinations as well:

> *orig.*   Professor Vance was a good lecturer and a good friend.

> *rev.*   Professor Vance was <u>both</u> a good lecturer <u>and</u> a good friend.

(or)

> *rev.*   Professor Vance was <u>not only</u> a good lecturer <u>but also</u> a good friend.

Use your ears
Your ears are probably your best critics: make good use of them. Before producing a final copy of any piece of writing, read it out loud in a clear voice. The difference between awkward and fluent passages will be easy to tell.

Revise early, revise often
It's hard to keep all of this writing advice in mind when preparing a first draft. Revision is the key to developing and solidifying your personal writing voice. Each time you come back to your draft, reread your previous paragraphs and make changes based on the suggestions provided in this chapter. You may find, for example, that you write primarily in the passive voice and have to go back and rework your sentences into the active voice. Use the checklist below to help guide you as you reread your writing:

Tone
I have avoided:
- ☐ colloquialisms
- ☐ frequent use of contractions
- ☐ overuse of the passive voice

Clarity

I have:

☐ chosen clear words
☐ avoided jargon
☐ been precise
☐ removed unnecessary qualifiers

Paragraph Style

I have:

☐ developed ideas fully
☐ used topic sentences
☐ maintained focus
☐ avoided monotony
☐ linked ideas

Succinctness

I have avoided:

☐ ambiguous pronouns
☐ abstract nouns
☐ vague qualifiers
☐ noun clusters
☐ worn-out expressions and circumlocutions

Force

I have:

☐ used active verbs
☐ used personal subjects
☐ provided concrete details

Strategy (Rhetoric)

I have:

☐ paid attention to the placement of key words
☐ subordinated minor ideas
☐ varied sentence structure and length
☐ used contrast and parallel phrasing

The Use of Neutral Language

The primary goals of scientific writing are *objectivity*—a term that implies a lack of bias—and *accuracy*, which means freedom from ambiguity. Although we tend to think of objectivity and accuracy in relation to the presentation and interpretation of data, they also have broader applications.

Years ago, relatively little attention was paid to the potential implications of using certain words. So, for example, referring to someone with a physical impairment as a *cripple* was not considered out of the ordinary. More recently, of course, there has been an increasing sensitivity to language that is not inclusive or that may cause offence. This is not the place to debate whether the pendulum of sensitivity has swung too far in one direction. However, you do need to think carefully about the words you use and what they might mean to another person.

Let's consider the word *cripple*. Suppose a student remarks that a particular professor was such a good instructor that she was able to help even the *math cripples* in the class. In this context, the term is not intended to show disrespect for individuals with physical disabilities; it is a metaphor to highlight the students' lack of math skills. However, it is possible that a person with a physical disability might take offence on hearing that remark. Do you feel that the student should not have used this term? What if the student was talking instead about his finances and remarked that by the time he graduated he would have a *crippling debt load*. Should such a comment also be avoided because it contains a term that is potentially offensive to someone?

The point of these examples is not to tell you whether you should use particular words or how far you should go to avoid giving offence. There is no correct answer to these questions, and there have been long and strenuous debates about political correctness. Rather than getting involved in such discussions, though, we would suggest that the most important thing is to think about the implications of what you say before you say it.

There are three areas that have attracted particular attention with respect to neutrality: the use of terms referring to men and women; the use of terms referring to different ethnic groups; and the use of terms referring to individuals with disabilities. We will discuss each of these in turn.

Terms referring to males and females

Until quite recently, *man* was widely used to refer to humans in general. It was not considered odd or inappropriate for Charles Darwin to write about *The Descent of Man*, and books with titles like *Man and Animal: Studies in Behaviour* or *Man and Beast: Comparative Social Behavior* were quite common. A quick search of the library catalogue at one university produced 462 items beginning with "*Man and . . .*" In almost all of these cases, the word *man* could be replaced by *humans* with no alteration in meaning. In contrast, there were only 76 listings for "*Woman and . . . ,*" and in most of these, *woman* referred specifically to human females.

Rather than asking whether this use of words is sexist, as some people argue, ask yourself if it meets the criteria of objectivity and accuracy. Clearly, the use of gender-specific terms in this fashion does not meet the criterion of accuracy, and may not meet the objectivity standard either. If you want to refer to the human species in general, then use *human, humankind*, or *people*.

The same guideline can be applied to job descriptions that traditionally were dominated by members of one sex—*fireman, policeman*, and *stewardess*, for example. In such cases, a slight modification allows the noun to cover both males and females: *firefighter, police officer*, and *flight attendant* are all perfectly acceptable alternatives.

You should be careful, though, not to carry these modifications to extremes. There are many words that contain the letters "m-a-n" that have a completely different etymology and do not refer to maleness. You should not be looking for alternatives for such words as *manufacture, manage*, or *manipulate*. You should also recognize that certain words that may originally have had a male connotation have become so fully integrated into the language that to change them would result in a convoluted or unintelligible rewording. *Manhole cover*, for example, has a specific referent and no longer implies that only men would go through the hole when it is uncovered. Although some people would argue that even these terms are sexist, the clarity achieved by using such a word seems more important than its etymology.

Another area of difficulty is the use of masculine pronouns to refer to someone who might be male or female. It was once conventional to use *he* or *his* when talking in general about an individual. So, each of the participants in an experiment was usually referred to as *he* even if some were female, as in, "Each of the participants had to complete his written questionnaire before he could be interviewed." Today, using *he* or *his* to refer to a person of either sex is not widely accepted.

You can get around this problem in a couple of ways. If you are writing a paper in which there are many references to individuals who may be male or female, then you might decide to use either the masculine or feminine pronouns exclusively; just be sure to acknowledge when you first use them that they will apply to both. This solution is not ideal, however: even with your acknowledgement that *he* and *his* will be used to refer to individuals of either sex, using the male pronouns hardly seems accurate, particularly if the majority of your participants are female.

If there will only be a few references of this type, then you can say *his or her* and *he or she*, as in, "each of the participants had to complete a written questionnaire before he or she could be interviewed." This solution is quite acceptable; however, compound pronouns are cumbersome, so if your report contains more than a few references of this sort, this solution might not be suitable.

The best solution may be to change your singular subject to a plural one, which would allow you to use the gender-neutral pronouns *they*, *them*, and *their*: "The participants had to complete *their* written questionnaires before *they* could be interviewed." We would advise against the use of *s/he*, which looks odd. Remember also that the term *no one* is singular, so it is incorrect to say something like "no one took *their* laptops to class." In this case, you would need a singular pronoun.

Finally, it is worth saying something about the use of the terms *sex* and *gender*. *Sex* refers to the biological distinction between males and females, and any discussion that deals with that distinction should refer to *sex*. For example, if it was not important whether you were testing males or females, you would say, "the sex of the participants was not relevant to this study." *Gender* refers either to a grammatical classification of words or to the cultural, social, or psychological dimensions of maleness or femaleness. Try to use these two terms appropriately.

Terms referring to different ethnic groups

Historically, Caucasian writers would refer to different ethnic groups using terms developed within the white community. Thus, terms like *Indian*, *Eskimo*, *Oriental*, *Coloured*, or *Negro* were used routinely, and often with a pejorative connotation. Little consideration was given to employing the terms used by members of these communities themselves.

Beginning in the 1960s with the rise of the civil rights movement in the United States, there was a concerted effort by different ethnic groups to promote descriptors that were accepted within their own communities. As a result, terms like *Afro-American* and *African American* have become the descriptors of choice. Similarly, the term *Eskimo* has been replaced by *Inuit*, the term *Oriental* by reference to specific country of origin, or more generally, *Asian*, and so on. You should be aware, though, that language is dynamic, so the preferred terms may change over time or vary depending on the context. A good example of this is the term *Indian* when used to refer to Native Americans and Canadians. It is still used in some official capacities: for instance, the US government still has a Department of Indian Affairs, and some Canadian legislation recognizes *status Indians* and *non-status Indians*, those who, respectively, are and are not members of bands that have signed treaties with the government. The Canadian constitution recognizes three groups of Aboriginal people: Indians, Métis, and Inuit. However, among these groups, the terms *First Nations* or *Indigenous Peoples* are generally preferred, and many individual groups favour, and have begun to promote, the use of more specific references—Anishnabe, Chippewa, Cree, Nisga'a, Oneida, and so on. When you are referring to a particular ethnic group, find out what name is used within the community you are discussing and use only that term.

Terms referring to functioning and disability

Just as there has been insensitivity in the way ethnic groups have been referenced, there used to be little recognition of people with disabilities as individuals. Instead, there was a tendency to use broad terms that perpetuated negative stereotypes: *deaf and dumb*, *cretin*, and *Mongoloid* were all used indiscriminately in both formal and informal writing. With respect to the criteria we set out above, these terms are neither objective nor accurate. Even the words *disability* and *handicap* are sometimes used inappropriately.

In 1980, the World Health Organization proposed a set of definitions to describe conditions that might limit a person's abilities. The framework discussed the consequences of disease and provided a tool for the classification of *impairments*, *disabilities*, and *handicaps*. The World Health Organization has since revised this framework to be more inclusive, and in 2001 the World Health Assembly unanimously endorsed the *International Classification of Functioning, Disability and Health* (ICF) to provide a more comprehensive classification of health and health-related states. This system discusses the health components of functioning and disability, setting this discussion in the context of environmental and personal factors that can influence a person's activities and participation in a wide variety of areas. In this respect, "*Functioning* is an umbrella term encompassing all body functions, activities and participation; similarly, *disability* serves as an umbrella term for impairments, activity limitations or participation restrictions" (WHO, 2001, p. 3). By stressing health and functioning at the body, individual, and societal levels, the ICF applies to all people and recognizes disability as a universal human experience.

The reason for this discussion is to help you realize that you must not categorize individuals purely on the basis of their clinically defined conditions. If you keep this in mind, then it becomes easy to see why you should use a phrase like "people with disabilities" instead of "the disabled," "a person with diabetes" instead of "a diabetic," or "profoundly hearing-impaired" instead of "deaf and dumb." You must remember to emphasize the person and not the condition.

One final point: if you are working with any group of participants from a clinical population or with individuals who have an impairment or disability, do not use the term *normals* to distinguish your non-clinical group from the others; it is demeaning.

Summary

Reading is enjoyable when the writer takes you along with her in whatever she writes. Although the subject matter may be complex, a well-written paper is one that the reader does not have to struggle through. If your reader has to read a sentence several times in order to understand what you are saying, then you have failed in your writing task. Good writing flows well because it is clear and does not contain unnecessary jargon. It is well-organized, and it fills in all the logical steps of an argument so that the reader does not have to make a guess at what you intended to say. Finally, it is unbiased. If a reader senses an attitude that comes across in your writing, then your writing will likely be perceived as biased. The question of what constitutes biased writing is a difficult one because there are so many different points of view. No matter how hard you try, it's unlikely that you will be able to satisfy everyone. The most successful strategy when you are writing is to make sure that you do not take traditional assumptions for granted. For example, it is no longer accurate to assume that all doctors or researchers are male or that nurses and research assistants are female. Wherever possible, you should use specific, neutral, or inclusive terms, and you should always be alert to the possibility that you may be misrepresenting a group. However, in our view, you should not tie your writing in knots to satisfy all demands for neutrality and correctness. You will have to use your judgment to determine what is acceptable and what is not. You should also be aware that what is acceptable now may change over time, so a word that is considered appropriate today may not be appropriate five years from now.

References

American Psychological Association (2010). *Publication Manual of the American Psychological Association* (6th ed.). Washington, DC: American Psychological Association.

Cluett, R., & Ahlborn, L. (1965). *Effective English prose: Writing for meaning, reading for style.* New York, NY: L. W. Singer.

Watson, J. D. & Crick, F. H. C. (1953). Molecular structure of nucleic acids: A structure for deoxyribose nucleic acid. *Nature, 171* (4356), 737–738.

Watson, J. D. (1968). *The double helix: A personal account of the discovery of the structure of DNA.* New York, NY: Atheneum.

World Health Organization. (1980). *International classification of impairments, disabilities, and handicaps: A manual of classification relating to the consequences of disease.* Geneva, Switzerland: Author.

World Health Organization. (2001). *International classification of functioning, disability and health.* Geneva, Switzerland: Author.

World Health Organization. (2002). *Towards a common language for functioning, disability and health: ICF* [Online document]. Retrieved from http://www.who.int/classifications/icf/training/icfbeginnersguide.pdf

Common Errors in Grammar and Usage

Objectives

- understanding sentence unity
- keeping subjects and verbs in agreement
- using proper verb tenses
- understanding pronouns
- using modifiers properly
- keeping pairs and parallels consistent

Introduction

This chapter is not a comprehensive grammar lesson; it's simply a survey of those areas where students most often make mistakes. It will help you keep a lookout for weaknesses as you are editing your work. Once you get into the habit of checking your work, it won't be long before you are correcting potential problems as you write.

The grammatical terms used here are the most basic and familiar ones; if you need to review some of them, see Glossary II. For a thorough treatment of grammar and usage, see Ruvinsky (2014).

Troubles with Sentence Unity

Sentence fragments

To be complete, a sentence must have both a subject and a verb in an independent clause; if it doesn't, it's a fragment. There are times in informal writing when it is acceptable to use a sentence fragment in order to emphasize a point, as in the following example:

✓ What is the probability of contracting AIDS through casual contact? Very low.

In this example, the sentence fragment *Very low* is clearly intended to be understood as a short form of *The probability is very low*. Unintentional sentence fragments, on the other hand, usually seem incomplete rather than shortened:

    ✗   The liquid was poured into a glass beaker. <u>Being a strong acid</u>.

The last "sentence" is incomplete because it lacks a subject and a verb. (Remember that a participle such as *being* is a verbal, or "part-verb," not a verb.) The fragment can be made into a complete sentence by adding a subject and a verb:

    ✓   <u>The liquid</u> <u>was</u> a strong acid.

Alternatively, you could join the fragment to the preceding sentence:

    ✓   The liquid was poured into a glass beaker because it was a strong acid.

    ✓   Because the liquid was a strong acid, it was poured into a glass beaker.

Run-on sentences

A run-on sentence is one that continues beyond the point where it should have stopped:

    ✗   The experiment went surprisingly well the participants agreed to come back for a second session.

This run-on sentence, also called a *fused sentence*, could be fixed by adding a period or semicolon after the word *well*.

Another kind of run-on sentence is one in which two independent clauses (phrases that can stand by themselves as complete sentences) are incorrectly joined by a comma:

    ✗   The study examined the health effects of fructose consumption, it was published in the *American Journal of Clinical Nutrition*.

This error is known as a *comma splice*. There are three ways of correcting it:

    1. by putting a period after *consumption* and starting a new sentence:

        ✓   . . . fructose consumption. It was . . .

2. by replacing the comma with a semicolon:

✓ ... fructose consumption; it was ...

3. by making one of the independent clauses subordinate to the other, so that it doesn't stand by itself:

✓ The study, which was published in the *American Journal of Clinical Nutrition*, examined the health effects of fructose consumption.

The one exception to the rule that independent clauses cannot be joined by a comma arises when the clauses are short and arranged in a tight sequence:

✓ I observed, I analyzed, I discovered.

This kind of sentence can create dramatic emphasis but should not be used very often.

Contrary to what many people think, words such as *however, therefore,* and *thus* cannot be used to join independent clauses:

✗ Two of my friends started out in chemistry, however they quickly decided they didn't like lab work.

The mistake can be corrected by beginning a new sentence after *chemistry* or (preferably) by putting a semicolon in the same place:

✓ Two of my friends started out in chemistry; however, they quickly decided they didn't like lab work.

Another option is to join the two independent clauses with a coordinating conjunction—*and, or, nor, but, for, yet,* and *so*:

✓ Two of my friends started out in chemistry, but they quickly decided they didn't like lab work.

Faulty predication

When the subject of a sentence is not connected grammatically to what follows (the predicate), the result is *faulty predication*:

✗ The <u>reason</u> he failed <u>was because</u> he couldn't handle multiple-choice exams.

The problem here is that *the reason* means essentially the same thing as *was because*. The subject is a noun and the verb *was* needs a noun clause to complete it:

✓ The <u>reason</u> he failed <u>was that</u> he couldn't handle multiple-choice exams.

Another solution would be to rephrase the sentence:

✓ He failed because he couldn't handle multiple-choice exams.

Faulty predication also commonly occurs with *is when* and *is where* constructions. This error can be corrected by following the verb *is* with a noun phrase or by changing the verb:

✗ The difficulty <u>is when</u> the two sets of data disagree.

✓ The difficulty <u>is the disagreement</u> between the two sets of data.

✓ The difficulty <u>arises when</u> the two sets of data disagree.

Troubles with Subject–Verb Agreement

Identifying the subject

A verb should always agree in number with its subject. Sometimes, however, when the subject does not come at the beginning of the sentence or when it is separated from the verb by other information, you may be tempted to use a verb form that does not agree:

✗ The <u>decrease</u> in funding for staff and equipment <u>were condemned</u> by the scientists.

The subject here is *decrease*, not *staff and equipment*; therefore, the verb should be singular:

✓ The <u>decrease</u> in funding for staff and equipment <u>was condemned</u> by the scientists.

Either, neither, each

The indefinite pronouns *either*, *neither*, and *each* always take singular verbs:

✓ <u>Either</u> of the questionnaires <u>has</u> to be completed.

✓ <u>Each</u> of the questions <u>was</u> read out loud.

Compound subjects

When *or*, *either . . . or*, or *neither . . . nor* is used to create a compound subject, the verb should usually agree with the last item in the subject:

✓ Neither the professor nor her students were able to solve the equation.

✓ Either the students or the TA was misinformed.

You may find, however, that it sounds awkward in some cases to use a singular verb when a singular item follows a plural item:

orig. Either my chemistry books or my biology text is going to gather dust this weekend.

In such instances, it's better to rephrase the sentence:

rev. This weekend, I'm going to ignore either my chemistry books or my biology text.

The word *and* creates a compound subject and therefore takes a plural verb. The phrases *as well as* and *in addition to* do not create compound subjects, so the verb remains singular:

✓ Organic chemistry and applied math are difficult subjects.

✓ Organic chemistry, as well as applied math, is a difficult subject.

Collective nouns

A collective noun is a singular noun that includes a number of members, such as *family*, *army*, or *team*. If the noun refers to the members as a unit, it takes a singular verb:

✓ The class is going on a field trip in June.

If, in the context of the sentence, the noun refers to the members as individuals, the verb becomes plural:

✓ The team are receiving their medals this week.

✓ The majority of bears hibernate in winter.

Titles

The title of a book or movie or the name of a business or organization is always treated as a singular noun, even if it contains plural words; therefore, it takes a singular verb:

✔ _The Thirty-Nine Steps_ is a fascinating book.

✔ Bausch and Lomb is a company that offers a wide range of eye health products.

Troubles with Verb Tenses

Native speakers of English usually know without thinking which verb tense to use in a given context. However, a few tenses can still be confusing.

The past perfect

If the main verb is in the past tense and you want to refer to something that happened before that time, use the _past perfect_ (_had_ followed by the past participle). The time sequence will not be clear if you use the simple past in both clauses:

✗ He hoped that she fixed the microscope.

✔ He hoped that she had fixed the microscope.

Similarly, when you are reporting what someone said in the past—that is, when you are using _past indirect discourse_—you should use the past perfect tense in the clause describing what was said:

✗ He told the TA that he wrote the essay that week.

✔ He told the TA that he had written the essay that week.

Using _if_

When you are describing a possibility in the future, use the present tense in the condition (_if_) clause and the future tense in the consequence clause:

✔ If she tests us on operant conditioning, I will fail.

When the possibility is unlikely, it is conventional—especially in formal writing—to use the subjunctive in the _if_ clause, and _would_ followed by the base verb in the consequence clause:

✔ If she were to cancel the test, I would cheer.

When you are describing a hypothetical instance in the past, use the past subjunctive (it has the same form as the past perfect) in the *if* clause and *would have* followed by the past participle for the consequence. A common error is to use *would have* in both clauses:

    ✗   If he <u>would have been</u> friendlier, I <u>would have asked</u> him to be my lab partner.

    ✓   If he <u>had been</u> friendlier, I <u>would have asked</u> him to be my lab partner.

Troubles with Pronouns

Pronoun reference

The link between a pronoun and the noun it refers to must be clear. If the noun doesn't appear in the same sentence as the pronoun, it should appear in the preceding sentence:

    ✗   The <u>textbook supply</u> in the bookstore had run out, so we borrowed <u>them</u> from the library.

Since *textbook* is used as an adjective rather than a noun, it cannot serve as referent or antecedent for the pronoun *them*. You must either replace *them* or change the phrase *textbook supply*:

    ✓   The <u>textbook supply</u> in the bookstore had run out, so we borrowed <u>the texts</u> from the library.

    ✓   The bookstore had run out of <u>textbooks</u>, so we borrowed <u>them</u> from the library.

When a sentence contains more than one noun, make sure there is no ambiguity about which noun the pronoun refers to:

    ✗   The faculty wants increased <u>salaries</u> as well as fewer <u>teaching hours</u>, but the administration does not favour <u>them</u>.

What does the pronoun *them* refer to: the salary increases, the reduced teaching hours, or both?

    ✓   The faculty wants increased <u>salaries</u> as well as fewer teaching hours, but the administration does not favour <u>salary increases</u>.

Using *it* and *this*

Using *it* and *this* without a clear referent can lead to confusion:

> ✗ Although the directors wanted to meet in January, it (this) didn't take place until May.

> ✓ Although the directors wanted to meet in January, the conference didn't take place until May.

Make sure that *it* or *this* clearly refers to a specific noun or pronoun.

Pronoun agreement and gender

A pronoun should agree in number and person with the noun that it refers to. However, an increasing awareness of sexist or biased language has changed what is considered to be acceptable over the last few decades. In the past, the following sentence would have been considered incorrect:

> When a student is sick, their classmates usually help out.

It would have been corrected to read:

> When a student is sick, his classmates usually help out.

This is because, traditionally, the word *his* has been used to indicate both male and female. Although many grammarians still maintain that *he* and *his* have dual meanings—one for an individual male and one for any human being—today this usage is increasingly regarded as sexist. As we pointed out in Chapter 11, an alternative to using *his* is to use *his or her*, as this handbook occasionally does, or *he/she*; however, these phrases can be awkward, particularly if they are used repeatedly in a passage. For this reason, using *their* or *they* to indicate an individual of either gender is becoming more common, and this trend appears to be gaining acceptance. As a result, the first sentence above would now be considered correct by many, though there are those who would still find it objectionable. Where possible, it's better to rephrase the sentence—in this case, by switching from the singular to the plural in both the noun and the pronoun:

> ✓ When students are sick, their classmates usually help out.

Using *one*

People often use the word *one* to avoid overusing *I* in their writing. Although in Britain this is common, in Canada and the United States frequent use of *one* may seem too formal and even a bit pompous:

> *orig.* If one were to apply for the grant, one would find oneself engulfed in so many bureaucratic forms that one's patience would be stretched thin.

In the past, a common way around this problem was to use the third-person *his* or (less often) *her* as the adjectival form of *one*:

> *rev.* One would find his (or her) patience stretched thin.

Today, this usage is regarded with less favour. As we saw in the preceding section, you may be able to substitute *his* with the plural *their*; just remember that some people still object to this usage. The best solution, again, may be to rephrase the sentence with a plural subject:

> *rev.* If researchers were to apply for grants, they would find themselves engulfed in so many bureaucratic forms that their patience would be stretched thin.

In any case, try to use *one* sparingly, and don't be afraid of the occasional *I*. The one serious error to avoid is mixing the third-person pronoun *one* with the second-person pronoun *you*.

> ✗ When one visits the cyclotron, you are impressed by its size.

In formal academic writing, *you* is not an appropriate substitute for *one*.

Using *me* and other objective pronouns

Remembering that it's wrong to say "Sherry and me were invited to present our findings to the delegates" rather than "Sherry and I were invited . . . ," many people use the subjective form of the pronoun even when it should be objective:

> ✗ The delegates invited Steve and I to present our findings.
> ✓ The delegates invited Steve and *me* to present our findings.

The verb *invited* requires an object; *me* is in the objective case. A good way to tell which form is correct is to ask yourself how the sentence would sound if the pronoun was used by itself. It will be obvious that the subjective form— "The delegates invited *I* . . ."—is not appropriate.

The same problem often arises with prepositions, which should also be followed by a noun or pronoun in the objective case:

✗ <u>Between</u> you and <u>I</u>, this result doesn't make sense.

✓ <u>Between</u> you and <u>me</u>, this result doesn't make sense.

✗ Eating well is a problem <u>for</u> <u>we</u> students.

✓ Eating well is a problem <u>for</u> <u>us</u> students.

There are times, however, when the correct case can sound stiff or awkward:

orig.   <u>To</u> <u>whom</u> was the award given?

Rather than keeping to a correct but awkward form, try to reword the sentence:

rev.   <u>Who</u> <u>received</u> the award?

Exceptions for pronouns following prepositions

The rule that a pronoun following a preposition takes the objective case has exceptions. When the preposition is followed by a clause, the pronoun should take the case required by its position in the clause:

✗ The students showed some concern <u>about</u> <u>whom</u> <u>would be selected</u> as Dean.

Although the pronoun follows the preposition *about*, it is also the subject of the verb *would be selected* and therefore requires the subjective case:

✓ The students showed some concern <u>about</u> <u>who</u> <u>would be selected</u> as Dean.

Similarly, when a gerund (a word that acts partly as a noun and partly as a verb) is the subject of a clause, the pronoun that modifies it takes the possessive case:

✗ We were surprised <u>by</u> <u>him</u> <u>dropping</u> out of school.

✓ We were surprised <u>by</u> <u>his</u> <u>dropping</u> out of school.

Troubles with Modifiers

Adjectives modify nouns; adverbs modify verbs, adjectives, and other adverbs. Do not use an adjective to modify a verb:

- ✗ He played <u>good</u>. (adjective with verb)
- ✓ He played <u>well</u>. (adverb modifying verb)
- ✓ He played <u>really</u> <u>well</u>. (adverb modifying adverb)
- ✓ He had a <u>good</u> <u>style</u>. (adjective modifying noun)
- ✓ He had a <u>really</u> <u>good</u> style. (adverb modifying adjective)

Squinting modifiers

Remember that clarity depends largely on word order: to avoid confusion, the relations between the different parts of a sentence must be clear. Modifiers should therefore be as close as possible to the words they modify. A squinting modifier is one that, because of its position, seems to look in two directions at once:

- ✗ She discovered <u>in the spring</u> she will receive government funding.

Is *spring* the time of the discovery or the time when she will receive government funding? The logical relation is usually clearest when you place the modifier immediately before or after the element it modifies:

- ✓ <u>In the spring,</u> she discovered that she will receive government funding.
- ✓ She discovered that she will receive government funding <u>in the spring</u>.

Other squinting modifiers can be corrected in the same way:

- ✗ Our biology professor gave a lecture on *Planaria*, <u>which was well illustrated</u>.
- ✓ Our biology professor gave a <u>well-illustrated</u> <u>lecture</u> on *Planaria*.

Dangling modifiers

Modifiers that have no grammatical connection with anything else in the sentence are said to be dangling:

- ✗ <u>Walking</u> around the campus in June, the river and trees made a picturesque scene.

Who is doing the walking? Here's another example:

> ✗ <u>Reflecting</u> on the results of the study, it was decided not to submit the paper for publication.

Who is doing the reflecting? Clarify the meaning by connecting the dangling modifier to a new subject:

> ✓ <u>Walking</u> around the campus in June, <u>Farah</u> thought the river and trees made a picturesque scene.

> ✓ <u>Reflecting</u> on the results of the study, <u>the research team</u> decided not to submit the paper for publication.

Troubles with Pairs and Parallels

Comparisons

Make sure that your comparisons are complete. The second element in a comparison should be equivalent to the first, whether the equivalence is stated or merely implied:

> ✗ Today's students have a greater understanding of calculus than their parents.

The sentence suggests that the two things being compared are *calculus* and *parents*. Adding a second verb (*have*) that is equivalent to the first one shows that the two things being compared are *parents' understanding* and *students' understanding*:

> ✓ Today's students <u>have</u> a greater understanding of calculus than their parents <u>have</u>.

A similar problem arises in the following comparison:

> ✗ The new text is a <u>boring book</u> and so are the lectures.

The lectures may be boring, but they are not a *boring book*; to make sense, the two parts of the comparison must be parallel:

> ✓ The new text is <u>boring</u> and so are the lectures.

Correlatives

Constructions such as *both . . . and, not only . . . but also*, and *neither . . . nor* are especially tricky. The coordinating term must not come too early or else the parts being compared will not be balanced. For the implied comparison to work, the two parts that come after the coordinating term must be grammatically equivalent:

✗ He <u>not only</u> studies music <u>but also</u> math.

✓ He studies <u>not only</u> music <u>but also</u> math.

Parallel phrasing

A series of items in a sentence should be phrased in parallel wording. Make sure that all the parts of a parallel construction are actually equivalent:

✗ We had to turn in <u>our</u> rough notes, <u>our</u> calculations, and finished assignment.

✓ We had to turn in <u>our</u> rough notes, <u>our</u> calculations, and <u>our</u> finished assignment.

Once you have decided to include the pronoun *our* in the first two elements, the third must have it too.

For clarity as well as stylistic grace, keep similar ideas in similar form:

✗ He <u>failed</u> genetics and <u>barely passed</u> statistics, but zoology <u>was</u> a subject he did well in.

✓ He <u>failed</u> genetics and barely <u>passed</u> statistics but <u>did well</u> in zoology.

Summary

In an era of Twitter and text messaging, and with limited instruction in grammar at the high school level, there is little pressure on students to develop their grammatical skills. This is not a failing limited to students. Professional writers, particularly in newspapers, seem to have lost the art of grammatical writing. It is not at all unusual to see newspaper articles that contain several grammatical errors. But this is not an excuse for you. As we discussed in Chapter 11, if you want to write well, your work must be easy to read through. If your reader is brought up short by a grammatical error, this can create a bad impression. Most grammatical errors can be avoided if you think about each sentence as you write it and then parse its structure. That is, you should try to break it down into its component parts. Consider the following sentence: "He gave a present to you and I." Break that down into two sentences: "He gave a present to you," and "He gave a present to I." Clearly the sentence should read as follows: "He gave a present to you and me." There are many sentence structures where this simple analysis will tell you if your grammar is correct.

Reference

Ruvinsky, M. (2014). *Practical grammar: A Canadian writer's resource* (3rd ed.). Don Mills, ON: Oxford University Press.

Punctuation

Objectives

- understanding how to correctly use different punctuation marks
- avoiding common errors in punctuation

Introduction

Punctuation causes students so many problems that it deserves a chapter of its own. If your punctuation is faulty, your readers will be confused and may have to backtrack; worse still, they may be tempted to skip over the rough spots. Punctuation marks are the traffic signals of writing; use them with precision to keep readers moving smoothly through your work. Most of the rules we give below are general, but when there are several possibilities (for example, when British and American usage differs), we have used the APA style guidelines.

Items in this chapter are arranged alphabetically: *apostrophe, brackets, colon, comma, dash, ellipsis, exclamation mark, hyphen, italics, parentheses, period, quotation marks,* and *semicolon.*

Apostrophe [']

1. **Use an apostrophe to indicate possession.** The possessive form is often used to refer to something "belonging" to someone. To figure out where to place the apostrophe, first think of the possessive as an *of* phrase:

     the house <u>of the Perkins</u>

     the fathers <u>of the girls</u>

     the parents <u>of the children</u>

     the plays <u>of Shakespeare</u>

If you want to shorten these phrases by using an apostrophe to indicate possession, follow these rules:

a. If the noun in the *of* phrase ends in *s*, add an apostrophe after the *s*:

the Perkins' house

the girls' fathers

b. If the noun in the *of* phrase does not end in *s*, add an apostrophe plus *s*:

the children's parents

Shakespeare's plays

2. **Use an apostrophe to show contractions of words:**

isn't; we'll; he's; shouldn't; I'm

Caution: don't confuse *it's* (the contraction of *it is*) with *its* (the possessive of *it*), which has no apostrophe. And remember that possessive pronouns never take an apostrophe: *yours, hers, its, ours, theirs.*

Brackets [ ]

Brackets are square enclosures, not to be confused with parentheses (which are round).

Use brackets to set off a remark of your own within a quotation. The brackets show that the words enclosed are not those of the person quoted:

Mitchell stated, "Several of the changes observed [in the cat] are seen also in the monkey."

Brackets are also used to enclose *sic*, which is used after an error, such as a misspelling, to show that the mistake was in the original. *Sic* should be italicized:

In describing the inhabitants of a tidal pool, he wrote that "it was almost impossible to loosen barnikles [*sic*] from the rock surface."

Colon [:]

A colon indicates that something is to follow.

1. **Use a colon before a formal statement or series:**

    ✓ The layers are the following: sclera, choroid, and retina.

    Do not use a colon if the words preceding it do not form a complete sentence:

    ✗ The layers are: sclera, choroid, and retina.

    ✓ The layers are sclera, choroid, and retina.

    On the other hand, a colon often precedes a vertical list, even when the introductory part is not a complete sentence:

    ✓ The layers are: sclera
                            choroid
                            retina

2. **Use a colon for formality before a direct quotation:**

    ✓ The instructor was adamant: "All students must take the exam today."

Comma [,]

Commas are the trickiest of all punctuation marks; even the experts differ on when to use them. Most people agree, however, that too many commas are as bad as too few because they make writing choppy and awkward to read. Certainly recent writers use fewer commas than earlier stylists did. Whenever you are in doubt, let clarity be your guide. The most widely accepted conventions are these:

1. **Use a comma to separate two independent clauses joined by a co-ordinating conjunction (*and, but, for, or, nor, yet, so*).** By signalling that there are two clauses, the comma will prevent the reader from confusing the beginning of the second clause with the end of the first:

    ✗ He finished working with the microscope and his partner turned off the power.

    ✓ He finished working with the microscope, and his partner turned off the power.

When the second clause has the same subject as the first, you have the option of omitting both the second subject and the comma:

✓ She writes well, but she never finishes on time.

✓ She writes well but never finishes on time.

If you mistakenly punctuate two sentences as if they were one, the result will be a *run-on sentence*; if you use a comma but forget the coordinating conjunction, the result will be a *comma splice*:

✗ He took his class to the zoo, it was closed for repairs.

✓ He took his class to the zoo, but it was closed for repairs.

Remember that words such as *however, therefore,* and *thus* are conjunctive adverbs, not conjunctions: if you use one of them the way you would use a conjunction, the result will again be a *comma splice*:

✗ She was accepted into medical school, however, she took a year off to earn her tuition.

✓ She was accepted into medical school; however, she took a year off to earn her tuition.

Conjunctive adverbs are often confused with conjunctions. You can distinguish between the two if you remember that a conjunctive adverb's position in a sentence can be changed:

✓ She was accepted into medical school; she took a year off, however, to earn her tuition.

The position of a conjunction, on the other hand, is invariable; it must be placed between the two clauses:

✓ She was accepted into medical school, but she took a year off to earn her tuition.

When, in rare cases, the independent clauses are short and closely related, they may be joined by a comma alone:

✓ I came, I saw, I conquered.

A *fused sentence* is a run-on sentence in which independent clauses are slapped together with no punctuation at all:

✗ He watched the hockey game all afternoon the only exercise he got was going to the kitchen between periods.

A fused sentence sounds like breathless babbling—and it's a serious error. This example could be fixed by adding a period or semicolon after the word *afternoon.*

✓ He watched the hockey game all afternoon. The only exercise he got was going to the kitchen between periods.

2. **Use a comma between items in a series.** Place a coordinating conjunction before the last item:

✓ The room that housed the animals was large, bright, and clean.

✓ There was a cage washer, a bottle washer, and a place for storing the clean glassware.

The comma before the conjunction is optional:

✓ We have an office, a lab and a clinic.

Sometimes, however, the final comma can help to prevent confusion:

✗ We arranged to move the rats, photographs of the lab and the gerbil food.

In this case, a comma can prevent the reader from thinking that *photographs* refers both to *the lab* and to *the gerbil food*:

✓ We arranged to move the rats, photographs of the lab, and the gerbil food.

3. **Use a comma to separate adjectives preceding a noun when they modify the same element:**

✓ It was a reliable, accurate scale.

When the adjectives do not modify the same element, you should not use a comma:

✗ It was an expensive, chemical balance.

Here *chemical* modifies *balance,* but *expensive* modifies the whole phrase *chemical balance.* A good way of checking whether you need a comma is to see if you can reverse the order of the adjectives. If you can reverse it (*reliable, accurate scale* or *accurate, reliable scale*), use a comma; if you can't (*chemical expensive balance*), omit the comma:

✓ It was an expensive chemical balance.

4. **Use commas to set off an interruption (or "parenthetical element"):**

- ✓ The outcome, he said, was a complete failure.
- ✓ My tutor, however, couldn't answer the question.

Remember to put commas on *both sides* of the interruption:

- ✗ My tutor however, couldn't answer the question.
- ✗ The equipment, they reported was obsolete.
- ✓ The equipment, they reported, was obsolete.

5. **Use commas to set off words or phrases that provide additional but non-essential information:**

- ✓ Her grade in statistics, her favourite course, was not very high.
- ✓ The new iPad, his pride and joy, was connected to his high-definition TV.

In these examples, *her favourite course* and *his pride and joy* are *appositives*: they give additional information about the nouns they refer to (*statistics* and *iPad*), but the sentences would be understandable without them. Here's another example:

- ✓ *Equinox* magazine, which is published locally, often contains material that I can use in my course.

The phrase *which is published locally* is called a *non-restrictive modifier* because it does not limit the meaning of the words it modifies (Equinox *magazine*). Without that modifying clause the sentence would still refer to the contents of the magazine. Since the information the clause provides is not necessary to the meaning of the sentence, you must use commas on both sides to set it off.

In contrast, a *restrictive modifier* is one that provides essential information; it must not be set apart from the element it modifies, and commas should not be used:

- ✓ The magazine that has the black cover is *Equinox*.

Without the clause *that has the black cover*, the reader would not know which magazine was *Equinox*.

To avoid confusion, be sure to distinguish carefully between essential and additional information. The difference can be important:

Students who are not willing to work should not receive grants. (Only those who are unwilling to work should be denied grants.)

Students, who are not willing to work, should not receive grants. (All students are unwilling to work and should not receive grants.)

6. **Use a comma after an introductory phrase when omitting it would cause confusion:**

   ✗ On the balcony above the students flew paper airplanes.

   ✓ On the balcony above, the students flew paper airplanes.

7. **Use a comma to separate elements in dates and addresses:**

   February 2, 2015. (Commas are often omitted if the day comes first: 2 February 2015.)

   117 Hudson Drive, Edmonton, Alberta.

   They lived in Dartmouth, Nova Scotia.

8. **Use a comma before a quotation in a sentence:**

   ✓ He stated, "We were able to isolate the *E. coli* bacterium."

   ✓ "The most difficult part of the procedure," she reported, "was finding the material to work with."

   For more formality, you may use a colon (see page 243).

9. **Use a comma with a name followed by a title:**

   D. Gunn, Ph.D.

   Patrice Lareau, M.D.

Dash [—]

A dash (also called an *em dash* because it's about the same width as a letter *m*) creates an abrupt pause, emphasizing the words that follow. Never use dashes as casual substitutes for other punctuation: overuse can detract from the calm, well-reasoned effect you want to create.

1. **Use a dash to stress a word or phrase:**

   The fire alarm—which was deafening—warned them of the danger.
   I thought that writing this paper would be easy—but I was wrong.

2. **Use a dash in interrupted or unfinished dialogue:**

> "We were going to try—" he said, as the bus drove by without stopping.
>
> "I was just thinking—" Donald began to explain, but Mario cut him off.

You can type two hyphens together, with no spaces on either side, to show a dash. Your word processor may automatically convert this to an em dash for you as you continue typing. Alternatively, you can insert an em dash from the list of special characters in your word-processing software.

En dash [–]

An en dash is shorter than a full dash and slightly longer than a hyphen (it is about the same width of a letter *n*).

Use an en dash instead of a hyphen to separate parts of inclusive numbers or dates:

> The years 1890–1914
>
> pages 3–10

Ellipsis [. . .]

1. **Use an ellipsis (three spaced dots) to show an omission from a quotation:**

> "The hormonal control of reproduction is modulated . . . ultimately by the production of gonadal steroids" (Millers, 2014, p. 108).

If the omission comes at the beginning or end of the quotation, an ellipsis is not typically used:

> Millers (2014) explained that reproductive control is modulated "by the production of gonadal steroids" (p. 108).

However, ellipsis points may be included to prevent misinterpretation or to emphasize that the quotation begins or ends in midsentence:

> She explained that "control of reproduction is modulated . . ." (Millers, 2014, p. 108).

2. **Use an ellipsis to show that a series of numbers continues indefinitely:**

> 1, 3, 5, 7, 9 . . .

Exclamation Mark [!]

An exclamation mark helps to show emotion or feeling. It is usually found in dialogue:

> "Woe is me!" she cried.

In scientific writing, there is virtually no time when you would need to use an exclamation mark.

Hyphen [-]

1. **Use a hyphen if you must divide a word at the end of a line.** When a word is too long to fit at the end of a line, it's better to start a new line than to break the word. This is rarely a problem these days now that word processors can format text automatically. If you must divide a word, however, remember these rules:

- Divide between syllables.
- Never divide a one-syllable word.
- Never leave one letter by itself.
- Divide double consonants except when they come before a suffix, in which case divide before the suffix:

> ar-rangement
> embar-rassment
> fall-ing
> pass-able

- When the second consonant has been added to form the suffix, keep it with the suffix:

> refer-ral
> begin-ning

2. **Use a hyphen to separate the parts of certain compound words:**

- compound nouns:

  sister-in-law; mother-of-pearl

- compound verbs:

  fine-tune; test-drive

- compound nouns and adjectives used as modifiers preceding nouns:

  a <u>well-designed</u> study; <u>sixteenth-century</u> science

Note that compound modifiers are hyphenated only when they precede the part modified; otherwise, omit the hyphen:

  The study was <u>well designed</u>.

  The object dates from the <u>sixteenth century</u>.

Also, do not hyphenate a compound modifier that includes an adverb ending in -*ly*:

✓ a well-written book

✗ a beautifully-written book

✓ a beautifully written book

Most hyphenated nouns and verbs lose the hyphen over time. When in doubt, check a dictionary.

3. **Use a hyphen with certain prefixes (*all-*, *self-*, *ex-*) and with prefixes preceding a proper name):**

  all-inclusive; self-imposed; ex-student; pro-nuclear; trans-Canada

4. **Use a hyphen to emphasize contrasting prefixes:**

  Both pre- and post-treatment measures were taken.

5. **Use a hyphen to separate written-out compound numbers from one to ninety-nine, and compound fractions.** Remember that in APA style, you should spell out the numbers one through nine, and

use numerals for numbers greater than nine. However, if you must start a sentence with a number, make sure you spell the number out.

eighty-one centimetres; seven-tenths full

Italics [*italics*]

There are several occasions when you should use italics:

1. **Use italics for the titles of books and journals:**

   Darwin's *Origin of Species* continues to attract widespread interest. The study was published in the *Journal of Applied Psychology*.

2. **Use italics for biological names:**

   This research examines the common or brown rat, *Rattus norvegicus*.

3. **Use italics (or quotation marks) to identify a word or phrase that is itself the subject of discussion:**

   They were asked to solve an anagram of the word *caveat*.

4. **Use italics to emphasize a word or idea:**

   It is important that all equipment be washed *immediately*.

   Keep in mind that you should not do this too often, or the emphasis will lose its force.

5. **Use italics for letters used as symbols or algebraic terms:**

   SD (standard deviation)

   df = 17 (degrees of freedom)

Parentheses [( )]

1. **Use parentheses to enclose an explanation, example, or qualification.** Parentheses show that the enclosed material is of incidental importance to the main idea. They make an interruption that is more subtle than one marked off by dashes but more pronounced than one set off by commas:

   The meerkat (a mongoose-like animal) is found in southern Africa.

> At least 30 people (according to the newspaper report) were under observation.

Remember that punctuation should not precede parentheses, but it may follow them if required by the sense of the sentence:

> There were some complaints (mainly from the less experienced students), but we decided to continue with the project anyway.

If the parenthetical statement comes between two complete sentences, it should be punctuated as a sentence, with the period, question mark, or exclamation mark inside the parentheses:

> I finished my last essay on April 3. (It was on long-term memory.) Fortunately, I had three weeks free to study for the exam.

2. **Use parentheses to enclose reference citations.** See Chapter 10 for details.

Period [.]

1. **Use a period at the end of a sentence.** A period indicates a full stop, not just a pause.

2. **Use a period with abbreviations.** British style omits the period in certain cases, but North American style usually requires it for abbreviated titles (Mrs., Dr., Rev., Ph.D., etc.). Abbreviations for place names may or may not use periods (B.C. or BC, N.W.T. or NWT, etc.) as long as you remain consistent within your document; however, in official postal use, two-letter state and provincial abbreviations do not require periods (BC, NT, PE, NY, DC, etc.). Although the abbreviations and acronyms for some organizations include periods, the most common ones generally do not (APA, CARE, CIDA, CBC, RCMP, etc.).

3. **Use a period at the end of an indirect question.** Do *not* use a question mark:

> ✗   He asked if I wanted a clean lab coat?
>
> ✓   He asked if I wanted a clean lab coat.

Quotation Marks [" " OR ' ']

Quotation marks are used for several purposes, as described below. Conventions regarding single or double quotation marks vary, but APA style recommends that you use double marks for quotations within the running text and single marks for quotations within quotations.

1. **Use quotation marks to signify direct discourse (the actual words of a speaker):**

   I asked, "What is the matter?"

   "I have a pain in my big toe," he replied.

2. **Use quotation marks to show that words themselves are the issue:**

   Quotation marks can be used to mark a slang word, an ironic comment, or an inappropriate usage to show that the writer is aware of the difficulty:

   Several of the "experts" did not seem to know anything about the topic.

   Use this device only when necessary. In general, it's better to let the context show your attitude or to choose another term.

3. **Use single quotation marks to enclose quotations within quotations:**

   He said, "several of the 'experts' did not seem to know anything about the topic."

Placement of punctuation with quotation marks

The *Publication Manual of the American Psychological Association* (2010) suggests the following guidelines:

- Periods and commas always go inside closing quotation marks:

  He said, "I think we can finish tonight," but I told him, "Marchael, it's time to go home."

- A semicolon or colon always goes outside the quotation marks:

  Lisa calls it "a masterpiece"; I call it junk.

- A question mark, dash, or exclamation mark goes inside the quotation marks if it is part of the quotation, but outside if it is not:

  She asked, "What *is* that, Lisa?"

  Did she really call it "a piece of junk"?

  You could hardly call it "a masterpiece"!

  I was just telling Mike, "*I* think it looks like—" when Lisa walked in the room.

- With a block quotation (one that is set off from the running text), you do not need to use any quotation marks, but for quotations within the block use double quotation marks.

Semicolon [;]

1. **Use a semicolon to join independent clauses (complete sentences) that are closely related:**

   ✓ For five days he worked non-stop; by Saturday he was exhausted.

   ✓ His lecture was confusing; no one could understand the terminology.

   A semicolon is especially useful when the second independent clause begins with a conjunctive adverb such as *however, moreover, consequently, nevertheless, in addition,* or *therefore* (usually followed by a comma):

   ✓ He tried to prove his hypothesis; however, his experiment was unsuccessful.

   It's usually acceptable to follow a semicolon with a coordinating conjunction if the second clause is complicated by other commas:

   ✓ Some of these animals, wolverine and lynx in particular, are rarely seen; but occasionally, if you are patient, you might catch a glimpse of one.

2. **Use a semicolon to mark the divisions in a complicated series when individual items themselves need commas.** Using a comma to mark the subdivisions and a semicolon to mark the main divisions will help to prevent mix-ups:

   ✗ He invited Professor Ludvik, the vice-principal, Christine Li, and Dr. J. Dexter Schokmann.

   Is the vice-principal Professor Ludvik, Christine Li, or a separate person?

   ✓ He invited Professor Ludvik; the vice-principal, Christine Li; and Dr. J. Dexter Schokmann.

   In a case such as this, the elements separated by the semicolon need not be independent clauses.

Summary

Many ancient writing systems had few punctuation marks. Similarly, other than exclamation marks many electronic messages make little use of punctuation. Perhaps due to lack of practice, many students have problems with punctuation. Some try to avoid the issue by writing in short sentences, but that only makes their writing seem choppy. If you're writing on a complex topic, then you'll need to produce longer and more carefully constructed sentences. When used correctly, punctuation will help you control the dynamics of your writing and guide your reader through your ideas. Commas tell your reader where to pause; parentheses let you provide some information that is not directly connected to your train of thought; and quotation marks allow you to highlight a passage or show that some words are not your own. When used properly, punctuation can be powerful. By learning just a few rules, you can create sentences that are direct and unambiguous. Proper punctuation can help your writing flow and give it a rhythm that will make the reader feel as if she is listening to someone talking.

Reference

American Psychological Association. (2010). *Publication manual of the American Psychological Association* (6th ed.). Washington, DC: Author.

Appendix A

Catchlist of Misused Words and Phrases

This chapter offers a catchlist of words and phrases that are often misused. A periodic read-through will refresh your memory and help you avoid needless mistakes.

accept, except. Accept is a verb meaning to *receive affirmatively*; **except**, when used as a verb, means to *exclude*:

> I accept your offer.

> The teacher excepted him from the general punishment.

accompanied by, accompanied with. Use **accompanied by** for people; use **accompanied with** for objects:

> He was accompanied by his wife.

> The brochure arrived, accompanied with a discount coupon.

advice, advise. Advice is a noun, **advise** a verb:

> He was advised to ignore the advice of others.

affect, effect. Affect is a verb meaning to *influence*; however, it also has a specialized meaning in psychology, referring to a person's emotional state. **Effect** can be either a noun meaning *result* or a verb meaning to *bring about*:

> The eye drops affect his vision.

> Because he was so depressed, he showed no affect when he heard the joke.

> The effect of higher government spending is higher inflation.

> People lack confidence in their ability to effect change in society.

all ready, already. To be **all ready** is simply to be ready for something; **already** means *beforehand* or *earlier*:

The students were <u>all ready</u> for the lecture to begin.

The professor had <u>already</u> left her office by the time Blair arrived.

all right. Write as two separate words: *all right*. This can mean *safe and sound, in good condition, okay*; *correct*; *satisfactory*; or *I agree*:

Are you <u>all right</u>?

The student's answers were <u>all right</u>.

(Note the ambiguity of the second example: does it mean that the answers were all correct or simply satisfactory? In this case, it might be better to use a clearer word.)

all together, altogether. All together means *in a group*; **altogether** is an adverb meaning *entirely*:

He was <u>altogether</u> certain that the children were <u>all together</u>.

allusion, illusion. An **allusion** is an indirect reference to something; an **illusion** is a false perception:

The rock image is an <u>allusion</u> to the myth of Sisyphus.

He thought he saw a sea monster, but it was an <u>illusion</u>.

a lot. Write as two separate words: *a lot*.

alternate, alternative. Alternate means *every other* or *every second* thing in a series; **alternative** refers to a *choice* between options:

The two sections of the class attended discussion groups on <u>alternate</u> weeks.

The students could do an extra paper as an <u>alternative</u> to writing the exam.

among, between. Use **among** for three or more persons or objects, **between** for two:

<u>Between</u> you and me, there's trouble <u>among</u> the team members.

amount, number. Amount indicates quantity when units are not discrete and not absolute; **number** indicates quantity when units are discrete and absolute:

A large <u>amount</u> of timber.

A large <u>number</u> of students.

See also **less, fewer.**

analysis. The plural is **analyses.**

anyone, any one. Anyone is written as two words to give numerical emphasis; otherwise it is written as one word:

<u>Any one</u> of us could do that.

<u>Anyone</u> could do that.

anyways. Non-standard English: use *anyway.*

as, because. As is a weaker conjunction than **because** and may be confused with *when*:

✗ <u>As</u> I was working, I ate at my desk.

✓ <u>Because</u> I was working, I ate at my desk.

✗ He arrived <u>as</u> I was leaving.

✓ He arrived <u>when</u> I was leaving.

as to. A common feature of bureaucratese. Replace it with a single-word preposition such as *about* or *on*:

✗ They were concerned <u>as to</u> the range of disagreement.

✓ They were concerned <u>about</u> the range of disagreement.

✗ They recorded his comments <u>as to</u> the effectiveness of the drug.

✓ They recorded his comments <u>on</u> the treaty.

bad, badly. Bad is an adjective meaning *not good*:

The meat tastes <u>bad</u>.

He felt <u>bad</u> about forgetting the dinner party.

Badly is an adverb meaning *not well*; when used with the verbs **want** or **need**, it means *very much*:

She thought he played the villain's part <u>badly</u>.

I <u>badly</u> <u>need</u> a new suit.

beside, besides. Beside is a preposition meaning *next to*:

She worked <u>beside</u> her assistant.

Besides has two uses: as a preposition it means *in addition to*; as a conjunctive adverb it means *moreover*:

<u>Besides</u> recommending the changes, the consultants are implementing them.

<u>Besides</u>, it was hot and we wanted to rest.

between. See **among**.

bring, take. One **brings** something to a closer place and **takes** it to a farther one:

<u>Take</u> it with you when you go.

Next time you come to visit, <u>bring</u> your friend along.

can, may. Can means to *be able*; **may** means to *have permission*:

<u>Can</u> you fix the lock?

<u>May</u> I have another piece of cake?

In speech, *can* is used to cover both meanings; in formal writing, however, you should observe the distinction.

can't hardly. A faulty combination of the phrases **can't** and **can hardly**. Use one or the other:

He <u>can't</u> swim.

He <u>can hardly</u> swim.

cite, sight, site. To **cite** something is to *quote* or *mention* it as an example or authority; **sight** can be used in many ways, all of which relate to the ability to *see*; **site** refers to a specific *location,* a particular place at which something is located.

complement, compliment. The verb to **complement** means to *complete* or *enhance*; to **compliment** means *to praise*:

Her ability to analyze data <u>complements</u> her excellent research skills.

I <u>complimented</u> her on her outstanding report.

The same rule applies when these words are used as adjectives. The adjective *complimentary* can also mean *free*:

Blue and yellow are <u>complementary</u> colours.

They gave me <u>complimentary</u> tickets.

compose, comprise. Both words mean to *constitute* or *make up*, but **compose** is preferred. **Comprise** is correctly used to mean *include, consist of,* or *be composed of*. Using **comprise** in the passive ("is comprised of")—as you might be tempted to do in the second example below—is usually frowned on in formal writing:

These students <u>compose</u> the group which will go overseas.

Each paragraph <u>comprises</u> an introduction, an argument, and a conclusion.

continual, continuous. Continual means *repeated over a period of time*; **continuous** means *constant* or *without interruption*:

The strikes caused <u>continual</u> delays in building the road.

Five days of <u>continuous</u> rain ruined our holiday.

could of. This construction is incorrect, as are **might of, should of,** and **would of**. Replace *of* with *have*:

✗ He <u>could of</u> done it.

✓ He <u>could have</u> done it.

✓ They <u>might have</u> been there.

✓ I <u>should have</u> known.

✓ We <u>would have</u> left earlier.

council, counsel. Council is a noun meaning an *advisory* or *deliberative assembly*. **Counsel** as a noun means *advice* or *lawyer*; as a verb it means to *give advice.*

The college <u>council</u> meets on Tuesday.

We respect her <u>counsel</u>, since she's seldom wrong.

As a camp <u>counsellor</u>, you may need to <u>counsel</u> parents as well as children.

criterion, criteria. A **criterion** is a standard for judging something. **Criteria** is the plural of *criterion* and thus requires a plural verb:

<u>These</u> are my <u>criteria</u> for grading the reports.

data. The plural of **datum**. The set of information, usually in numerical form, that is used for analysis as the basis for a study. Informally, **data** is often used as a singular noun, but in formal contexts it should be treated as a plural:

<u>These</u> data <u>were</u> gathered in an unsystematic fashion.

Because *data* often refers to a single mass entity, many writers now accept its use with a single verb and pronoun:

When the <u>data</u> is in we'll review it.

deduce, deduct. To deduce something is to *work it out by reasoning*; to **deduct** means to *subtract* or *take away* from something. The noun form of both words is **deduction.**

defence, defense. Both spellings are correct: **defence** is standard in Britain and is somewhat more common in Canada; **defense** is standard in the United States.

delusion, illusion. A **delusion** is a false belief; an **illusion** is a misleading perception:

One symptom of his schizophrenia was his paranoid <u>delusions</u>.

As the clouds passed in front of the moon, they created the <u>illusion</u> that the moon was moving.

dependent, dependant. Dependent is an adjective meaning *contingent on* or *subject to*; **dependant** is a noun.

Suriya's graduation is <u>dependent</u> upon her passing algebra.

Chedley is a <u>dependant</u> of his father.

device, devise. The word ending in **-ice** is the noun; the word ending in **-ise** is the verb.

different than, different from. Use **different from** to compare two persons or things; use **different than** with a full clause:

His plan is <u>different from</u> the others.

This city is <u>different than</u> it used to be.

diminish, minimize. To **diminish** means to *make* or *become smaller*; to **minimize** means to *reduce* something to the smallest possible amount or size.

disinterested, uninterested. Disinterested implies impartiality or neutrality; **uninterested** implies a lack of interest:

As a <u>disinterested</u> observer, he was in a good position to judge the issue fairly.

<u>Uninterested</u> in the experiment, he yawned repeatedly.

due to. Although increasingly used to mean *because of*, **due** is an adjective and therefore needs to modify something:

  ✗   <u>Due to</u> his impatience, we lost the contract. [Due is dangling.]

  ✓   The loss was <u>due to</u> his impatience.

e.g., i.e. E.g. means **for example**; **i.e.** means *that is*. It is incorrect to use them interchangeably.

entomology, etymology. Entomology is the study of insects; **etymology** is the study of the derivation and history of words.

exceptional, exceptionable. Exceptional means *unusual* or *outstanding*, whereas **exceptionable** means *open to objection* and is generally used in negative contexts.

His accomplishments are <u>exceptional</u>.

He was ejected from the game because of his <u>exceptionable</u> behaviour.

farther, further. Farther refers to distance, **further** to extent:

He paddled <u>farther</u> than his friends did.

She explained the plan <u>further</u>.

focus. The plural of the noun may be either **focuses** (also spelled **focusses**) or **foci.**

good, well. Good is an adjective that modifies a noun; **well** is an adverb that modifies a verb.

He is a <u>good</u> rugby player.

The experiment went <u>well</u>.

hanged, hung. Hanged means *executed by hanging.* **Hung** means *suspended* or *clung to*:

He was <u>hanged</u> at dawn for the murder.

He <u>hung</u> the picture.

She <u>hung</u> on to the boat when it capsized.

hereditary, heredity. Heredity is a noun referring to the biological process whereby characteristics are passed from one generation to the next; **hereditary** is an adjective describing those characteristics:

<u>Heredity</u> is a factor in the incidence of this disease.

Your asthma may be <u>hereditary</u>.

hopefully. Use **hopefully** as an adverb meaning *full of hope*:

She scanned the horizon <u>hopefully</u>, looking for signs of the missing boat.

In formal writing, using **hopefully** to mean *I hope* is still frowned upon, although it is increasingly common; it's better to use *I hope*:

✗   <u>Hopefully</u> the experiment will go off without a hitch.

✓   <u>I hope</u> the experiment will go off without a hitch.

i.e. Stands for "that is." This is *not* the same as **e.g.** See **e.g.**

illusion. See **delusion.**

incite, insight. Incite is a verb meaning to *stir up*; **insight** is a noun meaning (often sudden) *understanding*.

infer, imply. To **infer** means to *deduce* or *conclude by reasoning*. It is often confused with **imply**, which means to *suggest* or *insinuate*.

> We can <u>infer</u> from the large population density that there is a high demand for services.

> The large population density <u>implies</u> that there is a high demand for services.

inflammable, flammable, non-flammable. Despite its **in-** prefix, **inflammable** is not the opposite of **flammable**: both words describe things that are *easily set on fire*. The opposite of **flammable** is **non-flammable**. To prevent any possibility of confusion, it's best to avoid **inflammable** altogether.

irregardless. Irregardless is non-standard English; use *regardless*.

its, it's. Its is a form of possessive pronoun; **it's** is a contraction of *it is*. Many people mistakenly put an apostrophe in **its** in order to show possession.

> ✗ The cub wanted <u>it's</u> mother.

> ✓ The cub wanted <u>its</u> mother.

> ✓ <u>It's</u> time to leave.

less, fewer. Less is used when units are *not* discrete and *not* absolute (as in "<u>less</u> information"). **Fewer** is used when the units *are* discrete and absolute (as in "<u>fewer</u> details").

lie, lay. To **lie** means to *assume a horizontal position*; to **lay** means to *put down*. The changes of tense often cause confusion:

Present	Past	Past participle	Present participle
lie	lay	lain	lying
lay	laid	laid	laying

✗   I was <u>laying</u> on the couch.

✓   I was <u>lying</u> on the couch.

like, as. Like is a preposition, but it is often wrongly used as a conjunction. To join two independent clauses, use the conjunction **as:**

✗   I want to progress <u>like</u> you have this year.

✓   I want to progress <u>as</u> you have this year.

✓   Professor Dimitriou is <u>like</u> my old school principal.

might of. See **could of.**

minimize. See **diminish.**

mitigate, militate. To **mitigate** means to *reduce the severity* of something; to **militate** against something means to *oppose* it.

myself, me. Myself is an intensifier of, not a substitute for, *I* or *me*:

✗   He gave it to John and <u>myself</u>.

✓   He gave it to John and <u>me</u>.

✗   Jane and <u>myself</u> are invited.

✓   Jane and <u>I</u> are invited.

✓   <u>Myself</u>, I would prefer a swivel chair.

nor, or. Use **nor** with **neither**; use **or** by itself or with **either:**

He is <u>neither</u> overworked <u>nor</u> underfed.

The plant is <u>either</u> diseased <u>or</u> dried out.

off of. Remove the unnecessary **of:**

✗   The fence kept the children <u>off of</u> the premises.

✓   The fence kept the children <u>off</u> the premises.

phenomenon. A singular noun: the plural is **phenomena.**

plaintiff, plaintive. A **plaintiff** is a person who brings a case against someone else in court; **plaintive** is an adjective meaning *sorrowful*.

populace, populous. Populace is a noun meaning the *people* of a place; **populous** is an adjective meaning *thickly inhabited*:

> The populace of Hilltop village is not well educated.

> With so many people in such a small area, Hilltop village is a populous place.

practice, practise. Practice can be a noun, an adjective, or a verb; **practise** is always a verb. Note, however, that in Canada, **practise** is slightly preferred for the verb form:

> The soccer players need practice. (noun)

> That was a practice game. (adjective)

> The players need to practise (or practice) their skills. (verb)

precede, proceed. To **precede** is to *go before* (earlier) or *in front of* others; to **proceed** is to *go on* or *ahead*:

> The faculty will precede the students into the hall.

> The medal winners will proceed to the front of the hall.

prescribe, proscribe. These words are sometimes confused, although they have quite different meanings. **Prescribe** means to *advise the use of* or *impose authoritatively*. **Proscribe** means to *reject, denounce,* or *ban*:

> The professor prescribed the conditions under which the equipment could be used.

> The student government proscribed the publication of unsigned editorials in the newspaper.

principle, principal. Principle is a noun meaning a *general truth* or *law*; **principal** can be used as either a noun, referring to the *head of a school* or *a capital sum of money*, or an adjective, meaning *chief*.

rational, rationale. Rational is an adjective meaning *logical* or *able to reason*. **Rationale** is a noun meaning *explanation*:

That was not a <u>rational</u> decision.

The president sent around a memo explaining the <u>rationale</u> for her decision.

real, really. Real, an adjective, means *true* or *genuine*; **really**, an adverb, means *actually, truly, very,* or *extremely*.

The nugget was <u>real</u> gold.

The nugget was <u>really</u> valuable.

seasonable, seasonal. Seasonable means *usual* or *suitable for the season*; **seasonal** means *of, depending on,* or *varying with the season*:

It's quite cool today, but we can expect the return of <u>seasonable</u> temperatures later this week.

You must consider <u>seasonal</u> temperature changes when you pack for such a long trip.

should of. See **could of.**

their, there. Their is the possessive form of the third-person plural pronoun. **There** is usually an adverb, meaning *at that place* or *at that point*:

They parked <u>their</u> bikes <u>there</u>.

<u>There</u> is no point in arguing with you.

tortuous, torturous. The adjective **tortuous** means *full of twists and turns* or *circuitous*. **Torturous**, derived from *torture*, means *involving torture* or *excruciating*:

To avoid heavy traffic, they took a <u>tortuous</u> route home.

The concert was a <u>torturous</u> experience for the audience.

translucent, transparent. A **translucent** substance permits light to pass through, but not enough for a person to see through it; a **transparent** substance permits light to pass unobstructed, so that objects can be seen clearly through it.

turbid, turgid. Turbid, with respect to a liquid or colour, means *muddy, not clear*, or (with respect to literary style) *confused*. **Turgid** means *swollen*, *inflated*, or *enlarged*, or (again with reference to literary style) *pompous* or *bombastic*.

unique. This word, which means *of which there is only one* or *unequalled*, is both overused and misused. Since there are no degrees of comparison—one thing cannot be "more unique" than another—expressions such as *very unique* or *quite unique* are incorrect.

while. To avoid misreading, use **while** only when you mean *at the same time that*. Do not use **while** as a substitute for *although*, *whereas*, or *but*:

✗   While she's getting fair marks, she'd like to do better.

✗   I headed for home, while she decided to stay.

✓   He fell asleep while he was reading.

-wise. Never use **-wise** as a suffix to form new words when you mean *with regard to*:

✗   Sales-wise, the company did better last year.

✓   The company's sales increased last year.

your, you're. **Your** is a pronominal adjective used to show possession; **you're** is a contraction of *you are*:

You're likely to miss your train.

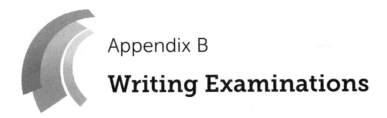

Appendix B

Writing Examinations

Introduction

Before your university career is over, you will have written many examinations. They will come in a variety of forms, ranging from true/false and multiple-choice tests to short-answer, problem-solving, and essay exams. No matter what type of examination you take, you need to be prepared. This does not mean sitting down a couple of nights beforehand and trying to read and remember everything in your textbook. Nor does it mean reading passively through your notes and texts once a week throughout the term. Studying is an active process, and if you develop good study skills you will be well on your way to success in whatever exams you may take.

The strategy suggested here is the one developed by the study-skills counsellors at Western University. You can adapt it to fit your own needs. The most important thing to remember is to be organized and to use your time effectively. For more information on study skills and exam writing, see Fleet, Goodchild, and Zajchowski (2006).

There are six steps to consider in preparing for an exam:

1. getting a perspective;
2. learning the material;
3. consolidating material and anticipating questions;
4. simulating the test;
5. filling in the gaps; and
6. doing a final review.

Getting a Perspective

Exam preparation has to begin long before the exam period itself. In fact, you should start organizing and collating your materials as soon as you have the course outline and know what kind of exams you will be taking. Then, as you progress through the term, you should be taking and organizing your notes in a way that will be the most useful when the exam finally comes around.

As the exam period approaches, gather together all the materials you have accumulated during the course—including textbooks and any notes you have made while reading, the course outline, lecture notes, and so on. Skim through this material to remind yourself of the main topic areas. Even at this stage, you should be able to identify general areas from which questions might be drawn.

Learning the material

You can make this stage much easier if you have spent some time after each lecture reviewing both your notes and the course textbook. Weekly reviews will help you remember important material and relate new information to old. If you don't review regularly, at the end of the year you'll be faced with relearning rather than remembering.

As you review, condense and focus the material by writing down key words or phrases that will trigger whole sets of details in your mind. The trigger might be a word that names or points to an important theory or definition, or it might be a quantitative phrase such as "three factors affecting the development of schizophrenia" or "four classes of operant conditioning."

Sometimes you can create an acronym or a nonsense sentence that will trigger an otherwise hard-to-remember set of facts—something like the mnemonic "**O**h, **O**h, **O**h, **T**o **T**ouch **A**nd **F**eel **A G**reen **V**iolet **A**t **H**ome" for the initial letters of the 12 cranial nerves. The difficulty of memorizing increases with the number of individual items you are trying to remember, so reducing the number of items to be memorized will increase your effectiveness. The more unusual the acronym, the more likely you are to remember it.

At this stage, you can benefit from rewriting and condensing your notes so that you can go through them quickly during your final review. Make sure you understand all the material. Trying to memorize something you don't understand is far more difficult than simply hanging facts on a well-understood framework.

Whatever your study plan, don't simply read through your text and other course materials without making notes, asking questions, or solving problems. Something that seems straightforward when you first read it may turn out to be much less clear when you have to write about it.

Consolidating and anticipating

You should think specifically about what questions may be on the exam. The best way to do this is to analyze the course material and then try to make up questions based on it. If you rephrase the material in the form of questions that might be asked, you should find it easier to remember what you've studied during the exam. If your instructor makes exams used previously in the course available to you, you can see the types of questions you might be asked, and you can check if you have prepared thoroughly. If old exams aren't available, you might get together with some of your classmates to ask each other possible exam questions. Just remember that the most useful review questions force you to analyze, integrate, or evaluate information, not simply to recall facts.

Simulating the test

Set a hypothetical exam for yourself, based on old exam questions and/or ones that you have made up. Then find a time when you will be free of interruptions and write the exam as if it were the real thing. Although this takes a lot of self-discipline, it's an excellent way to find out your strengths and weaknesses.

Filling in the gaps

By now you should have a good idea of which areas you know fairly well and which ones need further study. Go over these areas carefully. Don't waste time on things that you know well: just fill in the gaps.

Doing the final review

The day before the exam, go over your condensed notes and rehearse some possible questions. At this stage you should have done all of the basic work to make sure you understand and remember the material. What you need now is to get yourself into the best possible frame of mind to write the exam.

Test Anxiety

Most students feel nervous before tests and exams. Writing an exam of any kind imposes strong pressures. In an essay exam, because the time is restricted, you can't edit and rewrite the way you can in a regular essay; and because the questions are restricted, you must write on topics you might otherwise avoid. If you are writing a multiple-choice exam, often you might not know whether you are interpreting the questions correctly; and if there is a penalty for incorrect answers, you have the additional stress of deciding whether to mark an answer that you aren't sure is correct.

To do your best on an exam, you need to feel calm—but how? It may help to know that a moderate level of anxiety is beneficial: it keeps you alert. It's when you are overconfident or paralyzed with fear that you run into difficulties. There are many strategies for coping with test anxiety, but perhaps the best general advice is to try to control what makes you feel stressed. Give yourself lots of time to get to the exam so that you don't need to worry about traffic jams, transit delays, or last-minute room changes. At the exam, focus your attention on your own work rather than concerning yourself with how other students might be performing. Don't think about negative "what if" possibilities: if you have studied well, you should be well prepared for any exam question. Even if you can't turn off your worries, you can minimize them enough to perform well.

At the Exam

If you look at the question paper and your first reaction is "I can't do any of it," force yourself to keep calm; take several slow, deep breaths to relax, and then decide which questions you can answer best. Even if the exam seems impossible at first, you can probably find a few questions that look manageable. Begin with those. It will get you rolling and increase your confidence. By the time you have finished your first answer, your mind will have likely worked through the answer for another question.

Writing an Essay Exam

Read the exam

An exam is not a hundred-metre dash. Instead of starting to write immediately, take time at the beginning to read through each question and create a plan. A few minutes spent on thinking and organizing will bring better results than the same time spent writing a few more lines.

Apportion your time

Read the instructions carefully to find out how many questions you must answer and to see if you have any choice. Subtract five minutes or so for the initial planning, then divide the time you have left by the number of questions you have to answer. If possible, allow for a little extra time at the end to reread and edit your work. If the instructions on the exam indicate that not all questions are of equal value, apportion your time accordingly.

Choose your questions

Decide on the questions you will do and the order in which you will answer them. You don't have to answer the questions in the order they appear on the exam. Be sure to number your answers carefully so that your instructor knows which question you're responding to. If you have enough time and are organized enough, try to create a halo effect: put your best answer first, your poorest answers in the middle, and your second-best answer at the end in order to leave the reader on a high note. If you think you will be rushed, though, it's wiser to work from best to worst; that way you will be sure to get all the marks you can on your good answers, and you won't have to cut a good answer short at the end.

Read each question carefully

As you turn to each question, read it again carefully and underline all the key words. The wording will probably suggest the number of parts your answer should have; be sure you don't overlook anything—this is a common mistake when people are nervous. Since the verb used in the question is usually a guide for the approach to take in your answer, it's especially important that you interpret the key words in the question correctly. In Chapter 4, we summarized what you should do when you are faced with words like *explain, compare, discuss,* and so on; it's a good idea to review this list before you go to the exam (see page 57).

Make notes

Before you even begin to organize your answer, jot down key ideas and information related to the topic on rough paper or the unlined pages of your answer book. These notes will save you the worry of forgetting something by the time you begin writing. Next, arrange those parts you want to use into a brief plan, and use numbers to indicate their order (that way, if you change your mind, it will be easy to reorder them). At the end of the exam, you may have to submit any notes you've made along with your answer booklet, so be sure to cross out these notes—you don't want the person marking your paper to confuse them with your actual answers.

Be direct

Get to the points quickly and use plenty of examples to illustrate them. In an exam—as opposed to a term paper—it's best to use a direct approach. Don't worry about composing a graceful introduction: simply state the main points that you are going to discuss, then get on with developing them. Remember that your exam paper will likely be one of many read and marked by someone who has to work quickly; the clearer your answers are, the better they will be received.

For each main point, give the kind of specific details that will prove you really know the material. General statements will show you are able to assimilate information, but they need examples to back them up.

Write legibly

Poor handwriting makes readers cranky. When the marker has to struggle to decipher your writing, you may get poorer marks than you deserve. If your writing is not very legible, it's probably better to print. You should also write on every second or third line of your booklet: this will not only make your writing easier to read but also leave you space to make changes and additions if you have time later on.

Keep to your time plan

Keep to your plan and don't skip any questions. Try to write something on each topic. Remember that it's easier to score half marks for a question you don't know much about than it is to score full marks for one you could write pages on. If you find yourself running out of time on an answer and still haven't finished, summarize the remaining points and go on to the next question. Leave a large space between questions so that you can go back and add more if you have time. If you write a new conclusion, remember to cross out the old one—neatly.

Reread your answers

No matter how tired or fed up you are, reread your answers at the end if there's time. Check especially that you've been clear. Just as you would when you're writing a research paper, try to imagine yourself as your marker and ask if she would understand what you've written. Try to get rid of confusing sentences, and improve your transitions so that the logical connection between your ideas is as clear as possible. Revisions that make answers easier to read are always worth the effort.

Writing a Multiple-Choice Exam

Many students are terrified of multiple-choice exams. They worry that they will need to know every minute detail about the material, or that the questions will be ambiguous. In some cases this is true, but the problem is often related more to the way students approach the test than to their knowledge of the material or to the test itself. The suggestions below are based on the strategies for writing multiple-choice exams proposed by Fleet, Goodchild, and Zajchowski (2006):

1. **Cover up the answers.** This will force you to concentrate all of your attention on the question. One of the most common mistakes students make is misreading the question because they read it through too quickly.

2. **Read and process the question.** Take your time. Make sure you understand *exactly* what the question is asking. If necessary, rephrase it in your own words. Pay attention to qualifying words such as *always*, *only*, or *never*.

3. **Predict a possible answer.** Before looking at the alternatives, see if you can answer the question on your own. If you can recall a possible answer, then you're less likely to be fooled by the alternatives that are listed. Although your memory may be jogged by seeing the alternatives, sometimes they are very similar and can be confusing.

4. **Check the format of the question.** Are there combinations of alternatives, such as "all of the above," or "*a* and *c*"? If there are, you need to consider them very carefully. Test-setters sometimes make these combinations the right answer because they know that students with a patchy knowledge of course material will latch on to one fact they know, and that only those with a thorough knowledge of the material will recognize that some or all of the answers listed are correct.

5. **Process each alternative answer.** Work your way through each alternative, asking yourself two questions. First, is the statement true, regardless of its relation to the question? Sometimes the alternatives are factually incorrect. Second, what is the relationship of the alternative to the question? A statement may be true, but not relevant to the question.

6. **Eliminate the wrong answers.** If you have been successful in step 5, you may be able to narrow down the field by excluding the alternatives that cannot be correct.

7. **Identify the correct answer.** At this point you may be in a position to select the correct answer. If not, go to step 8.

8. **Reread the question.** If you're still not certain of the best answer, go back to the question again, now that you have had more time to think about it. Sometimes a second reading will make the correct answer much more obvious.

9. **Guess.** If there is no penalty for guessing, then be sure to select an alternative. If you have eliminated more than one alternative, then even a random choice has better odds of earning you marks than leaving the question blank does. More important, your guess is likely to be an "educated" one, increasing your chance of success even further. If there is a penalty for guessing—that is, if points are deducted for an incorrect answer—then you need to be more careful with this strategy. If you have at least some idea about the question, a guess is almost always worth taking the chance.

Writing an Open-Book Exam

If you think that permission to take your books into the exam room is a guarantee of success, be forewarned: do not fall into the trap of relying too heavily on your reference materials. You may spend so much time flipping through pages and looking things up that you won't have time to write good answers. The result may be worse than if you had been allowed no books at all.

If you want to do well, use your books only to check information and look up specific, hard-to-remember details for a topic you already know a good deal about. For instance, if your subject is biochemistry, you can look up chemical formulae; if it is statistics, you can look up equations; if it is psychology, you can look up specific terms or experimental details. In other words, use the books to make sure your answers are precise and well illustrated. Never use them to replace studying and careful exam preparation.

Writing a Take-Home Exam

The benefit of a take-home exam is that you have time to plan your answers and to consult your texts and other sources. The catch is that the amount of time you have to do this is usually less than you would have for an ordinary essay. Don't work yourself into a frenzy trying to respond with a polished research essay for each question. Keep in mind that you were given this assignment to test your overall command of the course: your marker is likely to be less concerned with how much you can pull out of the text than with evidence that you have understood and assimilated the material.

The guidelines for a take-home exam are similar to those for a regular exam; the only difference is that you don't need to keep such a close eye on the clock:

- Keep your introduction short and get to the point quickly.
- Organize your answer in a straightforward and obvious way so the reader can easily see your main ideas.
- Use concrete examples to back up your points.
- Where possible, show the range of your knowledge of course material by referring to a variety of sources rather than constantly using the same ones.
- Try to show that you can analyze and evaluate material—that you can do more than simply repeat information.
- If you are asked to acknowledge the sources of any quotations or data you use, be sure to jot them down as you go; you may not have time to do so at the end.

Reference

Fleet, J., Goodchild, F., & Zajchowski, R. (2006). *Learning for success: Effective strategies for students* (4th ed.). Scarborough, ON: Thomson Nelson.

Appendix C

Writing a Resumé and Letter of Application

Introduction

Whether you are looking for a summer job, applying to graduate school, or seeking permanent employment, eventually you will have to write a resumé and letter of application. The person who reads your application will be looking at many others and will not spend much time initially on each one, so you need to prepare something that is concise but designed to make a good first impression.

Preparing a Resumé

A resumé is much more than a summary of facts about you; you should think of it as a marketing tool designed to fit an individual employer's or organization's needs. You will need to supply some basic information, but how you organize it and which details you emphasize are up to you. One good strategy is to put your most important qualifications first so that they are noticed at first glance. For most students this means leading with educational qualifications, but for others it may mean starting with work experience. Within each section of your resumé, use reverse chronological order so that the most recent item is at the beginning.

Whatever arrangement you choose, your goal is to keep the resumé as concise as possible while including all the specific information that will help you "sell" yourself. A reader will lose interest in a resumé that goes on and on, mixing pertinent details with trivial ones. On the other hand, experience or skills that may seem irrelevant might actually demonstrate an important attribute or qualification. For example, working as a part-time short-order cook may be significant if you state that this was how you paid your way through university.

Here is a list of common resumé information, along with some suggestions on how to present it:

- **Name.** Your name is usually placed in capital letters and centred at the top of the page.

- **Addresses and telephone numbers.** Give your most current information, which will ensure you can be reached while your application is in process. Include both your home and cell numbers, as well as your email address. If you have several email accounts, use the one linked to your institution if possible; partyanimal@awesomemail.com will not create a good impression.

- **Career objectives (optional).** It's often helpful to let the employer know your career goals, or at least your current employment aspirations.

- **Education.** Include any degrees or related diplomas or certificates along with the institution that granted them and the dates they were granted. If it will help your case, and if you are short of other qualifications, you may also list courses you have taken that are relevant to the job.

- **Awards or honours.** These may be in a separate section or included with your education information.

- **Work experience.** Give the name and location of your employer, along with your job title and the dates of employment. Instead of outlining your duties (which an employee may or may not carry out well), list your accomplishments on the job, using point form and action verbs. For example:

  - Designed and administered a public awareness survey.
  - Supervised a three-member field crew.

- **Specialized skills.** This is a chance to list information that may give you an advantage in a competitive market, such as specific information technology skills or software suites you're experienced with, or knowledge of a second language. If you have worked as a research assistant, be sure to state the type of work you did and for whom you worked. For example:

  - Assisted Professor William James in a research project on social learning in gerbils, Lakehead University, Summer 2014.

- **Other interests (optional).** Depending on the amount of information you have already included, and on the type of employer, you may choose to omit this section. Sometimes, however, including a few achievements or interests, such as athletic or musical accomplishments, will show that you are well-rounded or especially disciplined. Avoid making a long list of items that merely show passive or minimal involvement.

- **References (optional).** If asked to supply the names of people who can give references, be sure to give the complete title, address, phone number, and email address of each one. If you are not asked for references, you don't need to supply names—instead, write "References available upon request." Increasingly, employers are waiting until they are serious about hiring an individual before they consider references. If you do supply names, check with your potential references beforehand to be sure they are willing to provide one, and ask which contact information they would prefer you to list.

Standard resumé

Joanne Smith

Present Address (until 30 April 2014):	Permanent Address:
500 University Avenue	RR#5
London ON N6A 2V3	Ilderton ON N0M 2A0
Home: (519) 555-1234	(519) 777-4321
Cell: (860) 233-5450	
email: jsmith27@uwo.ca	

Career Objective: An entry-level position in human resources, where my background in organizational psychology would be an asset

Education:

- B.A. (Hons) Psychology, Western University (expected June 2014)

(Honours thesis: "Dilbert in Academia: Job Satisfaction among University Professors")

Honours and Awards:

- Dean's Honour List, 2011–2013, Western University
- President's Entrance Scholarship, 2011 ($5,000), Western University

Work Experience:

Summer 2013—Research assistant for Professor G. Humphrey Hall (Project title: "Social interactions among graduate students in different disciplines")

- helped develop questionnaire and conduct interviews
- assisted in statistical analysis of data
- drafted *Method* and *Results* sections of final report

Summer 2010—Summer intern, United Nations, New York

- maintained and organized general filing
- provided office support
- maintained computer database

Summer 2008—Sales associate and cashier, Walmart, London

- assisted customers with finding and purchasing products

Specialized Skills and Experience:
- Strong computer skills. Knowledge of Windows 8; basic knowledge of Linux. Familiarity with the following programming languages: HTML, JavaScript, C++. Extensive experience with word-processing, database, spreadsheet, and presentation software.
- Custom designed web pages for businesses in both Canada and the United States. Used knowledge of HTML, JavaScript, FTP, database, image and sound manipulation software.
- Strong statistical background. Took several advanced statistics courses and was able to use these skills in my research assistant position.

Other Interests and Achievements:
- Participated in competitive gymnastics at provincial level for six years. Member of Ontario Provincial Gymnastics Team for three years. Gymnastics coach. Assisted gymnasts aged 4–14 in advancing through the CanGym Levels System, while helping them gain new skills and confidence.
- Active interest in theatre arts. Member of Theatre Ontario, London Community Players, Theatre Western. Principal roles in several productions.

References:
Available upon request

A resumé with these traditional categories is not the only kind that works, however. Even if your experience is not directly related to the position you want, you can still write an effective *functional resumé*. Most functional resumés have categories for experience in different functions (for example, Research, Administration, Sales). Others may focus on personal attributes such as initiative, teamwork, analytic ability, or communication skills. If you choose to write a functional resumé, it's a good idea to include at the bottom a brief record of employment with dates, so that the reader has a firm grasp of when you did what.

Functional resumé

Sandra Cargill

RR#2
Granton ON
N0M 1V0
Home: (519) 777-4321
Cell: (647) 555-2468
email: cargill3@newserver.com

Career Objective: Work in a public-relations or media organization dealing directly with clients or the public

Profile: Excellent communicator with extensive experience working in front of an audience and a proven record of initiative

Communications and Public Appearance Experience:

- Reporter for the *Gazette* newspaper at Western University, Sept 2012– April 2014.
- Announcer on CHRW ("Radio Western") at Western University, 2010–2012. Hosted weekly show "Awful Oldies," Jan–Dec 2010.
- Member of Theatre Ontario, London Community Players, Theatre Western. Principal roles in several productions.
- Singer and guitarist at local clubs.

Initiative:

- Founded my own business as a web page designer for local businesses
- Developed a website and bulletin board service for tropical bird owners to exchange information
- Supported myself throughout university with contract web design and computer programming jobs

Education:

B.A. (Hons) Psychology and English, Western University (June 2012). Specialized in industrial and organizational psychology, and in drama.

Other Achievements and Activities:

- Vice-President (Communications), University Student Council, 2011–12
- Participated in World Triathlon Championships, Lausanne, Switzerland, 2010

References:

Available upon request

The tone of the resumé should be upbeat: don't draw attention to any potential weaknesses you might have, such as a lack of experience in a particular area. Never list a category and then write "None"—you don't want to suggest that you lack something! Remember to reorder your list of special skills to suggest a fit with each particular job you apply for, so that the reader will see at a glance that you have the needed skills. Finally, never claim more for yourself than is true; putting something into a resumé that is not true will guarantee that you will not get the job if your potential employer finds out and it could be grounds for dismissal if it is discovered later.

You are not required to state anything about your age, place of birth, race, religion, or sex (which you can obscure if you use your initials rather than your given names). Keep in mind, though, that if you are completing an application form with set questions, it is a good idea to provide all the information requested; if you don't, your application may be ignored.

Preparing a Letter of Application for a Job

Do not use the same letter for all applications: craft each one to focus directly on the particular job and company in question and to catch the attention of each particular reader. In a sense, both the resumé and the letter of application are intended to open the door to the next stage in the job hunt: the interview. The key is not just to state information but to link your skills to the position. What matters is not what *you want* but what the *employer needs*.

One challenge in writing a letter of application is to write about yourself and your qualifications without seeming egotistical. Two tips can help:

1. Limit sentences beginning with *I*. Instead, try burying *I* in the middle of some sentences, where it will be less noticeable; for example, "For two months last summer, I worked as a . . ."
2. As much as you can, avoid making unsupported, subjective claims. Instead of saying, "I am a highly skilled manager," say something like, "Last summer, I managed a $50,000 field study with a crew of seven assistants." Rather than claim, "I have excellent research skills," you might say, "Based on my previous work, Professor Miriam Badani selected me from among ten applicants to help with her summer research work."

Here is an example (not to be copied rigidly), of an application letter that tries to connect the applicant's background with the needs of the company:

---

1 April 2014

Mr. Steven Nazar
Personnel Director
MegaDrug Corporation
110 Xenon Street
Toronto ON M6Z 9Q1

Dear Mr. Nazar

I am writing in response to your advertisement in the *Globe and Mail* on 15 March for a position as a Research Associate at MegaDrug Corporation. This entry-level position matches my career interests and fits well with my skills and experience. It is clear from the reports I have read that your company is well known as a leader in research into the development of new therapeutic agents, and I am very interested in becoming a member of such a highly regarded research team.

I will be graduating in May from Queen's University with a combined honours degree in physiology and psychology. The courses I have taken in these two disciplines have provided me with a strong background in basic human physiology as well as extensive experience in the design, running, and analysis of behavioural experiments involving both humans and animals. I have also had the opportunity to work as a research assistant for the last two summers in both the physiology and psychology departments.

The enclosed resumé and university transcript will provide you with a more comprehensive account of my background, achievements, and interests.

I look forward to meeting with you to discuss the position.

Sincerely,

Sandra Cargill

Sandra Cargill

Final Words of Advice

When you apply for a job, your application is likely to be one of many. This means that it must pass an initial screening process before it is considered seriously. For that reason, it is *absolutely essential* that you submit a package that looks professional. First impressions count. Poor spelling, bad grammar, and a sloppy layout are guarantees that your application will end up in a wastepaper basket. Before you send out your application, go through the following checklist to be sure that everything is as it should be:

- ☐ Have I spell checked both my resumé and my covering letter? Have I double-checked the spelling of the name of the person I am writing to on both the cover letter and the envelope (or email)?
- ☐ Have I made sure that there are no grammatical errors in my cover letter?
- ☐ Are both my resumé and my cover letter printed on good-quality paper?
- ☐ Does my resumé include everything about me that might be relevant to *this* job?
- ☐ Is the layout of my resumé neat, clear, and logically organized?

Glossary I

Key Terms and Abbreviations in Psychology

analysis of variance (ANOVA). A statistical test that compares the means of several samples to determine whether the difference between them could have occurred by chance.

applied research. Research intended to provide decision-makers with practical, action-oriented recommendations to solve a problem. (Compare **basic research**.)

baseline. A measure of conditions or behaviour before experimental manipulation is carried out.

basic (or pure) research. Research that is intended to obtain a greater understanding of a phenomenon without considering what the practical applications might be. (Compare **applied research**.)

between-subject variables. Experimental treatment conditions in which each group of subjects receives a different treatment. (Compare **within-subject variables**.)

confidence interval (CI). A range of values expressing the likelihood that the mean estimated from a sample represents the true mean of a population. A "95 per cent confidence limit" means that there is only a 5 per cent chance that the true value is *not* included within the span of the error.

control (for). Examine the influence on the dependent variable of changes in one independent variable while holding constant (i.e., *controlling for*) other independent variables.

control group. Those subjects who are not exposed to the experimental manipulations. (Compare **experimental group**.)

deduction. Drawing a specific conclusion by reasoning from more general information. (Compare **induction**.)

dependent variable. The variable that is measured in an experiment. This is what you expect to change as a result of an experimental manipulation. (Compare **independent variable**.)

experimental group. Those subjects who are exposed to the experimental manipulations. (Compare **control group**.)

F-ratio. The test statistic in an analysis of variance whose value will indicate whether the differences between means are statistically significant.

hypothesis. A statement of an expected relationship between two or more variables.

independent variable. The variable that is manipulated in an experiment. This is the experimental treatment that is imposed on a subject to produce a change in behaviour. (Compare **dependent variable**.)

induction. Drawing a general conclusion on the basis of specific facts. (Compare **deduction**.)

intervening variable. A characteristic or condition that explains the link between a cause and an effect; a variable *through which* the independent variable acts on the dependent variable.

logarithm. The exponent or power to which a base must be raised to yield a given number. So, for common, or base-10, logarithms, the value of the logarithm is the power to which 10 must be raised to give that number: e.g., $10^2 = 100$, therefore $\log_{10} 100 = 2$. A very wide range of numbers is sometimes converted to logarithmic values to compress the scale.

mean (M or $\overline{X}$). The average of a set of scores, calculated as the total of all the scores added together, and then divided by the number of scores in the sample.

model. A theoretical "picture" of the relations among causes and effects.

population. The entire collection of individuals from which a sample is drawn. In a typical psychology experiment in which first-year students are the participants, the population might be first-year university students, or all university students, or all individuals between 18 and 30 years of age. Which of these applies depends on whether the individuals in the sample may be assumed to possess the relevant characteristics that may be generalized to the broader population.

qualitative data. Data that cannot be satisfactorily described by numbers and must be described in words.

quantitative data. Data that can be satisfactorily described by numbers.

regression line. A "line of best fit," representing the *trend* of a set of data. It is calculated using a regression equation and represents the line that passes closest to all the points in a data set. Depending upon the trend (i.e., linear or curvilinear) of the data, different regression equations may be used.

sample. The subset of individuals who are tested in an experiment and whose data may be generalized to a wider population.

significance (or **statistical significance**). The likelihood that the result obtained in a study was not due to chance, but was a result of the experimental manipulation.

significance level. A quantitative estimate of the likelihood that the obtained result could have occurred by chance. A result that is significant at the .05 level indicates that the probability of a chance result is 5 out of 100.

standard deviation (SD). A measure of the variability of scores in a sample. It tells you how closely a set of scores cluster around the mean of a set of data and is calculated as the square root of the average squared deviation of each score from the mean.

standard error of the mean (SEM). An estimate of the variability of scores in a population, based on data from a single sample. Mathematically, it is the standard deviation of the sampling distribution of means.

theory. A set of interconnected statements or propositions that attempts to explain a causal relationship.

within-subject variables. Experimental treatment conditions in which a single group of subjects receives each different treatment. (Compare **between-subject variables**.)

Glossary II

Key Terms in Grammar

abstract. A summary accompanying a formal scientific report or paper, briefly outlining its contents.

abstract language. Language that deals with theoretical, intangible concepts or details: e.g., *justice, goodness, truth.* (Compare **concrete language**.)

acronym. A pronounceable word made up of the first letters of the words in a phrase or name: e.g., *NATO* (from *North Atlantic Treaty Organization*). A group of initial letters that are pronounced separately is an **initialism**: e.g., *CBC, NHL.*

active voice. See **voice**.

adjectival phrase (or **adjectival clause**). A group of words modifying a noun or pronoun: e.g., *the dog that belongs to my brother.*

adjective. A word that modifies or describes a noun or pronoun: e.g., *red, beautiful, solemn.*

adverb. A word that modifies or qualifies a verb, adjective, or adverb, often answering a question such as *how? why? when?* or *where?*: e.g., *slowly, fortunately, early, abroad.* (See also **conjunctive adverb**.)

adverbial phrase (or **adverbial clause**). A group of words modifying a verb, adjective, or adverb: e.g., *The dog ran with great speed.*

agreement. Consistency in tense, number, or person between related parts of a sentence: e.g., between subject and verb, or noun and related pronoun.

ambiguity. Vague or equivocal language; meaning that can be taken two ways.

antecedent (or **referent**). The noun for which a following pronoun stands: e.g., *cats* in *Cats are happiest when they are sleeping.*

appositive. A word or phrase that identifies a preceding noun or pronoun: e.g., *Mrs Jones, my aunt, is sick.* The second phrase is said to be **in apposition to** the first.

article. See **definite article, indefinite article**.

assertion. A positive statement or claim: e.g., *The data are inconclusive.*

auxiliary verb. A verb used to form the tenses, moods, and voices of other verbs: e.g., *am* in *I am swimming.* The main auxiliary verbs in English are *be, do, have, can, could, may, might, must, shall, should,* and *will.*

bibliography. (1) A list of works used or referred to in writing an essay or report. (2) A reference book listing works available on a particular subject.

case. Any of the inflected forms of a pronoun (see **inflection**).
  Subjective case. *I, we, you, he, she, it, they*
  Objective case. *me, us, you, him, her, it, them*
  Possessive case. *my/mine, your/yours, our/ours, his, her/hers, its, their/theirs*

circumlocution. A roundabout or circuitous expression, often used in a deliberate attempt to be vague or evasive: e.g., *in a family way* for "pregnant"; *at this point in time* for "now."

clause. A group of words containing a subject and predicate. An **independent clause** can stand by itself as a complete sentence: e.g., *I bought a hamburger.* A **subordinate** (or **dependent) clause** cannot stand by itself but must be connected to another clause: e.g., *Because I was hungry, I bought a hamburger.*

cliché. A phrase or idea that has lost its impact through overuse and betrays a lack of original thought: e.g., *slept like a log, gave 110 per cent.*

collective noun. A noun that is singular in form but refers to a group: e.g., *family, team, jury.* It may take either a singular or plural verb, depending on whether it refers to individual members or to the group as a whole.

comma splice. See **run-on sentence**.

complement. A completing word or phrase that usually follows a linking verb to form a **subjective complement**: e.g., (1) *He is my father;* (2) *That cigar smells terrible.* If the complement is an adjective it is sometimes called a **predicate adjective**. An **objective complement** completes the direct object rather than the subject: e.g., *We found him honest and trustworthy.*

complex sentence. A sentence containing a dependent clause as well as an independent one: e.g., *I bought the ring, although it was expensive.*

compound sentence. A sentence containing two or more independent clauses: e.g., *I saw the accident and I reported it.* A sentence is called **compound-complex** if it contains a dependent clause as well as two independent ones: e.g., *When the fog lifted, I saw the accident and I reported it.*

conclusion. The part of an essay in which the findings are pulled together or the implications revealed so that the reader has a sense of closure or completion.

concrete language. Specific language that deals with particular details: e.g., *red corduroy dress, three long-stemmed roses.* (Compare **abstract language**.)

conjunction. An uninflected word used to link words, phrases, or clauses. A **coordinating conjunction** (e.g., *and, or, but, for, yet*) links two equal parts of a sentence. A **subordinating conjunction**, placed at the beginning of a subordinate clause, shows the logical dependence of that clause on another: e.g., (1) *Although I am poor, I am happy;* (2) *While others slept, he studied.* **Correlative conjunctions** are pairs of coordinating conjunctions (see **correlatives**).

conjunctive adverb. A type of adverb that shows the logical relation between the phrase or clause that it modifies and a preceding one: e.g., (1) *I sent the letter; it never arrived, however.* (2) *The battery died; therefore, the car wouldn't start.*

connotation. The range of ideas or meanings suggested by a certain word in addition to its literal meaning. Apparent synonyms, such as *poor* and *underprivileged*, may have different connotations. (Compare **denotation**.)

context. The text surrounding a particular passage that helps to establish its meaning.

contraction. A word formed by combining and shortening two words: e.g., *isn't* from "is not"; *we're* from "we are."

coordinate construction. A grammatical construction that uses correlatives.

coordinating conjunction. Each of a pair of correlatives.

copula verb. See **linking verb**.

correlatives (or coordinates). Pairs of co-ordinating conjunctions: e.g., *either/or, neither/nor, not only/but (also).*

dangling modifier. A modifying word or phrase (often including a participle) that is not grammatically connected to any part of the sentence: e.g., *Walking to school, the street was slippery.*

definite article. The word *the*, which precedes a noun and implies that it has already been mentioned or is common knowledge. (Compare **indefinite article**.)

demonstrative pronoun. A pronoun that points out something: e.g., (1) *This is his reason*; (2) *That* looks like my lost earring. When used to modify a noun or pronoun, a demonstrative pronoun becomes a **demonstrative adjective**: e.g., *this hat, those* people.

denotation. The literal or dictionary meaning of a word. (Compare **connotation**.)

dependent clause. See **clause**.

diction. The choice of words with regard to their tone, degree of formality, or register. Formal diction is the language of orations and serious essays. The informal diction of everyday speech or conversational writing can, at its extreme, become slang.

direct object. See **object**.

discourse. Talk, either oral or written. **Direct discourse** (or **direct speech**) gives the actual words spoken or written: e.g., *Donne said, "No man is an island."* In writing, direct discourse is put in quotation marks. **Indirect discourse** (or **indirect speech**) gives the meaning of the speech rather than the actual words. In writing, indirect discourse is not put in quotation marks: e.g., *He said that no one exists in an island of isolation.*

ellipsis. Three spaced periods indicating an omission from a quoted passage. At the end of a sentence use four periods.

essay. A literary composition on any subject. Some essays are descriptive or narrative, but in an academic setting most are expository (explanatory) or argumentative.

euphemism. A word or phrase used to avoid some other word or phrase that might be considered offensive or too harsh: e.g., *pass away* for *die*.

expletive. (1) A word or phrase used to fill out a sentence without adding to the sense: e.g., *To be sure, it's not an ideal situation.* (2) A swear word.

exploratory writing. The informal writing done to help generate ideas before formal planning begins.

fused sentence. See **run-on sentence**.

general language. Language that lacks specific details; abstract language.

gerund. A verbal (part-verb) that functions as a noun and is marked by an *-ing* ending: e.g., *Swimming can help you become fit.*

grammar. The study of the forms and relations of words and of the rules governing their use in speech and writing.

hypothesis. A supposition or trial proposition made as a starting point for further investigation.

hypothetical instance. A supposed occurrence, often indicated by a clause beginning with *if*.

indefinite article. The word *a* or *an*, which introduces a noun and suggests that it is non-specific. (Compare **definite article**.)

independent clause. See **clause**.

indirect discourse (or indirect speech). See **discourse**.

indirect object. See **object**.

infinitive. A type of verbal not connected to any subject: e.g., *to ask*. The **base infinitive** omits the *to*: e.g., *ask*.

inflection. The change in the form of a word to indicate number, person, case, tense, or degree.

initialism. See **acronym**.

integrate. Combine or blend together.

intensifier (or **qualifier**). A word that modifies and adds emphasis to another word or phrase: e.g., *very tired*, *quite happy*, *I myself*.

interjection. An abrupt remark or exclamation, usually accompanied by an exclamation mark: e.g., *Oh dear! Alas!*

interrogative sentence. A sentence that asks a question: e.g., *What is the time?*

intransitive verb. A verb that does not take a direct object: e.g., *fall, sleep, talk.* (Compare **transitive verb.**)

introduction. A section at the start of an essay that tells the reader what is going to be discussed and why.

italics. Slanting type used for emphasis or to indicate the title of a book or journal.

jargon. Technical terms used unnecessarily or in inappropriate places: e.g., *peer-group interaction* for "friendship."

linking verb (or **copula verb**). A verb such as *be, seem,* or *feel,* used to join subject to complement: e.g., *The apples were ripe.*

literal meaning. The primary, or denotative, meaning of a word.

logical indicator. A word or phrase—usually a conjunction or conjunctive adverb—that shows the logical relation between sentences or clauses: e.g., *since, furthermore, therefore.*

misplaced modifier. A word or group of words that can cause confusion because it is not placed next to the element it should modify: e.g., *I only ate the pie* [Revised: *I ate only the pie.*]

modifier. A word or group of words that describes or limits another element in the sentence.

mood. (1) As a grammatical term, the form that shows a verb's function.
> **Indicative mood:** *She is going.*
> **Imperative mood:** *Go!*
> **Interrogative mood:** *Is she going?*
> **Subjunctive mood:** *It is important that she go.*

(2) When applied to literature generally, the atmosphere or tone created by the author.

non-restrictive modifier (or **non-restrictive element**). See **restrictive modifier**.

noun. An inflected part of speech marking a person, place, thing, idea, action, or feeling, and usually serving as subject, object, or complement. A **common noun** is a general term: e.g., *dog, paper, automobile.* A **proper noun** is a specific name: e.g., *Martin; Sudbury; Ski-Doo.*

object. (1) A noun or pronoun that completes the action of a verb is called a **direct object**: e.g., *He passed the puck.* An **indirect object** is the person or thing receiving the direct object: e.g., *He passed Simon* (indirect object) *the puck* (direct object). (2) The noun or pronoun in a group of words beginning with a preposition: e.g., *at the house, about her, for me.*

objective complement. See **complement**.

objectivity. A position or stance taken without personal bias or prejudice. (Compare **subjectivity.**)

outline. With regard to an essay or report, a brief sketch of the main parts; a written plan.

paragraph. A unit of sentences arranged logically to explain or describe an idea, event, or object. The start of a paragraph is sometime marked by indentation of the first line.

parallel wording. Wording in which a series of items has a similar grammatical form: e.g.,

At her marriage my grandmother promised <u>to</u> <u>love</u>, <u>to honour</u>, and <u>to obey</u> her husband.

paraphrase. Restate in different words.

parentheses. Curved lines enclosing and setting off a passage; not to be confused with square brackets.

parenthetical element. A word or phrase inserted as an explanation or afterthought into a passage that is grammatically complete without it: e.g., *My musical career, <u>if it can be called that</u>, consisted of playing the triangle in kindergarten.*

participle. A verbal (part-verb) that functions as an adjective. Participles can be either **present**, usually marked by an *-ing* ending (e.g., *taking*), or **past** (e.g., *having taken*); they can also be **passive** (e.g., *being taken* or *having been taken*).

part of speech. Each of the major categories into which words are placed according to their grammatical function. Traditional grammar classifies words based on eight parts of speech: verbs, nouns, pronouns, adjectives, adverbs, prepositions, conjunctions, and interjections.

passive voice. See **voice**.

past participle. See **participle**.

periodic sentence. A sentence in which the normal order is inverted or in which an essential element is suspended until the very end: e.g., *Out of the house, past the grocery store, through the school yard, and down the railway tracks raced the frightened boy.*

person. In grammar, the three classes of personal pronouns referring to the person speaking (**first person**), the person spoken to (**second person**), and the person spoken about (**third person**). With verbs, only the third-person singular has a distinctive inflected form.

personal pronoun. See **pronoun**.

phrase. A unit of words lacking a subject-predicate combination, typically forming part of a clause. The most common kind is the **prepositional phrase**—a unit consisting of a preposition and an object: e.g., *They are waiting <u>at the house</u>.*

plural. Indicating two or more in number. Nouns, pronouns, and verbs all have plural forms.

possessive case. See **case**.

prefix. An element placed in front of the root form of a word to make a new word: e.g., *pro-, in-, sub-, anti-* (Compare **suffix**.)

preposition. A short, introductory word in a unit of words containing an object, thus forming a **prepositional phrase**: e.g., *<u>under</u> the tree, <u>before</u> my time.*

pronoun. A word that stands in for a noun. A **personal pronoun** stands for the name of a person: *I, he, she, we, they*, etc.

punctuation. A conventional system of signs (e.g., comma, period, semicolon, etc.) used to indicate stops or divisions in a sentence and to make meaning clearer.

reference works. Sources consulted when preparing an essay or report.

referent. See **antecedent**.

reflexive verb. A verb that has an identical subject and object: e.g., *Isabel <u>taught herself</u> to skate.*

register. The degree of formality in word choice and sentence structure.

relative clause. A clause introduced by a relative pronoun: e.g., *The man <u>who came to dinner</u> is my uncle.*

relative pronoun. *Who, which, what, that,* or their compounds, used to introduce an adjective or noun clause: e.g., *the house that Jack built*; *whatever you say*.

restrictive modifier (or **restrictive element**). A phrase or clause that identifies or is essential to the meaning of a term: e.g., *The book that my aunt gave me is missing*. It should not be set off by commas. A **non-restrictive modifier** is not needed to identify the term and is usually set off by commas: e.g., *This book, which my aunt gave me, is one of my favourites*.

rhetorical question. A question asked and answered by a writer or speaker to draw attention to a point; no response is expected on the part of the audience: e.g., *How significant are these findings? In my opinion, they are of the utmost importance for the following reasons. . . .*

run-on sentence. A sentence that goes on beyond the point where it should have stopped. The term covers both the **comma splice** (two sentences incorrectly joined by a comma) and the **fused sentence** (two sentences incorrectly joined without any punctuation).

sentence. A grammatical unit that includes both a subject and a verb. The end of a sentence is marked by a period, a question mark, or an exclamation mark.

sentence fragment. A group of words lacking either a subject or a verb; an incomplete sentence.

simple sentence. A sentence made up of only one clause: e.g., *Joaquim climbed the tree.*

slang. Colloquial speech considered inappropriate for academic writing; it is often used in a special sense by a particular group: e.g., *stoked* for "excited"; *diss* for "disrespect."

split infinitive. A construction in which a word is placed between *to* and the base verb: e.g., *to completely finish*. Many still object to this kind of construction, but splitting infinitives is sometimes necessary when the alternatives are awkward or ambiguous.

squinting modifier. A kind of misplaced modifier that could be connected to elements on either side, making meaning ambiguous: e.g., *When he wrote the letter finally his boss thanked him.*

standard English. The English currently spoken or written by literate people and widely accepted as the correct and standard form.

subject. In grammar, the noun or noun equivalent with which the verb agrees and about which the rest of the clause is predicated: e.g., *They swim every day when the pool is open.*

subjective complement. See **complement**.

subjectivity. A stance that is based on personal feelings or opinions and is not impartial. (Compare **objectivity**.)

subjunctive. See **mood**.

subordinate clause. See **clause**.

subordinating conjunction. See **conjunction**.

subordination. Making one clause in a sentence dependent on another.

suffix. An element added to the end of a word to form a derivative: e.g., *prepare, preparation*; *sing, singing*. (Compare **prefix**.)

synonym. A word with the same dictionary meaning as another word: e.g., *begin* and *commence*.

syntax. Sentence construction; the grammatical arrangement of words and phrases.

tense. A set of inflected forms taken by a verb to indicate the time (i.e., past, present, future) of the action.

theme. A recurring or dominant idea.

thesis statement. A one-sentence assertion that gives the central argument of an essay.

topic sentence. The sentence in a paragraph that expresses the main or controlling idea.

transition word. A word that shows the logical relation between sentences or parts of a sentence and thus helps to signal the change from one idea to another: e.g., *therefore, also, however.*

transitive verb. A verb that takes an object: e.g., *hit, bring, cover.* (Compare **intransitive verb.**)

usage. The way in which a word or phrase is normally and correctly used; accepted practice.

verb. That part of a predicate expressing an action, state of being, or condition that tells what a subject is or does. Verbs are inflected to show tense (time). The principal parts of a verb are the three basic forms from which all tenses are made: the base infinitive, the past tense, and the past participle.

verbal. A word that is similar in form to a verb but does not function as one: a participle, a gerund, or an infinitive.

voice. The form of a verb that shows whether the subject acted (**active voice**) or was acted upon (**passive voice**): e.g., *He stole the money* (active). *The money was stolen by him* (passive). Only transitive verbs (verbs taking objects) can be passive.

Index